HITLER'S
V-Weapon Sites

Philip Henshall

SUTTON PUBLISHING

First published in the United Kingdom in 2002 by
Sutton Publishing Limited · Phoenix Mill
Thrupp · Stroud · Gloucestershire · GL5 2BU

British Library Cataloguing in Publication Data
A catalogue record for this book is available from the British Library.

ISBN 0-7509-2607-4

Typeset in 10.5/13.5pt Times.
Typesetting and origination by
Sutton Publishing Limited.
Printed and bound in England by
J.H. Haynes & Co. Ltd, Sparkford.

Contents

Tables

TABLE 1: LOCATION OF SITES: CALAIS–SOMME AREA (MAP 1)

Site No.	Site Location	Original Purpose	Site No.	Site Location	Original Purpose
1	Hames Boucres	Hottot type	26	Bientques	V1 modified
2	Lostebarne/Ardres	V1 ski	27	Blanc Pigeon Ferme	V1 modified
3	Bois du Rossignol	Hottot type	28	Thiennes	V2 storage/launch
4	Cocove	V1 ski	* 29	Ferme du Forestel	V1 modified
5	Watten	V2 bunker	30	Linghem	V1 ski
6	Mimoyecques	HDP bunker	* 31	Rely	V1 modified
7	Zederzeele (Middel Straete)	V1 ski	32	Drionville	V1 ski
* 8	Wemaers Cappel (La Ferme du Tom)	V1 modified	33	Erny St Julien	V1 modified
9	Le Breuil	Hottot type	34	Febvin Palfart	V1 ski
10	Westhove	V1 modified	35	Bois d'Enfer	V1 ski
11	Forêt Nationale de Tournehem	V1 ski	36	Audincthun	V1 ski
12	Cormette	V1 ski	37	Bois de Renty	V1 ski
13	Zudausques	V1 ski	38	Beaumetz-les-Aire	V1 modified
14	Le Nieppe	V1 ski	* 39	Vincly	V1 modified
15	Wisques	V1 ski	40	Livossart	V1 ski
16	Renescure	V1 storage, original	41	Rimeaux	V1 modified
17	La Longeville	V1 ski	* 42	Ferfay	V1 modified
* 18	Fromental	V1 modified	* 43	Fiefs	V1 modified
19	Wizernes	V2 bunker	44	Fruges, Bois de Coupelle	V1 ski
20	Heuringhem	V1 ski	45	Bellevue	V1 ski
21	Coubronne	V1 modified	46	Prédefin	V2 radar tracking for Walten
22	Lottinghen	V1 bunker	47	Maisoncelle	V1 ski
23	La Belle-Hôtesse	V1 modified	48	Crepy	V1 ski
* 24	Bois des Huit Rues	V1 ski	49	Bergeneuse	V2 storage, original
25	Rocquetoire	V2 guidance for Wizernes	50	Ruisseauville	V1 ski
			* 51	Crepieul	V1 ski
			52	Bois de la Justice	V1 ski

TABLE 2: LOCATION OF SITES: THE SOMME TO THE RIVER SEINE (MAP 2)

Site No.	Site Location	Original Purpose	Site No.	Site Location	Original Purpose
1	Marquenneville	V1 ski	38	Les Grandes Ventes, Les Petits Moreaux	V1 ski
2	Behen	V1 ski	39	Ardouval, Val Ygot ou la Grande Volée	V1 ski
3	Bois Cocquerel	V1 ski	40	Fresles, Haut de Fresles	V1 modified
4	Neuville au Bois	V1 storage	41	Esclavelles, La Chênaie	V1 ski
* 5	Fresnoy	V1 modified	42	Beaumont-le-Hareng, Le Mont Rouge	V1 ski
6	Moyenville/Mesnil Trois Foetus	V1 ski	43	Cropus, Freval	V1 ski
7	Bouillancourt	V1 ski	44	Croixdalle, Les Hallots	V1 modified
8	Campneuseville, Beaulieu	V1 ski	* 45	Baillolet	V1 modified
9	Campneuseville, Prestaux	V1 ski	46	Lucy	V1 modified
10	Richemont, Coquereaux	V1 modified	47	Menonval	V1 modified
11	St-Léger-aux-Bois, Mesnil-Allard	V1 modified	* 48	Esclavelles, Les Hayons	V1 ski
12	Callengeville (Bosc-Geffroy), Le Coudroy	V1 modified	* 49	Maucomble, Carrefour 118 et Maison Forestière	V1 modified
13	Callengeville (Bosc-Geffroy), La Hêtroye	V1 modified	* 50	Ardouval, Le Châtelet	V1 modified
14	Saint-Pierre-des-Jonquieres	V1 ski	* 51	Les Grandes Ventes, Route de la Loge	V1 modified
15	Preuseville	V1 ski	* 52	Les Grandes Ventes, Le Chemin Coursier	V1 modified
16	Fresnoy-Foiny (Bois de Tous Vents)	V1 modified	* 53	Les Grandes Ventes, La Route Charlemagne	V1 modified
* 17	Melleville, Montauban	V1 modified	* 54	Les Grandes Ventes, Le Fond des Six Frères	V1 modified
* 18	Millebosc, Rond de Namours	V1 modified	* 55	Les Grandes Ventes, La Mare du Four	V1 modified
* 19	Guerville, Château de la Haye	V1 modified	* 56	Les Grandes Ventes, La Laie Madame	V1 modified
20	Dancourt, Le Goulet ou Val de l'Eau	V1 modified	57	Muchedent, Pubel	V1 modified
* 21	Saint Riquier-en-Rivière, Poteau Maitre Jean	V1 modified	* 58	Freulleville, Le Croc	V1 modified
* 22	Realcamp, Les Hauts Buissons	V1 modified	59	Rocquemont, Le Grand Parc	V1 ski
* 23	Realcamp, Le Grand Marché	V1 modified	60	Estouteville, Ecalles	V1 ski
* 24	Campneuseville, La Houssaye	V1 ski	* 61	Bosc-Roger-sur-Buchy, Les Grands Bordeaux	V1 ski
* 25	Saint Léger aux Bois, Les Sapins	V1 modified	* 62	Beaubec-la-Rosière, Le Bois de Leon	V1 modified
26	Richemont, Le Transformateur	V1 modified	63	Le Fossé, Forêt de Montadet	V1 modified
* 27	Richemont, Les Cateliers	V1 modified	64	Beauvoir-en-Lyons, Les Routieux	V1 modified
* 28	Aubermesnil, Les Erables le Mont Gournoy	V1 modified	65	Mesnil-Lieubray, La Vente	V1 modified
29	Retonval, Le Bout du Haut	V1 modified	* 66	Mont Cauvaire, Parc de College de Normandie	V1 modified
30	Retonval, La Ventillette	V1 modified	* 67	St André-sur-Cailly, Carqueleu	V1 modified
* 31	Les Essarts Varimpré, Les Barres Bleues	V1 modified	68	St André-sur-Cailly, Route de Cailly	V1 modified
32	Vatierville, Bremont	V1 modified	69	Saint Germain-des-Essourts	V1 modified
* 33	Les Landes, Piste D60	V1 modified	* 70	La Vieux Rue, Parc du Château	V1 modified
* 34	Nullemont, Le Val Gay	V1 modified	* 71	Quincampoix, Les Haquets	V1 modified
35	Aumale, Bois de la Vierge	V1 modified	* 72	Quincampoix, La Mare aux Loups	V1 modified
36	Notre-Dame-d'Aliermont, Le Bout d'Amont	V1 ski	* 73	St Jean-du-Cardonnay, Château de Polignac	V1 modified
37	Notre-Dame-d'Aliermont, Les Champ Dubost	V1 modified			

Site No.	Site Location	Original Purpose	Site No.	Site Location	Original Purpose
74	Montigny, Clos à Paons	V1 modified	110	Ocqueville, Catteville	V1 modified
* 75	Montigny, Château	V1 modified	111	Rocquefort, Bois du Château	V1 modified
* 76	Henouville, Maresogne	V1 modified	112	Bois-Himont, Château Himont	V1 modified
77	La Vaupatière, Château des Parquet	V1 modified	113	Allouville-Bellefosse, Château de Bellefosse	V1 modified
78	Saint Pierre de Varengeville, Château Lebreton	V1 modified	114	Bolleville, Château de Beaunay	V1 modified
79	Quevillon	V1 modified	*115	Trémauville, Ferme Barbaray	V1 modified
80	La Londe, Carrefour d'Orival	V1 modified	*116	Tocqueville-les-Murs, Château le Romé	V1 modified
81	Mauny, Le Château	V1 modified	117	Angerville-Bailleul, Le Château	V1 modified
82	Yville-sur-Seine	V1 modified	118	Gommerville, Château de Filières	V1 modified
83	Saint-Paër, Château d'Aulnay	V1 modified	119	Saint-Romain-de-Colbosc, Château de Gromesnil	V1 modified
84	Sainte Margarite sur Duclair, La Grande Planitre	V1 modified	120	Saint-Jean-de-Folleville	V1 modified
* 85	Houppeville, La Coudrette	V1 modified	121	Saint-Arnoult	V1 modified
* 86	Houppeville, Les Cinq Frères	V1 modified	122	Villequier – Château La Guerche	V1 modified
* 87	Houppeville, Les Cotrets	V1 modified	123	La Mailleraye – Caveaumont	V1 modified
* 88	Houppeville, Belle Image	V1 modified	124	Beaumont I	V1 warhead storage/ servicing, final
89	Belmesnil	V1 ski	125	Longuemort	V1 ski
90	Saint Ouen le Mauger, Herbouville	V1 ski	126	St Martin l'Hortier	V1 storage, original
91	Belleville en Caux	V1 ski	127	Biennais	V1 storage, original
92	Tôtes, Bonnetot	V1 ski	128	Monville	V1/V2 storage, final
93	Auffay, Bosmelet	V1 ski	129	Authieu-Ratiéville	V1/V2 storage, final
94	Varneville-Bretterville, Bel-Event	V1 modified	130	Beaumont II	V1 storage, final
95	Torp-Mesnil, Heudieres	V1 modified	131	Inval Boiron	V1/V2 storage, final
* 96	Bertreville-Saint-Ouen, Bois Famille Garam	V1 ski	132	Bois d'Etrejust	V1/V2 storage, final
* 97	Bacquerville en Caux, Mont Candon	V1 modified	133	Salouel	V1/V2 storage, final
98	Sainte Geneviève en Caux	V1 modified	134	Forêt du Helle(t)	V1 and site, spares storage
99	Ancretteville Saint Victor	V1 modified			
100	Hugieville	V1 modified	*135	Val des Joncs	V1 modified
*101	Limesy, Château de Bagneux	V1 modified	136	La Breteque	V1 modified
*102	Fresquenne, Château	V1 modified	*137	Bois de la Haie	V1 modified
103	Grémonville, La Vatine	V1 modified	138	Beatot	V1 ski
104	Boudeville	V1 modified	*139	La Grand Vallée	V1 modified
105	Prétot-Vicquemare, Le Bois de Beville	V1 modified	*140	Avesnes-Chaussoy	V1 modified
106	Motteville, Le Château	V1 modified	*141	Chateau Bernapre	V1 modified
107	Hautot-l'Auvray, Château de la Menaongère	V1 modified	142	Clères	V2 railway turntable, final
108	Breteville Saint Laurent, La Hallière	V1 modified	143	La Musette	V1/V2/Rh launch
109	Angiens, Bois du Château de Silleron	V1 modified	144	Caumont	LOX production/ storage, final
			145	Canteleu-Dieppedalle	LOX production/ storage, final

*Operational sites

TABLE 3: LOCATION OF SITES: RIVER SEINE TO CHERBOURG PENINSULA (MAP 3)

Site No.	Site Location	Original Purpose	Site No.	Site Location	Original Purpose
1	Elbeuf	V2 storage, original	22	St Croix-sur-Mer	Hottot type
2	La Prée	V1 modified	23	Claironde Ferme	Hottot type
3	Malleville sur-le-Bec	V1 modified	24	Hottot les Bagues	Hottot type
* 4	Bretigny	V1 modified	25	Château Molay	V2 field launch, original
5	Le Petit Boisney	V1 modified			
6	Boissy Lamberville	V1 modified	26	Château de Beaumont	Hottot type
7	Giverville	V1 modified	27	La Meauffe	V2 and A9/A10 storage/ launch, final
8	Barville	V1 modified			
9	Bourdainville Fa veròlles	V1 modified	28	Vaubadon	V2 MT service/ maintenance
10	Berville	V1 modified			
11	Coupersarte	V1 modified	29	Château Cloay	V2 field launch, original
12	Lessard et le Chêne	V1 modified			
13	Castillon-en-Auge	V1 modified	30	Lison	V2 field launch, original
14	Les Authieux	V1 modified			
15	Mesnil Mauger	V1 modified	31	Bretteville-sur-Laize	V2 and A9/A10 MT service/maintenance
16	Quétiéville	V1 modified			
17	La Conardière	V1 modified	32	Bois de Baugy	V2 storage, final
18	Louvagny	V1 modified	33	Bois de Villers	Hottot type
19	Fierville la Campagne	V1 modified	34	St. Marc d'Ouilly	V2 forward oxygen storage, original
20	Vimont	V1 modified			
21	Haut Mesnil	V2 and A9/A10 storage/ launch, final	35	Authou	V1 storage, final
			36	Conde sur Risle	V1 storage, final

*Operational sites

TABLE 4: LOCATION OF SITES: CHERBOURG PENINSULA (MAP 4)

Site No.	Site Location	Original Purpose	Site No.	Site Location	Original Purpose
1	Sottevast	V2 bunker	28	Rauville la Bigot (I)	V1 modified
2	Brécourt	V1 bunker	29	Rauville la Bigot (II)	V1 modified
3	Silos	Rh launch silo	30	Rauville la Bigot (III)	V1 modified
4	Couville	V1 bunker	31	Bricqueboscq	V1 modified
5	Hardinvast	V1 ski	32	Bonnetot	V1 modified
6	La Motterie	V1 ski	33	La Haulle	V1 modified
7	Le Pivot	V1 ski	34	Château Golleville	V1 modified
8	La Croix Rouge	V1 ski	35	Le Quênoy	V1 modified
9	La Flague	V1 ski	36	Château de Sainte-Colombe	V1 modified
10	Château Pannelier	V1 ski			
11	La Sorellerie	V1 ski	37	Le Hameau Margot	V1 modified
12	Lorion	V1 ski	38	Hameau Piquet	V1 modified
13	Le Bel Hamelin	V1 modified	39	Bois de Denneville	V1 modified
14	Tonneville	V1 modified	40	Crossville-sur-Douve	V1 modified
15	L'Epinay Ferme	V1 modified	41	Hautmesnil	V1 modified
16	Lillerie Ferme	V1 modified	42	Cadets	V1 modified
17	La Vacquerie	V1 modified	43	Valognes	V1 storage, original
18	Montaigu la Bisette	V1 modified	44	Bricquebec	V1 storage, new
19	Les Semis	V1 modified	45	Le Poteau	V2 MT service/ maintenance
20	Le Bécot	V1 modified			
21	Hameau de Haut	V1 modified	46	Tamerville	V1 bunker
22	Château de Beaumont	V1 modified	47	Beaumont Hague	V2 launch
23	Les Fosses	V1 modified	48	Château de Chiffrevast	V2 MT service/ maintenance
24	Châteaux l'Hermitage and Rochemont	V1 modified	49	La Bordonnerie	V2 MT service/ maintenance
25	La Capitainerie, Saussemesnil (I)	V1 modified	50	Teurthéville-Bocage	V2 launch
26	Vaugoubert, Saussemesnil (II)	V1 modified	51	La Croix Frimot	V2 transit storage
27	Breuville	V1 modified			

TABLE 5: V-WEAPONS STORAGE, REAR. FINAL ORGANISATION (MAP 5)

Site	Purpose and History	Site	Purpose and History
La Bouille	V2 storage	Nogent sur Oise	V2 storage
Orival	V2 storage	Aumont	V2 storage – targetted
Nucourt	V1 storage – targetted and bombed	Ytres	V1 storage – targetted
Le Coudray	V2 storage – targetted	Renaix	V1 storage
Méry-sur-Oise	V2 storage – targetted and bombed	Bouvines	V1 storage
Forêt de l'isle Adam	V2 storage – targetted and bombed	Bernagousse	V2 storage
Villiers Adam	V2 servicing/storage/launch – targetted	Vauxaillon	V2 storage – targetted
		Billy-sur-Aisne	V2 storage
Tavernay	V2 storage – targetted	Vierzy	V2 storage
Bois de Cassan	V2 storage – targetted and bombed	Rilly la Montague	V1 storage – targetted and bombed
Parmain	V1 spares storage – targetted	Sompius	V2 storage – targetted
St Vaast les Mello	V2 storage – targetted	Tavannes	V2 storage
Thiverny	V1 storage – targetted and bombed	Commercy/Euville	V2 storage
Montataire	V2 storage	Tiercelet	V2 storage
St Leu d'Esserent	V1 storage – targetted and bombed	Peltre	V2 storage
Savonnieres en		Floreffe	V2 storage
Perthois	V2 storage – targetted	Hollogne	V2 storage
Trossy/St. Maximin	V2 storage – targetted and bombed	Bar le Duc	V2 storage

TABLE 6: ACIU LIST OF V-WEAPONS SITES, AUGUST 1944 (MAP 6)

Site Number	Site Location	Site Number	Site Location
X1/A/10A	Flottemanville-Hague I	46	St Agathe d'Aliermont
10B	Flottemanville-Hague II	47A	Puchervin
11	Bois d'Esquerdes	48	Le Mesnil-Allard
14	Valognes	49	St Martin l'Hortier
15A	Croisette	50	Drionville
17	Domléger	51	Bellevue
19	St Josse au Bois	52	Le Petit Bois Robert
20	Gueschart	53	Bois Rempre
21A	Maison Ponthieu I	54	Bois Pottier
21B	Maison Ponthieu III	55	Maisoncelle
22	Labroye	56	Pommerval
24	Brunehaut Pre Fme	57	Cormette
25	Yvrencheux/Bois de Waripel	58	Agenvillers
26A	La Glacerie	59	Behen
26B	La Sorellerie III	60	Bois Coquerel
26C	Hardinvast/La Motterie	61	Mesnil Trois Foetus
26D	Bristellerie	62	Petit Bois Tillencourt
27	Bonnetot	63	Longuemont
28	St Pierre des Jonquieres	64	Hambures
29	Preuseville	65	Ruisseauville
30	Freval	66	Le Plouy Fme
31	Bailly-La-Compagne	67	Fruges/Bois de Coupelle
32	Heuringhem	68	Lostebarne/Ardres
34	Forêt d'Hesdin	70	Cocove
36	Domart en Ponthieu	71	Vacquerie le Boucq
37	Gorenflos	72	Linghem
38	Ailly-la-Haut Clocher	73	Bois de Huit Rues
39	Bois Carré	74	Bois de la Justice
40	Ligescourt/Bois de St Saulve	75	Le Meillard
41	Mesnil au Val	76	Eclimeux
42	Herbouville	77	Belleville-en-Caux
43	Neuville-au-Bois	78	Marquenneville
44	Noyelle-en-Chausee	79	Beauvoir
45	Campneuseville	80	Quoeux

Site Number	Site Location	Site Number	Site Location
81	Montorgueil	149	Middel Straete
82A	Bois de Crequy	150	La Grande Maison
83	Vacqueriette	151	Hottot
84	Bouillancourt	152	Le Veram
85	Bonnieres	153	Claironde Fme
86	Le Nieppe	154	Vignacourt
87	Febvin Palfart	155	La Conardiere
88	Forêt Nationale de Tournehem	156	Flers
89	Les Petits Moraux	157	Fressin
90	Renescure	158	Bachimont
91	Beaulieu Ferme	159	Les Fosses
92	Château de Bosmellet	160	Château de Beaumont
93	La Sorellerie II	161	Regnauville
94	Audincthon	162	St Crois sur Mer
95	Le Grisemont	163	La Lande
96	Wisques	164	Cadets
97	Sautrecourt	165	Crepieul
99	Bois d'Enfer	166	Le Breuil
100	Zudausques	167	Le Manoir
101	Ecalles-s-Buchy	168	Breuville
102	Bois de Renty II	169	Hames Boucres
105	Belmesnil	170	La Prèe
106	Heudiere	171	Haute Côte I
107	Grand Parc	172	Le Petit Boisney
108	Les Hayons	173	Prédefin
109	St Airien	174	Coubronne
110	Ardouval	175	Le Grand Rossignol
112	Notre Dame Ferme	176	Ligescourt II
114	Bois Mecle	177	Wadicourt
115	Beaumont le Hareng	178	Blangermont
116	Biennais	179	Linzeux
117	La Longeville	180	Prouville
120	Livossart	181	Mont Louis Fme
121	Le Groseillier	182	Anderbelck
124	Beautot	183	Vaugoubert
127	Briquebec	184	L'Hey
* 128	Belhamelin – La Granchette	185	Cauches d'Ecques
129	L'Epinay Ferme	186	Bernaville
131	Fienvillers	187	Fresnoy
132	Autheux	188	Gappennes
133	Les Fontames	189	Bois de Denneville
134A	Rauville-le-Bigot	190	Haut Cote II
134B	Rauville-le-Bigot	191	Coulonvillers
135	Vauvicard	192	Remaisnil
136	Margot	193	Erny St Julien
137	Le Quesnoy	194	Le Becot
138	L'Epinette	195	Belloy sur Somme
139	Fleury	196	Fme du Forestel
140	Crepy	197	Hameau des Blonds
141	Fiefs	198	Lillerie
142	Grosville	199	Bois du Rossignol
143	Beaumetz-lès-Aire	200	Belle Croix les Bruyeres
144	Enguinegatte	201	Rimeaux
145	Piquet	202	La Belle-Hôtesse
146	Lambus	203	Noyelle en Chaussee
147	Bamieres	204	Rely
148	Bientques		

Note: * First V1 modified identified. Most V1 sites after this are modified sites.

TABLE 7: ACIU VI LAUNCH SITE LOCATIONS, HOLLAND AND GERMANY 1944–45

	Site	Location		Site	Location
1	Wallscheld	North West Germany	21	Puttershoek	North East Holland
2	Brocksheld	North West Germany	22	Ypenburg	West Holland
3	Buchel	North East Holland		(Airfield)	
4	Alfen	North East Holland	23	Rijssen/	North East Holland
5	Rohr	North West Germany		Tichedveld	
6	Greimerath	North West Germany	24	Rijssen/Haspel	North East Holland
7	Hellendoorn/	North East Holland	25	Tusveld	North East Holland
	Holterberg		26	Wierden/	North East Holland
8	Hellendoorn/	North East Holland		Kippershoek	
	Spoorwegdoch		27	Almelo/	North East Holland
9	Eckfield	North West Germany		Berkwoode	
10	Huize Joppe	North East Holland	28	Almelo/	North East Holland
11	Schoonheten	North East Holland		Kollenveld	
12	Oolden	North East Holland	29	Falkenberg I	North West Germany
13	Joppe	North East Holland	30	Falkenberg II	North West Germany
14	Lettele	North East Holland		(Tondorf)	
15	Lommdspdorf	North West Germany	31	Heiroth	North West Germany
16	Braakhek	North East Holland	32	Kelberg	North West Germany
17	Billenbfuren	North East Holland	33	Gelenberg	North West Germany
18	Rotterdam A	West Holland	34	Willwerscheld	North West Germany
	(North)		35	Rotterdam/	West Holland
19	Rotterdam B	West Holland		Vlaardingen	
	(South)		36	Delf/Hamwoning	West Holland
20	Urschmitt	West Holland			

≠   Altenwalde – British V2 launches, Operation 'Backfire'

MAPS NOTE:

IGN – Institute Graphique Nationale is the French equivalent of the OS large-scale maps in the UK.

KEY TO FEATURES OF VI SITE PLANS (CHAPTER 4)

1 Compass alignment pad
2 Launch pad
3 Launch bunker
4 Garage/workshop
5 Concrete parking
6 Additional parking or passing place
7 Sentry post
8 Launch ramp support blocks
9 Water tank

Prologue

France is a vast open-air museum of military architecture. Like the United Kingdom, it has medieval castles, but, from the Middle Ages onwards, it also has a unique record of military history. From 1660 to 1700 Louis XIV's military engineer, Vauban, fortified the towns and cities on France's borders and his expertise ensured that France became virtually impregnable on land. Vauban's designs ushered in a new era of reliable artillery and the musket, and the remains of his work are still visible around France, and were still being used in the First World War.

Over two hundred years later Minister of War André Maginot spearheaded the 1930 Bill to finance the new fortifications along France's eastern frontier with Germany. But the 'Maginot Line' was obsolete before it was completed, and this vast system has become a museum exhibit in its own right. Only ten years after Maginot's Bill, Hitler and the Organisation Todt made their own contribution to this open air museum: first, the 'West Wall' of Fortress Europe, quickly followed by the vast complex of sites built for the V-weapons.

From the halcyon days of the Third Reich in 1942 the V-weapons offensive was organised on a grand scale, with little thought that anyone would, or could, interfere with those plans that would usher in another new era of weaponry. But by 1943 everything was coming unstuck, including the V-weapons offensive. What had begun in a methodically planned fashion quickly turned into a deadly game of hide and seek with Allied air power and agents.

Despite this, the V1 and its new 'modified' launch sites were ready in June 1944 for the signal to GO. In addition the V2 sites were almost ready to play their part in the offensive. But once again circumstances changed. D-Day ensured that virtually all the French sites were quickly lost or became unusable and the V-weapons offensive was cut short. Had this not been the case, there is no doubt that, left to their own devices, the V-weapons would have had the capability to reduce southern England, including its ports, to an impotent spectator to the war against Russia.

Although England was the main target for these weapons, Peenemünde had designed a two-stage rocket capable of reaching America, the A9/A10 and although Dornberger and Von Braun and other members of the team claimed that the weapon only existed on the drawing board, evidence has now come to light which shows this to be another 'Peenemünde lie'.

The vast complex of sites is still there. Some are now museums, but all are worthy of investigation, and all of them are now part of this unique landscape.

Introduction

In the Second World War Germany built four long-range, unmanned weapons capable of reaching targets in the UK from mainland Europe. Undoubtedly the main driving force behind the development of these weapons was the failure of the Wehrmacht to conquer or subdue Britain in 1940 and 1941. The Luftwaffe had been unable to deliver the knock-out blow that Goering had promised and the fact was that the Royal Navy was still intact and capable of destroying any invasion fleet protected by Hitler's new navy. Only the U-boats were having any measure of success – but no country had been forced to surrender solely by the action of submarines, and it was unlikely that even Doenitz believed his force alone could provide the answer where others had failed.

The spectre haunting Hitler and his military planners as they put the finishing touches to Operation Barbarossa, the invasion of Russia in July 1941, was the prospect of fighting on two fronts. Warnings against this went back to the early 1800s and the influential Prussian military general and strategist Karl von Clausewitz. In his book *On War*, which had become the basis for the total war concept used in Germany up to the First World War, he emphasised the perils of fighting on two fronts and insisted that it must be avoided at all costs.

One new group of weapons in Hitler's armoury did offer the possibility of a solution to the problem in the West. Even if they were not actually able to defeat Great Britain, these new weapons with the help of the U-boats, should be able to render Britain militarily impotent and incapable of influencing any of the German military plans in the foreseeable future. Ever since Hitler's rise to power in 1933, military minds in Germany had been allowed to investigate any new methods of warfare, especially as the hated Versailles 'Diktat' had banned or severely restricted most types of conventional military forces. Within this framework of military freedom, unmanned long-range weapons offered many advantages over their conventional relations. The more obvious advantages were the lack of a human crew and the possibility of the missiles travelling at unheard-of speeds, unencumbered by the trappings of aircraft and able to outrun enemy aircraft.

By 1940 two of these new weapons were well into their development programme, the Luftwaffe and the Army working on what became known as the V1 and V2 respectively. In addition two other weapons were also arriving on the scene, the Rheinböte (Rhine messenger), which was the back-up to the V1, and Rochling's 'Hochdruckpumpe' (High Pressure Pump), the original version of the 'super-gun'. All four weapons had at least

Opposite: The V2 test site at Blizna, Poland, 1944. This tower was used for pre-launch assembly and testing. (PRO)

one basic similarity, even in their original concepts: they had a range of at least 150 miles which meant that they were all capable of reaching the principal target area: Great Britain. Coverage stretched from the Channel coast to a line drawn across the country from Bristol in the west to Norwich in the east – an area that included the capital London and all the main ports which could be used to launch an invasion of Europe.

The conquest of Holland, Belgium and France in the spring and summer of 1940 meant that a huge potential site area for the new weapons suddenly became available. Northern France especially, with its Channel coastline and extensive rural and wooded areas, was the obvious choice for the launching, servicing and storage of the new weapons. Sites from Calais to Caen could cover the whole of Southern England, including London, while the Cherbourg Peninsula, jutting out into the Channel, was the ideal location for sites covering the West as far as Bristol. Another advantage of the northernmost area of France was its industry, especially cement – a crucial ingredient for the ever more ambitious building programme. France's industrial heartland lay in the north, in an area from Calais inland to Lille, Mons down to Cambrai and Arras and back to the coast; it was a vast jungle of factories producing coal, steel, cement and power. In addition there was a rail network linking the area with the rest of Europe. As the V-weapons offensive got under way this area of northern France was turned into one gigantic weapons site covering over 3,000 square miles.

WITH GRATEFUL THANKS. . . .

A great many organisations helped me to research this book, among them the National Air and Space Museum, Washington DC, and the Imperial War Museum, London. Special thanks must go to the Public Records Office, London, whose archives hold most of the official material on the V-weapons sites and whose staff always give a friendly and helpful service. The French naval authorities at Cherbourg were of great assistance when inspecting the Brécourt and Castel Vendou sites.

Space does not permit me to acknowledge in person, the kindness and long memories of all the many wartime survivors whom I met in the course of my extensive site visits; ex-members of the RAF and the Allied Central Interpretation Unit (ACIU), various fellow enthusiasts around the world and, not least, my wife Jean and our children, who might well have preferred to holiday somewhere sunnier.

Finally, we should remember those men and women of the RAF, USAF and other Allied forces and the bravery of Resistance workers and SOE agents who risked torture and death to ensure the ultimate failure of Hitler's V-weapons. In the forest near Les Hallots V1 launch site is a memorial to two young men, shot on 24 June 1944: 'They fought and died in the shadows'.

CHAPTER I

The V-Weapons –
A Brief History

1.1 THE V1 – 'DOODLEBUG'

The original interest of the German Air Ministry (*Reichs LuftMinisterium*, RLM) had been in unmanned target drones and battlefield surveillance aircraft – little more than powered model aircraft – but as war approached potential enemy targets became more clearly defined. The specification changed in the late 1930s to an unmanned aircraft carrying a 1-ton bomb load over a maximum range of 300 miles, a huge leap forward for the technology of the day. The RLM project was given the codenames 'Flakzielgerat 76' (Flak target equipment) and 'Kirschkern' (cherry stone), later to be referred to as Vengeance Weapon 1, or V1. Contractors working on the project were Argus for the fuselage-mounted ram (pulse) jet, Arado for the airframe and Lorenz for the guidance/control system, and the whole emphasis was on simplicity and the use of basic, non-strategic materials such as wood and mild steel. By June 1942, when the design was finalised, Fieseler were in charge of the overall project and Askania the guidance/control system.

By this time the V1 was a mid-wing monoplane having a wingspan of 17ft 3in, a tailplane span of 6ft 9in, overall length 27ft, maximum fuselage diameter 2ft 9in and a fully loaded weight of 4,800lb, of which 1,800lb was the high-explosive warhead. The ram jet motor, 11ft 3in long and 1ft 11in maximum diameter, sat on top of the fuselage and used low-octane petrol, producing a maximum thrust of 800lb. The ram jet is simplicity itself, with a minimum of moving parts. The front of the motor tube was occupied by a spring-loaded square grid valve, looking like a car radiator, into which fuel was injected and ignited initially by a single sparkplug. The vanes on the grid valve opened and closed at a frequency of around 50 cycles/second, giving the V1 its characteristic buzzing sound (someone once said it sounded like a Model T Ford going up-hill). The main disadvantage of the ram jet is that the air-fuel mixture has to be compressed in the combustion chamber, hence the V1 needed to be in forward motion before full thrust could be achieved. This meant that either a ramp launch was required, using an external power source to propel it along the ramp until flying speed was reached, or it could be launched from an aircraft, but the latter method added a complication that contradicted the original concept of the weapon – its freedom from manned aircraft. Nevertheless aircraft launch was an option that was kept in mind for the future as a means of extending the weapons range.

The only really complicated part of the V1 was the auto-pilot which utilised two gyros: a vertical reference gyro linked to an aneroid barometer controlled elevators in the tail to provide height control and a directional gyro linked to a magnetic compass controlled the rudder via servo motors. Power for the system was provided by compressed air stored in two wire-wound spheres located in the fuselage behind the main spar. With the only directional control being provided by the rudder, this meant that if side-winds were encountered during flight the V1 adopted a crab-like attitude to maintain its bearing. Strong side-winds caused problems with target accuracy. In normal manned aircraft, ailerons in the wing-tips move in opposite directions to produce a rolling movement which is then combined with rudder movement to produce a change in direction – the 'twist and steer' principle – but with the V1 simplicity was the overriding factor. This simplicity produced a weapon that was far from perfect, as the directional gyro could be 'tumbled' if the fuselage was rotated through more than ±85 deg., a fact discovered by Allied fighter pilots who found that by raising the V1's wing-tips with those of their own aircraft, the V1 eventually became unstable and dived into the ground. In addition, in theory at least, the V1 could not change direction owing to its lack of ailerons. However, if the wings were given some positive dihedral (that is, when viewed from the front the wing-tips were higher than the wing centres), and the wings were placed slightly above the fuselage centre-line, this provided the ability to produce a small amount of roll. Later in the V1 offensive some V1s were equipped with a timer device which used this turn and roll sequence to give a few degrees change in direction, which meant that the launch ramp need not be directly aligned on the target. (It was this ramp alignment that had originally confirmed to the Allies that the main target was London.)

Flight testing of the ram jet started in 1941 with the motor slung beneath the fuselage of a Gotha 145 biplane. In early 1942 this was supplemented by testing at operational speeds using Me 109 and 110 aircraft, with full-size launches from Fw 200s, using the Luftwaffe research establishment at Peenemünde-West. Two launch ramps were built at Peenemünde-West, originally using Rheinmetal-Borsig solid-fuel boosters to accelerate the V1 along the ramp. Due to various problems, this method was changed to a catapult using high-pressure steam generated by hydrogen peroxide (HTP) and a catalyst, potassium or calcium permanganate, a system developed by the firm of Herman Walter of Kiel.

The first successful launch using the new Walter catapult took place on 24 December 1942, the V1 flying on for 130 miles along the Baltic coastline from Peenemünde. On 19 June 1942, at a top level RLM meeting chaired by Field Marshal Erhard Milch, it was decided to give the V1 maximum priority to produce an operational weapon, with all testing being transferred to Peenemünde-West. Work started on the formation of a group capable of launching the V1 as an operational weapon in the field.

By May 1943 testing was progressing satisfactorily but performance was down on specification. Originally it was intended to fly at 450–500mph over a range of 300 miles, but this was now reduced to 350–400mph over a maximum range of 200 miles, mainly because of increased weight and drag. Nevertheless, a relatively cheap and easily manufactured weapon was now being produced, eminently suitable for mass-production using semi-skilled labour, and if the few loose ends could be tidied up the Luftwaffe believed they had a successful weapon. Mass-production was planned to begin at the Volkswagen plant at Fallersleben in September 1943; the target was to make 1,400 V1s by January 1944, rising to 8,000 per month by September 1944.

For the operational ramp launches in northern France a new Luftwaffe organisation was formed. FlakRegiment 155(W), under the command of Colonel Max Wachtel, had a total staff of 3,500, comprising four Abteilung (Companies), each with two services and supply sections and four launch firing teams. Each firing team was capable of manning four launch sites and hence, in theory at least, a maximum of 64 V1s could be launched simultaneously. The operational group moved down the coast from Peenemünde to Zinnowitz and launch training was carried out from two ramps located at nearby Zempin. In addition, air-launches were not forgotten and in 1943 Gruppe III of Kampfgeschwader 3 was formed for this purpose and equipped with 40 He 111H-22s. This bomber was then being phased out of front-line service, but its sturdy structure and docile flying qualities proved

Peenemünde, the Zinnowitz V1 training site at Zempin for Luftwaffe teams using the weapon in France. (PRO)

ideal for carrying a single V1 under the port wing. This aspect of the testing programme went ahead smoothly as the V1 proved to be extremely stable when air-dropped, developing no pitching oscillations, but only a slight lateral movement that quickly damped itself out.

By the start of 1943 the original site building programme had begun in northern France and the initial date for the offensive against the UK was set for 15 February 1944, by which time it was expected that 1,400 V1s would be available for the offensive. However, the Allied bombing campaign intervened with both the Fieseler works at Kassel and the Volkswagen plant at Fallersleben being on the target list and by the end of 1943 it was obvious that the 15 February date was unrealistic. In addition, Peenemünde had been bombed by the RAF on 17 August 1943. Although both Zinnowitz and Zempin were untouched, after a meeting with Himmler only two days later, Hitler decided that all mass-production facilities for both the V1 and the V2 should be moved to a new underground factory, Mittelwerke or Central Works as it became known, in the Hartz Mountains at Kohnstein near Nordhausen. The SS were to supervise the enlargement of some existing tunnels using forced labour from the concentration camps. Buchenwald, for example, was nearby.

The move to Nordhausen in March 1944 disrupted production again and not until April 1944 did the number of V1s available for operations reach the 1,000 mark. But in the

V1s being moved out of storage. RH trolley is as used for general site movements. LH trolley is the double, spring mounted trolley used to place the V1 onto the ramp. (IWM)

bomb proof atmosphere, mass-production of the relatively simple V1 increased dramatically, to such an extent that by the middle of June, when the offensive finally started from the French sites, almost 12,000 missiles were ready for use and production was running at 8,000 per month. The total production for 1944 was over 26,000. Although the transfer of FlakRegiment 155(W) and Colonel Wachtel to France in October 1943 had been premature, their time was put to good use in making sure that the sites available in France were fully operational and ready for use on 12/13 June 1944, the start of the offensive.

1.2 THE V2 AND A9/A10 AMERICA ROCKET

The V2 rocket also had humble beginnings in the early 1930s. Interest in rockets could trace its ancestry back to the Berlin amateur rocket society, the Verein fur Raumschiffart (VfR), which included most of the early rocket experts in Germany such as Hermann Oberth, Max Valier, Rudolf Niebel, Willy Ley and Klaus Riedel. They fired their crude rockets from the Berlin suburb of Reinickerdorf and in 1930 they were joined by the 18-year-old student Wernher von Braun. The Army, in particular the Ordnance Branch of the

V1, assembly of wings to fuselage. (IWM)

Ballistics and Weapons Office led by General Becker, was also interested in rocketry and Captain Walter Dornberger was appointed to lead a team investigating the military potential of this new device. In 1932 the VfR demonstrated a liquid-fuelled rocket to Dornberger and other officers at the Army's Kummersdorf firing range and shortly afterwards the VfR was shut down by the Gestapo and its members disbanded. From now on rockets were a military secret.

Dornberger was convinced that liquid- not solid-fuel rockets were the way forward and from 1933 he rapidly started building a team of specialists in the various disciplines required. They included civilian personnel, among them the newly qualified von Braun. In 1933–4 work at Kummersdorf near Berlin was concentrated on producing a reliable liquid-fuelled rocket motor, using liquid oxygen (LOX) as the main propellant, to power the first rocket design from Dornberger's new team. It was given the designation A1. Completed at the end of 1933, the A1 was 5ft long, 15in diameter and powered by the now reliable 650lb thrust motor. Unfortunately the A1 was unstable, but by December 1934 its successor, the A2, was ready for launch. It was similar in size to the A1, but gyroscopes were used in the control system to make it more stable. During tests on the island of Borkum in the North Sea, two A2s were successfully launched, reaching a height of 1.5 miles. By 1936 the team had increased to 150 specialists and in March the new 3,500lb thrust motor was demonstrated before Army personnel including the Commander-in-Chief, General Frisch. This demonstration, which showed how a powerful rocket motor could be switched off at the flick of a switch, proved to be the turning-point for Dornberger. Funds were allocated to his project and permission given to build a new rocket facility in a suitably remote part of Germany. Von Braun suggested the island of Usedom in the Baltic. After inspections by the Army and Luftwaffe, it was agreed that they would use the tip of the island, near the village of Peenemünde, to build both Dornberger's new rocket base and a Luftwaffe research establishment, complete with airfield, costs being divided between the two services with the Luftwaffe's construction branch looking after most of the building work.

With building work at Peenemünde well advanced by the middle of 1937, Dornberger's team had progressed to the A3 rocket but they were perhaps over-confident after the success of the A2 and the A3 proved to be a step too far for their existing knowledge. The A3 was 25ft long, with a maximum diameter of 2ft 6in, and used the latest liquid-fuel motor of 3,500lb thrust. With launch pads not yet available at Peenemünde-East, a makeshift launch facility was built on the neighbouring island of Greifswald Oie. Four A3s were launched from Oie in the winter of 1937/8 and all were failures. After climbing to a few hundred feet, they lost stability and crashed into the sea, and it was realised that the step from the small A2 to the A3 had been carried out without the necessary testing, which should have included a systematic programme of scale-model trials to confirm all the important design features.

With the A4, later to be called the V2, already in the planning stage, a new test vehicle was rapidly introduced to the development programme. The A5 was of the same overall dimensions as the A3 but had new control surfaces, and the electrical firm Siemens was contracted to produce a more reliable gyro control system. The Zeppelin company's subsonic wind tunnel at Friedrichshafen and the University of Aachen's small supersonic tunnel were both used to produce a more refined aerodynamic design and to carry out testing on the control and stability of the new rocket design. A flight test programme started in 1938 with the dropping of inert one-fifth scale-models of the A5 from He 111s, from heights of up to 20,000ft. With the rockets tracked by cine-theodolite cameras from the ground, the speed of sound, Mach 1, was exceeded in steep dives at heights below 5,000ft. The test rockets deployed parachutes in the tail and were very often available for re-use in the test programme. Due to delays in Siemens producing the control system, four inert full-size A5s with fixed control surfaces were launched from aircraft in July 1938 to confirm the basic stability of the design and all these test vehicles performed satisfactorily over flights of up to 5 miles at subsonic speeds.

In the final series of tests in March 1939 one-fifth scale-models with fixed controls were launched from Peenemünde, powered by a new HTP rocket motor developed by the Walter company. These successful trials, at which supersonic speeds were reached, provided the final data required by Dornberger for the full-scale A5 tests. In October 1939 two uncontrolled A5s using the 3,500lb motor were launched from Peenemünde, and this time there were no problems, both rockets reaching heights of 7.5 miles. The third A5 was fitted with the Siemens control gear which rotated the vertical axis of the pitch gyroscope towards the horizontal position four seconds after launch. This axis change was fed back via servo motors to the control surfaces which applied the necessary movements to bring the rocket's pitch axis in-line with those of the gyroscope. This resulted in the rocket's trajectory following a gradual curve until a position was reached which produced the required range.

Over the next two years, from October 1939 to 1941, twenty-five A5s were launched without a single failure. All were recovered by parachute, and some were used several times in the test programme. These trials covered all aspects of the later A4 (V2), including the use of the Würzburg Riese radar situated on the mainland a few miles behind the launch pad. The A5 differed in one major aspect from the A4: the alcohol/oxygen fuel mixture was injected into the combustion chamber using pressurised nitrogen. The A4 developed a thrust of 56,000lb at launch and used 7.5 tons of fuel a minute, so obviously compressed nitrogen would not be suitable in these circumstances. Two very powerful fuel pumps were needed, but they had to be small enough to fit within the crowded motor compartment of the rocket. Eventually the Kiel firm of Hellmuth Walter produced a miniature turbine with rotating blades; only 19in in diameter, it was powered by steam generated by HTP and a catalyst, this driving the pumps supplying fuel to the motor.

By 1941 the construction work at Peenemünde-East, Dornberger's rocket base, was largely complete and all the facilities were operational including the very advanced supersonic wind tunnel, capable of operating at between Mach 1.2 and Mach 4.5, speeds unimaginable in 1941. Peenemünde had its own docks, power station, liquid oxygen plant, workers and PoW camps, plus everything associated with a town of 20,000 inhabitants. Despite the progress at Peenemünde, Dornberger was engaged in a constant battle with the military planners and this became particularly heated after the early successes of the conventional military forces against Poland and France up to June 1940. The failure of the Luftwaffe later in 1940 and 1941 to defeat the RAF improved the situation for Dornberger and removed any possibility of his establishment being shut down. Even its priority ratings for materials, etc., the project's life-blood, gradually improved as the military situation slowly deteriorated from late 1942 onwards.

The first A4 launch was scheduled for 13 June 1942 and, as was usual for occasions such as this, the 'launch' of a new weapon on which a vast amount of resources had been spent, there was a large gathering of VIPs to witness the event, including military and political leaders including Albert Speer the new Armaments Minister. The 46ft A4 must have been an impressive sight to the visitors, most of whom were seeing the

A V2 launch under British control, Operation 'Backfire', 1945 (PRO)

rocket for the first time. Despite the extensive pre-launch checks, just two seconds after motor ignition A4-001 fell back on to the pad and exploded as 10 tons of volatile fuel ignited in a massive fireball. On 16 August 1942 002 was launched successfully, minus the VIPs, only to break up after 45 seconds when travelling at Mach 3. Telemetry records indicated that the motor had stopped abruptly, the resulting rapid deceleration causing structural failure. No A4s were ever recovered intact owing to the supersonic impact velocity, but the point of impact in the sea was indicated by coloured dye carried in the dummy warhead.

Despite these failures 003 was prepared for launch on 3 October 1942 and this time the rocket made a perfect flight, falling into the sea 120 miles along the coast, only 2.5 miles from the predicted impact point. The success of this flight confirmed a vast amount of theoretical data and claimed a number of 'firsts'. When it reached Mach 1 at 26 seconds, it was the first time any guided missile had exceeded the speed of sound. At 58 seconds the motor was shut down by a radio signal and the rocket, travelling at Mach 5 at a height of 100,000ft, carried on as a ballistic missile, reaching an apex height of 60 miles before plunging downwards in an arc towards the ground. Re-entering the Earth's atmosphere at over 3,000mph, the outside skin temperature rose to 650°C as drag slowed it down to 2,000mph, Mach 3, at which speed it hit the sea. The plotting of the rocket's trajectory was carried out by two systems, both using the Würzburg Riese radars, initially from the set located behind the launch pad on the mainland and during the trajectory from a string of stations along the Baltic coastline. During the flight, information on temperatures, pressures and so on was transmitted from the rocket via a coded telemetry link to a ground receiver near the first Würzburg Riese.

Following this successful launch Dornberger and von Braun, who was now Peenemünde's scientific head, issued a report detailing the progress to date and the possible plans for the use of the A4 as a military weapon, with an expected output of 4,000 V2s in the first year of operations. This report, issued in November 1942, was circulated to military, political and industrial leaders and, despite some adverse comment from Dornberger's superiors, it was generally agreed that mass-production should go ahead. This was endorsed by Armaments Minister Albert Speer, who appointed Gerhard Degenkolb as director of the mass-production programme. Degenkolb was chosen because he had transformed locomotive production at the Krupp and Henschel works by using standardised designs in place of traditional production methods, increasing production from 1,900 locomotives in 1941 to 5,500 by 1943. Despite the enthusiastic statements made by Dornberger and von Braun, the fact was that the V2 had never been designed for mass-production. Each rocket was assembled by hand by a skilled workforce, and no mass-production plans or equipment existed at that time. However, Degenkolb quickly produced plans for 300 V2s to be manufactured in October 1943, rising to 900 per month by December. These V2s were to be produced at the pre-production works at Peenemünde, originally intended for small-scale production, at the Zeppelin GmbH works at Friedrichshafen and at the Henschel-Rax works at Wiener-Neustadt.

On 26 May 1943 a joint demonstration was held at Peenemünde for both military and civilian VIPs at which both the V1 and V2 were to be launched during the day's activities. In the event, both the V1s launched crashed soon afterwards but both V2s made perfect flights. The timing of this demonstration was undoubtedly linked to the worsening fortunes of the German military machine. The mass-bombing attacks on the Third Reich had started in 1942 with raids on Lübeck and Rostock, followed by those on Kiel and Dortmund, with the first 1,000-bomber raid taking place on Cologne on 30 May 1942. These heavy air-raids continued through to 1943 with Hamburg and Berlin being regular targets. At sea the U-boats had lost the initiative in the battle of the Atlantic as Allied countermeasures improved, to such an extent that between April and May 1943 Doenitz was losing almost one U-boat for every Allied ship sunk. This was an unacceptable ratio and it forced a complete review of the U-boat campaign. On land, 1943 had started badly and was getting worse. On 30 January Field Marshal Paulus and what was left of the Sixth Army surrendered at Stalingrad and on 12 May the Afrika Korps surrendered to the Allies in Tunisia with the loss of over 240,000 German and Italian troops and most of their equipment. This was bad enough, but worse was to come. In the winter of 1942/3 the Russians recaptured the city of Kursk and in the early summer of 1943 they gathered together a massive armoured force to recapture the Briansk–Orel region and the capital of the Ukraine, Kharkov.

To Hitler, in his East Prussian headquarters, the 'bulge' in the Russian line seemed to present an ideal opportunity to repeat one of the classic encirclement movements of

1941/2 and destroy the very same armies that had been victorious at Stalingrad, before continuing the advance towards Moscow and Stalingrad. Despite amassing a huge amount of armour, guns, aircraft and men of the 2nd, 9th and 4th Armies, when the Battle of Kursk started on 5 July 1943 the German commander Field Marshal Manstein quickly realised that there was to be no repeat of earlier victories. After four days the bulge had only been dented by 10 miles in the north and 30 miles in the south and the tips of the two German pincers were still 100 miles apart. On 12 July the main Russian counter-attack started when it became clear that the German offensive had run out of steam. Orel was recaptured on 4 August and Kharkov on the 23rd, gaining a gradual momentum that would carry the Russian armies to Berlin. Operation Zitadelle cost the Germans heavy losses, which in many cases they were unable to replace. Some 70,000 men were killed or wounded, and 3,000 tanks, 1,000 guns, 1,300 aircraft and 5,000 other vehicles were destroyed.

On 7 July 1943, just two days after the start of Operation Zitadelle, Dornberger and von Braun were ordered to Hitler's Rastenburg headquarters, together with films, models and displays of the V2 and its development. After watching the complete presentation, Hitler ordered immediate changes to the V2 mass-production programme, increasing the original Degenkolb figure of 900 V2s per month to 2,000 by December 1943 with the extra production being carried out at the Demag works at Falkensee. Karl Saur, one of Speer's department heads and an old Nazi Party confidant of Hitler's, was given the job of coordinating the new mass-production programme. Colonel Dornberger was promoted on the spot to major-general and von Braun was given the title of Professor. They returned to Peenemünde with a new sense of urgency and the highest possible priority rating for V2 development work, Dringende Entwicklung (DE). The following day Albert Speer and Degenkolb also arrived at Rastenburg, to hear about the changes to the V2 programme direct from Hitler. Speer's success at increasing armaments production despite the Allied air-raids had earned Hitler's respect and hence, with Speer's knowledge of the problems regarding mass-producing the V2, the production figures were amended again on the 9th. The 900 target was moved forward to October, with 1,300 being produced by December with a gradual increase to 1,800 per month by April 1944.

These new plans were thrown into disarray on the night of 17 August 1943 when 597 bombers of the RAF attacked Peenemünde for the first time. Despite the marker flares being slightly off-target and the main damage being done to civilian accommodation, some of the rocket facilities were damaged and two senior members of von Braun's team were killed, including Dr Thiel who was in charge of rocket motor development. In addition, the raid on Peenemünde had been preceded by raids on Friedrichshafen and Wiener-Neustadt, seriously affecting the mass-production plans for these sites. The pre-production building at Peenemünde escaped virtually undamaged and it was from here that the first operational V2s were produced and passed to the new field training organisation set up by Dornberger, Lehr und Versuchs Batterie 444, which moved to Zinnowitz for its initial training. Batterie 444 was established to instruct personnel in the operational use of the V2, and training included the handling of live warheads where necessary. The bombing of Peenemünde on 17 August 1943 and the worsening military

The elliptical launch pad, Test Stand VII, at Peenemünde. A V2 is just visible on a trailer. Inset: The same view after bombing raids in August/September 1943.

Fitting a live warhead at a test site, probably Blizna. The V2 warhead was codenamed 'Elefant'. (PRO)

situation produced another highly significant result. Heinrich Himmler, head of the SS, had visited Peenemünde on at least one occasion early in 1943, and two days after the Peenemünde raid he flew to Rastenburg to discuss the whole V-weapons programme with Hitler. It would not have been difficult to convince Hitler that further changes were needed if the V2 in particular was going to be an effective weapon. It was quite likely that Peenemünde and the V2 mass-production sites would be visited again by Allied bombers and Himmler offered an alternative. He suggested that a new testing and launch base should be set up at an SS training ground at Blizna in Poland, between Cracow and Lvov, known to the SS as Heidelager. Here, surrounded by pine forests and remote from Allied bombers, all future launches and test work could be carried out in safety and the SS would provide a back-up role, including security. In addition, mass-production could

A standard V2 produced by slave labour at the Central Works, Nordhausen, ready for transport by rail to the Dutch launching sites, November 1944. (IWM)

be moved to some underground mine workings, then used for storing strategic chemicals, at Kohnstein near Nordhausen in the Hartz Mountains. The existing tunnels could be enlarged to provide ample production space for the V2, V1 and any other essential war *matériel*, in a secure, bomb-proof environment. The nearby Buchenwald concentration camp would provide the labour force to enlarge the tunnels, and once again the SS would look after security. The area was already under SS administration through SS Colonel Dr Wagner, which would simplify the administration of the move. Hitler approved Himmler's plans and by 22 August 1943, following meetings between Hitler, Speer, Saur and Himmler, the necessary orders were put into effect.

The SS now had a major executive role in the V2 project and, although there was little technical input at that time, eventually the whole project would be under SS control. The man chosen by Himmler to take up this executive role was one of the rising stars of the SS organisation, SS Brigadeführer und General der Waffen SS Dr Ing. Hans Kammler. An SS technocrat with a low-profile public image but who wielded a vast amount of power behind the scenes, Kammler was eventually personally appointed by Hitler to be in charge of the whole V-weapons programme and jet aircraft production. Before Nordhausen was completed, the original V2 production facilities were repaired and in September and October 1943 the first mass-produced V2s were transported to the Blizna range for test and training purposes.

The Army had also made arrangements for the operational use of the V1 in the field for, although the V1 was strictly a Luftwaffe weapon, the Luftwaffe had no ground organisation suitable for this purpose. Two experienced artillery officers were involved:

Lieutenant-General Erich Heinemann was in overall control of both the V2 and V1 operations, while Major-General Richard Metz was in charge of the V2.

By January 1944 Nordhausen was in production and up to the end of February the total production was 140 V2s, rising to 300 by April and 600 in August. The figures for October and November were 650, December 618, January 1945 700, February 615 and March 490, these numbers being supplemented by production from the original sites. The human cost of the Nordhausen project was huge. Dornberger, von Braun and other senior members of the Peenemünde team were all involved in the project from day one, attending meetings when necessary, but after the war they denied any knowledge of the harsh treatment of the forced labour. A new concentration camp for the workers, Dora, was built adjacent to the main works entrance and over 15,000 prisoners were brought in from Buchenwald camp. Eventually the workforce totalled 32,000, housed in 31 sub-camps to the main Dora camp, which had its own crematorium. It has been estimated that during construction of the site at Nordhausen the death rate was 17,000 per year, and the tunnel complex stretched for 22 miles and housed a Junkers' aero engine plant and factories making U-boat and aircraft components.

By the middle of 1944 there were sufficient V2s coming off the production lines for an offensive to be scheduled to start later in the year. By now there were four Army operational groups, Batteries 444, 485, 836 and 191 Motorised, and in addition the SS had also formed its own group, SS-Werfer Batterie 500. All five groups were now stationed at Blizna, putting the finishing touches to their training before moving to northern France. With the SS playing an ever-increasing role in both the V1 and V2 projects, Himmler had von Braun and two of his senior engineers, Riedel and Gottrup, arrested on 15 March 1944 and it was only after the personal intervention of Albert Speer that they were released after two days. It was a sign of what was to come.

On 20 July 1944 another event took place that virtually ensured that the SS would soon be in complete control of the V-weapons programme. An attempt was made on Hitler's life at his Rastenburg headquarters. A briefcase bomb was placed under a conference table and at precisely 12.50 p.m. it exploded. However, because of the hot weather the daily conference was taking place in a wooden building among the pine trees, with the windows open to admit fresh air. This reduced the effect of the blast, as did the solid structure of the table. Stenographer Berger was killed outright, and General Gunther Korten, Luftwaffe Chief of Staff, General Rudolf Schmundt, Chief Adjutant of the Armed Forces and Colonel Heinz Brandt died later of their injuries. Hitler himself was not seriously injured, although his hair was singed, his right arm and leg were bruised and his eardrums were affected by the blast. Action against conspirators, real or imaginary, was swift and ruthless, and one of those implicated was General Friedrich Fromm, Commander-in-Chief of the Reserve Army and also Chief of the Heereswaffenamt, the Army Weapons Office, which controlled all the Army's rocket and weapons projects including the V2. With Fromm arrested, Himmler wasted no time in making sure that he took over his responsibilities. Indeed, Hitler actually appointed Himmler as Fromm's successor on the same day as the failed bomb plot.

On 6 August Kammler was promoted to lieutenant-general by Himmler and on the same day Hitler appointed Kammler as Plenipotentiary (General Commissioner) for all aspects of the Army's V-weapons projects. Complaints from Speer, Dornberger and von Braun that these moves usurped their authority and responsibilities on the projects were dismissed and now the SS had almost complete control of all the V-weapons projects.

Even before the V2 had made its first successful flight on 3 October 1942, Peenemünde was working on the next generation of long-range rockets. The relatively simple task of adding swept-back wings of 20ft (6.1m) span to the V2 increased the maximum range from 200 miles to between 350 and 400 miles, the final trajectory being a high-speed glide: this was the A4(b). But the real prize was a rocket capable of flying the Atlantic, the 'America rocket'. The U-boats had failed to stop supplies reaching Britain from American soil; untouched by war, a rocket offensive, with suitable warheads, could be the decisive factor in preventing the inevitable invasion of northern France.

The experts at Peenemünde already appreciated that to obtain a range of several thousand miles, the only solution was a multi-stage rocket, the first stage providing the boost for the rocket to reach the required height and velocity for the second stage's intercontinental flight. By 1941 drawings were being produced of the A9/A10 two-stage rocket, the A10 being the booster and the A9 being similar to the A4(b) but with reduced wing span to fit inside the A10's body. The main details known about the A9/A10 are shown in the table. For simplicity, the A10 booster appears to have been equipped with a scaled-up version of the V2's rocket motor, although a six-motor version had been considered.

	Combined A9/A10	V2
Max. body diameter:	13.6ft (4.2m)	5.4ft (1.7m)
Max. diameter over fins:	29.5ft (9m)	11.6ft (3.5m)
Overall length:	85.8ft (26m)	46.6ft (14.1m)
Take-off weight:	93.9 tons (93,900 kg)	12.7 tons (12,700kg)
Maximum thrust:	200 tons (70,000 kg)	8.8 tons

Trajectory details reveal that, after 60 sec and at an altitude of 120 miles, the A9 would deploy, when the A10 was expected to parachute back to earth. At a maximum all-burnt altitude of 200/250 miles the A9 would continue on an extended glide, giving a range of up to 3,500 miles. A large number of heavily populated and industrial areas on the eastern side of the USA, including New York, would have been within reach of the A9/A10, especially from launch sites in western France. The 'official' Peenemünde history of the long-range versions of the V2 is brief. Two A4(b)s were launched on 8 and 24 January 1945, the first was a failure but the second reached a height of 50 miles, but according to Dornberger and von Braun, the A9/A10 never progressed beyond the drawing board stage. However, documentation in the PRO, Kew shows that in 1944 new underground facilities were being built in France to handle rockets twice the size of the V2. The SS and in particular General Kammler were now in charge of the V-weapons programme and white elephant sites such as Watten, Hitler's showpiece rocket base, had been ruthlessly scrapped. In fact the whole V-weapons site organisation was being radically overhauled in light of the new military situation the Third Reich found itself in, from late 1943 onwards. Time had now become a critical factor and in these circumstances the probability that General Kammler was authorising the use of valuable resources for the building of new sites for paper rockets was less than zero.

But what of Peenemünde itself. Drawings exist of the A9/A10 dated 1941, before the first launch of the V2. By 1941 therefore, construction must have started on a new launch complex for the 86ft America rocket. It needed completely new handling, testing and launching equipment for the extra weight and height, plus the thrust of the A10 was almost ten times that of the V2, with all the problems that implied regarding the rocket exhaust before it cleared the pad. So where was this new facility to be built. Here we encounter another Peenemünde lie. A few miles inland, behind the V2 pre-production works, are three large circular emplacements. Dornberger described the centre one as Test Stand XI, intended for launching production V2s. Below is a photograph from the PRO archives (AIR 14/3722), which shows an aerial view of Test Stand XI, taken by the RAF on 19 February 1944. The ACIU specialists studying this photograph noted the large amount of activity, the pipework and various buildings, and came to the conclusion it was part of an HTP production plant. The ACIU had compared some of the plant items with those on a photograph of Ober Raderach, the main HTP production centre near Friedrichshafen in southern Germany. Looking at a photograph of Ober Raderach, the conclusions reached by the ACIU experts appear very strange. In fact there are many significant features at the Test Stand which have nothing in common with Ober Raderach. The Test Stand pipework and other buildings are clearly visible, but we know they didn't exist for HTP production.

The Allied concern about HTP was based on the original belief that the V2 used HTP as a fuel, but by June/July this had been abandoned when it was discovered that the V2

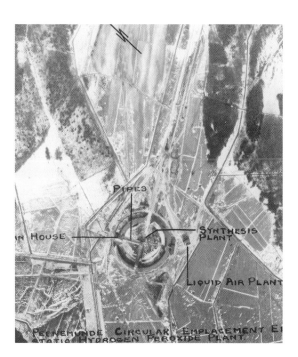

Peenemünde Test Stand XI. Allied Intelligence mistakenly identified this as an HTP production site, but it is almost certainly the America rocket launch complex. (PRO)

STORAGE TANKS

COOLING
TOWER

LIQUID AIR PLANT

SYNTHESIS
PLANTS

CONTROL HOUSE

Ober Raderach 6,000 tons/year HTP production plant near Friedrichshafen in Southern Germany. The photograph that mistakenly convinced Allied Intelligence that Test Stand XI at Peenemünde was also for the manufacture of HTP. (PRO)

used liquid oxygen and an alcohol/water mixture for its rocket fuel. However, Test Stand XI was bombed by the USAF on 18 July and 4 and 25 August 1944, the 'official' reason being to destroy the (non-existent) HTP production facilities. David Irving, in his book *The Mare's Nest*, is puzzled by these three bombing raids, 'long after the A4's true fuel had been established' and goes on to say that no HTP was ever produced at Peenemünde, which is correct.

If British Intelligence was not aware of the A9/A10 developments, American Intelligence probably was. For this information to have leaked to their Press, that the Germans had produced a rocket capable of reaching the East Coast of the USA and beyond would have been political dynamite, especially once the inevitable subject of warheads was discussed. The original concerns about HTP, therefore, provided a convenient 'excuse' to subject Test Stand XI to three of the heaviest bombing raids Peenemünde had seen, leaving the site completely obliterated – as the photo in Dornberger's book *V2* shows.

Looking at the emplacement, a broad, pale line, at least 50ft wide, bisects the top part of the circle, joining three other darker lines to form a cross in the centre. The pale line, which is several hundred feet long, is on exactly the same alignment as the launch direction used for the V1 and V2 launches along the Baltic coast. The Test Stand also has many similar features to the early launch complexes at Cape Kennedy and based on comparisons between these sites it is virtually certain that the 'Fan House' is the rocket service tower and the 'Pipes' are a runway to allow the tower to move to and from the launch stand. The 'Synthesis Plant' is the actual launch stand, with the rocket support tower adjacent to the pad. The lower section of the 'cross' is the rocket motor exhaust flame path, covered over to obscure the cooling water reservoirs. The 'Liquid Air Plant' is a vehicle/engine shed containing equipment for transferring the rocket to the launch stand. The actual emplacement is huge, the diameter inside the outer walls is at least 400ft, far larger than anything built for the V2 and the various items visible are completely different to those on the other rocket test stands. After the first bombing of Peenemünde on 17 August 1943, the whole situation changed almost overnight. The SS took an ever-increasing role in the organisation and most of the test and development work was moved to other locations out of range of Allied bombers. These included the SS site at Blizna in Poland. Just as the A9/A10 complex was separated from the V2 test stands at Peenemünde, a new location was also required for the America rocket. There is some evidence that at least one A9/A10 complex was built near Rudisleben in what was East Germany and it is believed that at least one full-sized test vehicle was launched from this location in 1945.

1.3 THE RHEINBÖTE (RHINE MESSENGER)

The heavy engineering and armaments firm of Rheinmetal-Borsig had considerable experience in solid-fuel rockets, short-range weapons for the Army and rocket-assisted take-off (RATO) devices for the Luftwaffe. Hence it was natural that it would be approached when initial studies were being carried out for long-range weapons in the late 1930s. By May 1942, with the V1 and V2 still waiting for their first successful launch, Rheinmetal-Borsig (R-B) had produced plans for a multi-stage solid-fuel rocket with a range of 150 miles and a payload of 2,700lb. (Clearly R-B had been working to a similar specification to that of the V1 and V2.) The project was given the codename Raketsprenggranate 4831 (high-explosive grenade rocket) and the name Rheinböte (Rhine Messenger). Although a contract was issued on this basis, it was soon realised by R-B and the Army that development of such a rocket would take some time and therefore, as an operational weapon might be required sooner rather than later, work commenced immediately on a series of single- and multi-stage rockets with much smaller warheads. The final accepted design was a four-stage solid-fuel rocket designated the Rh-Z-61/9, having an overall length of 42ft 7in, a launch weight of 3,700lb and a warhead of 88lb, the maximum range being just under 150 miles. Each stage of the rocket had six swept-back fins and, as no guidance or control system was fitted, it was spin-stabilised with the rocket slowly rotating during its trajectory. Like the V1, the Rheinböte had to be aligned accurately on the target before launch and its maximum velocity was slightly higher than that of the V2 at over Mach 5.

Initial trials took place at Ludwigsfelde, 20 miles south of Berlin, but later tests were transferred to the Army range at Leba, 160 miles down the coast from Peenemünde, with the rockets launched towards the island of Bornholm, which was also used by the Army as a range and tracking station. The final firing tests took place at Posen late in 1944.

From recently discovered information in the PRO archives at Kew, London, we now know more about the background to the Rheinböte. This new information is based on interviews carried out by British Intelligence in 1945 with senior R-B personnel working on the Rheinböte project. Perhaps the most significant new information is that the Rheinböte was originally intended as a reserve weapon in case the V1 failed. This helps to explain why the Rheinböte always appeared to lag behind the V1 and V2 in its development work. It was not until the middle of 1943 that demonstrations of the Rh-Z-61/9 took place before the Heereswaffenamt and by this time it included the SS, usually with Kammler present. Kammler himself appears to have been in favour of the project, despite reservations expressed by the Army, mainly because, Dornberger claimed, of its small warhead. But if the Rheinböte were held in reserve for the V1, it could have also had the same role for the V2 – in which case it would be natural for Dornberger to regard it as a competitor. The V2 was still unreliable and the airburst problem was not finally cured until 1945, and hence nothing was assured. The Rheinböte III had a 1,700lb warhead and a range of 150 miles, placing this version in a similar category to both the V1 and V2, and of course it was far less complicated than either of these two weapons. After the bomb plot of 20 July 1944 the Rheinböte project also came under the control of the SS and Kammler, and at another demonstration of the Rh-Z-61/9 on 16 November 1944 at the Leba range Kammler ordered R-B to produce 500 Rheinböte III rockets per month. By the end of December 1944 a total of 115 rockets were available and a dedicated launch battery was formed, Batterie 709, under the direct control of the SS. One of the results of the slow progress of the Rheinböte was that specialised mobile launching equipment for field operations had been delayed so much that eventually a Meillerwagen V2 transporter was modified for this purpose. The 42ft 7in Rheinböte was a long, slender, flexible rocket, and it was essential that a rigid platform was used at launch to obtain an accurate trajectory; however, the Meillerwagen was not ideal in this respect.

Additional information from the interviews with R-B personnel also revealed that plans were under way to use a smooth bore 50ft tube, of 31.5in internal diameter, to act as a launcher. The first stage was to be discarded in favour of a gun-type first stage and gyroscopic stabilisation was to be used for the final stage. These modifications were expected to increase the target accuracy of the rocket over the 125-mile-plus ranges, giving a dispersion of 80 per cent within 1.6 miles in range and 0.6 miles in line.

One final relevant piece of information produced from the interviews was that 'Dr Klein stated that at the request of Generals Dornberger and Kammler, four launching ramps were sent to Holland and in January 1945 he heard that about twelve rockets with 25kg explosive warheads had been fired'. The use of the term 'launching ramps' gives the impression that perhaps these were not the modified Meillerwagen transporters and suggests that dedicated transportable launch equipment may have eventually been available.

1.4 THE HOCHDRUCKPUMPE (HIGH PRESSURE PUMP): HITLER'S 'SUPER-GUN'

The fourth and last weapon in Hitler's V-weapon armoury was perhaps the most bizarre, but it is also the one which has lived on into the present day.

As a long-range weapon (that is, with a range of greater than 20 miles), conventional artillery is limited because there is a practical limit to the length of the barrel and the size of the explosive charge that can be used to propel the shell. One possible solution was to have a very long barrel, over 400ft in length, and arrange a series of explosive charges to be fired in sequence immediately behind the shell as it passed along the barrel. The French had considered such an idea in 1917 when Paris was being shelled from a distance of 81 miles by Krupp's rail-mounted Pariskanone, but this bombardment lasted only twenty weeks and so the French project was not pursued.

In the Second World War Hermann Rochling of the Rochling Eisen und Stahlwerke in the Saar, known as the Krupp of the Saar, was a member of the Reichsvereingung Eisen (Reich Iron Association); the other two members were Alfred Krupp and Walter 'Panzer' Rohland of the Deutsche Edelstahlwerke. These three men were among the most powerful industrialists in the Third Reich and their companies supplied Hitler with most of the raw materials for his armaments. Although Rochling was not in the missile business, he must have felt that he was missing out on some of the action of his fellow 'barons' and decided to make a contribution to Hitler's long-range armoury. One of his senior engineers, August Coenders, dug out the plans for the original French 'super-gun', and within a few weeks model testing was being carried out with a 20mm diameter shell. Gaining Hitler's approval for the project was not a problem since Rochling had ready access to both Hitler and Speer, and was able to bypass the usual Army Weapons Office approval system. The project undoubtedly appealed to Hitler for its novelty and the fact that it involved little outlay in terms of resources. In addition, there was the pleasing prospect of firing 500 or so shells an hour at London from the French coast.

By August 1943 Rochling had a contract which bypassed all the usual Army channels of approval and he also had access to the Army firing ranges and their personnel. The codename of Hochdruckpumpe (High Pressure Pump) was chosen for the project, although the Army later gave it two other names, *Fleischiges Lieschen* (Busy Lizzie) and *Tausendfussler* (Millipede), the first one derived from its intended high rate of fire and the second from the multitude of side-branches on the long barrel when viewed from above.

After model testing confirmed that the concept worked, two full-size test rigs were built at the Army ranges at Hillersleben near Magdeburg and Misdroy on the island of Wolin near Peenemünde. The initial trials used a smooth-bore barrel, since the shell velocities were too high for rifling, with a total length of 405ft. Because there were no rifling grooves in the barrels and thus the shell had no rotational motion to provide stability, small fins were provided, either fixed or arranged to deploy as the shell emerged from the nozzle. As the shell moved along the barrel, twenty-eight sequential charges were fired electrically from side branches, each one accelerating the shell from its initial firing velocity in the breech. Various shell configurations were tried, with typically an overall length of 9ft and a maximum diameter of 5.9in over the stabilising fins. Although full-scale testing showed the system worked in principle, the shell velocities necessary to reach London (at least 5,000ft/sec) had not been achieved, the best results in testing being some 3,600ft/sec, which was comparable with conventional artillery. Only Krupp's 11-in K5 railway gun had exceeded this figure. In an attempt to incease shell velocity the side-branch charges were increased in size, but two major problems immediately revealed themselves.

First, isolated sections of the main barrel started to fail owing to faults in the steel and secondly, as the shell exit velocity increased, the shells lost stability and started 'toppling', resulting in a vastly reduced range. It was obvious that insufficient testing had been carried out. When aerodynamicists at the University of Gottingen were consulted, their advice was that in the time available the only solution was to reduce the weight of the shell. The Army HWA was now advising that the project should be cancelled, although Hitler was convinced it could still be made to work. Speer and Saur did manage to have the shell production figures reduced from the 10,000 per month agreed on 25 January 1944 to 5,000 per month while the problems were investigated. In addition to Rochling, Peenemünde had also been carrying out research for Krupp to extend the range of conventional artillery. This was based on Krupp's own family of 11-in railway guns produced under the codename Bruno. Different barrel lengths extended the range, but eventually barrel flexing and rifling problems resulted in Krupp considering a similar idea to Rochling's. Two Bruno barrels were bored out to 12.2in and the rifling removed. Peenemünde supplied a shell design similar to the HDP shell, 71in long and 4.7in diameter, the shell being steadied in the barrel by a sabot ring, which was discarded at the muzzle when four fins deployed, for spin-stability. This shell was fired from the normal railway-mounted barrel and achieved a maximum range of only 90 miles. Plans were also being considered to provide a small rocket motor in the base of the shell to boost the velocity.

Kammler had inherited the HDP project along with the V1, V2 and Rheinböte, and following demonstrations at Misdroy on 29 November and 22 December 1944, using a shortened barrel of 197ft and production versions of the shell, it was decided that an effort should be made to produce an operational weapon, although by this time the original site earmarked for the HDP was in Allied hands. An alternative site was quickly made ready near Trier, on the banks of the River Ruwer, just across the German border not far from Strasbourg, and here Artillery Abteilung HAA 705 assembled two of the short-barrel versions. Their target was the eastern area of France from Luxembourg to Strasbourg, and on 30 December 1944 both HDP barrels commenced firing in the direction of the advancing Allied forces. By 13 January 1945 just over 100 shells had been fired. Kammler ordered two more barrels from Rochling, but the rapidly worsening military situation meant that on 12 February 1945 the two existing barrels were dismantled and moved back into Germany, spelling the end for the HDP project.

1.5 THE WARHEADS

All four weapons had an offensive capability of varying potential effectiveness, depending to a large extent on the weight of their payload and their vulnerability to counter-measures. This was despite post-war claims from Dornberger, von Braun and just about everyone else who worked at Peenemünde that their main interest in rockets, especially the V2, was for space travel, reaching the moon and increasing man's knowledge of science. These claims were made most strongly by survivors of the original Peenemünde team who had been employed on the US weapons and space program projects after the war. The facts were, however, that the V1, V2, Rh and HDP were all able to carry a payload of either conventional high explosives or perhaps some other material equally or more deadly. As far as conventional explosives were concerned, by 1943 Germany and the Allies had developed such substances to a fine art with explosives such as TNT and Amatol, a mixture of 50 per cent ammonium nitrate and 50 per cent TNT and the new RDX (cyclotrimethylenetrinitramine) plus aluminium powder. Germany developed its own version of this explosive, called Trialen, composed of 70 per cent TNT, 15 per cent RDX and 15 per cent aluminium powder. (The aluminium powder increased the blast effect by a factor of two, but its use was restricted in Germany owing to the shortage of aluminium.) Both the V1 and the V2 had warhead weights of about 1,800lb, depending on the type of explosive used. Amatol was more dense than Trialen, and so maximum warhead weights using these two materials were 1,800lb and 2,000lb respectively. The V1 was actually a more deadly conventional weapon than the V2: the V2 impacted at Mach 3 and dissipated some of its explosive energy inside the crater, while the V1 impacted at around 200mph and the blast effects were consequently greater. With the V1 the killing over-pressure (that is, the pressure above normal atmospheric that would kill a human being) was produced at a radius of 50ft for an Amatol warhead. The radius at which houses would normally be destroyed was 225ft and the radius at which some structural damage would occur was 600ft. This is, of course, not the whole story, as death or serious injury could be caused not only from direct blast effects but also by being hit by flying debris and the collapse of buildings. These were the effects of conventional high explosive warheads carried by the V1 and V2. The Rheinböte had an offensive warhead weight of 55lb and the HDP an explosive weight of about 20lb.

Apart from high-explosive warheads, Germany was also working on biological weapons, battlefield gases and nuclear weapons. The nerve gases Tabun and Sarin had been produced by IG Farben for a top-secret organisation headed by the Army's General Hermann Oschner and by 1945 many hundreds of tons of these substances were available for use. The poison gases phosgene and chlorine were also being produced, and in this respect very little had changed since the First World War. Chlorine had been the first gas used in that war and this, together with phosgene, was the cheapest and most usable gas available. Both are heavier than air, chlorine 2.5 times and phosgene 3.5 times, but phosgene is the most easily stored in bulk since it is a liquid below 46.8°F (8.2°C), whereas chlorine is a liquid only below −29°F (−34°C). The extra density of phosgene reduces its dilution at the target and both chemicals were sometimes mixed together before use.

Nuclear weapons were also being worked on. The scientists working on the nuclear programme had to choose between using radioactive material mixed with some heavier-than-air dust or ash, which would cover the ground with a radioactive blanket of varying intensity and duration, or using a fission weapon comprising uranium U235 or plutonium Pu239.

For any of these unconventional warheads modifications were required to the original V-weapons, although the physical size of the Rh and HDP warheads meant that only a small package of biological, chemical or nuclear material could be used, distributed at the target by conventional explosives. The V1 and the V2, owing to their much larger warhead size, were capable of carrying any of the above materials, plus they could also be used for an active nuclear weapon, similar in size to the US 'Little Boy' and 'Fat

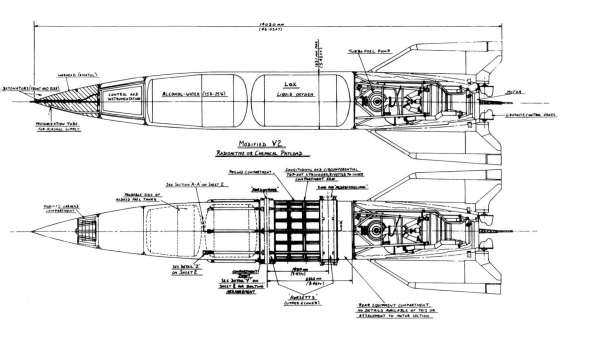

Details of standard and modified versions of the V2. (PRO/Author)

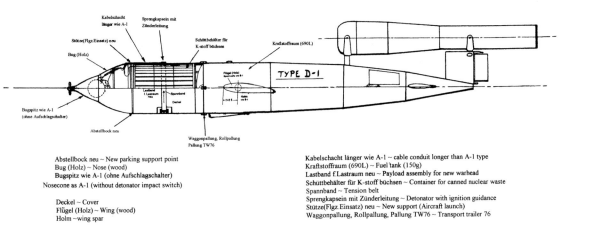

Abstellbock neu ~ New parking support point
Bug (Holz) ~ Nose (wood)
Bugspitz wie A-1 (ohne Aufschlagschalter)
Nosecone as A-1 (without detonator impact switch)

Deckel ~ Cover
Flügel (Holz) ~ Wing (wood)
Holm ~wing spar

Kabelschacht länger wie A-1 ~ cable conduit longer than A-1 type
Kraftstoffraum (690L) ~ Fuel tank (150g)
Lastband f.Lastraum neu ~ Payload assembly for new warhead
Schüttbehälter für K-stoff büchsen ~ Container for canned nuclear waste
Spannband ~ Tension belt
Sprengkapsein mit Zünderleitung ~ Detonator with ignition guidance
Stütze(Flgz.Einsatz) neu ~ New support (Aircraft launch)
Waggonpallung, Rollpallung, Pallung TW76 ~ Transport trailer 76

Details of a V1 modified for nuclear/alternative warhead. (NASM Washington/Author)

Man' bombs dropped on Hiroshima and Nagasaki respectively. It is interesting to note that the 'Little Boy' U235 bomb dropped on Hiroshima had a weight (less armoured casing) of 1,700lb, almost exactly the same weight as the V1/V2 warhead.

Drawings of 'modified' V1s and V2s were produced and both were capable of carrying unconventional warheads. The drawings on page 22 show variations of the standard V1 and V2, the original being dated September 1944 and March 1943 respectively. The V1 drawing is based on an original held in the National Air and Space Museum (NASM), Washington, USA. The most significant difference between the standard V1 and the type D-1 is that the high-explosive warhead is replaced with a container labelled 'Schuttenbehalter fur K-stoff buschen', which translates as 'Container for canned nuclear waste'. The German word for nuclear is Kern and Kern-stoff is nuclear material. Other changes from the conventional explosive version are:

(i)   Deletion of the nose-mounted detonator switch and replacement of the internal detonator with an external detonator 'corsett' to ensure maximum distribution of the contents at the target.
(ii)   The use of a 150-gallon fuel tank, the smallest tank used on the V1, to ensure the maximum payload weight.
(iii) The replacement of the heavy mild-steel nose-cone and wing covering with wood to ensure the maximum possible range.

The VI's container could have been used for any type of payload, including poison/ nerve gas.

The V2 drawings, opposite show a 'standard' V2 with the normal high-explosive warhead and the modified V2 with a container positioned behind the fuel tanks. These drawings are from a collection of over 2,000 miscellaneous V2 drawings held at the PRO, Kew, which were seized by the Allied authorities in 1945. The modified V2 provided a storage compartment that was 6ft long and 5ft in diameter and was inserted behind the fuel tanks using quick-release fasteners and attachments. The new compartment was an extremely strong, rigid structure and it was attached to the V2 in such a way that, in the event of a launch failure, it would break free from the rocket fuselage and thus survive the subsequent fuel explosion. The original high-explosive warhead in the nose was replaced by ballast weights and the new compartment was positioned as far back in the structure as possible, so that the contents would not be buried in the impact crater but distributed at the target as widely as possible. The fuel capacity of the modified V2 would have been reduced but calculations indicate that with only minor modifications to the fuel the original range of the V2 could have been regained. Without any modifications to the fuel, the range was reduced from 200 miles to 125 miles, but this was still sufficient to reach London from the Calais area. In 1943 Peenemünde was carrying out considerable research on rocket fuels and a contract was issued to the Research Division of the German Post Office, which was also engaged in nuclear research, to investigate the possibility of using nuclear fuels or fission as a rocket propellant.

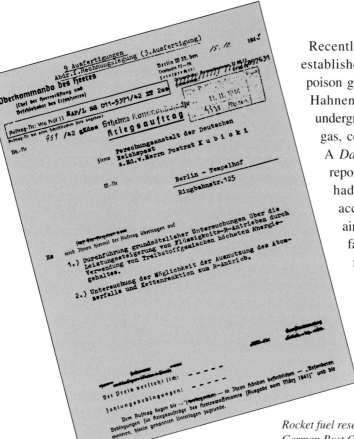

Recently discovered information has established a link between the V2 and poison gas. North-west of Hanover, in the Hahnenberg forest near Leese, an underground plant was producing poison gas, completely unknown to the Allies. A *Daily Mail* article of 19 April 1945 reported that advancing British troops had stumbled on the factory by accident, it was invisible from the air. V2s were found adjacent to the factory entrances and in the forest, minus warheads and with some destroyed by the retreating Germans. The photograph, below shows one of the destroyed V2s of which some may have been modified to carry a gas payload in the fuselage compartment.

Hahnenberg Forest, Leese, Germany. Site of poison gas factory, V2 blown up by retreating Germans.(IWM)

CHAPTER 2

The Sites

2.1 INTRODUCTION

To support the four V-weapons during the planned offensive against the UK, a comprehensive system of sites was required in northern France, the most suitable launching area for the weapons. These sites would need to be able to provide storage, servicing and launch facilities for the weapons plus storage for the fuel, spare parts and consumable items such as batteries. In 1941–2, when the project was in its early planning stages, the military situation in the Third Reich looked extremely rosy. The whole of Europe, except for Britain, was either under German domination, a German ally or neutral. A large area of Russia was occupied and despite some set-backs in the winter of 1941/2, the situation in the East was still very encouraging. The RAF had started bombing raids against German targets but these were little more than isolated events and nothing like the regular mass-raids that were to come later, and in any case the Luftwaffe had already inflicted much greater damage on British towns and cities. In December 1941, following the Japanese attack on Pearl Harbor, Hitler had declared war on the United States. If this were intended to encourage Japan to attack Russia via the back door, it was a mistake – but in any case the USA was going to be fully occupied in the Pacific for some time to come.

It was in this positive atmosphere that the German planners set to work devising the details of the V-weapons offensive against the UK and perhaps targets further afield. In normal circumstances project planners tend to exist in a somewhat unreal state and can easily get carried away by ever more optimistic predictions of the potential success and requirements for a particular project. In some respects this is what happened to the V-weapons, with the exception of perhaps the Rheinböte, which was by far the simplest of the V-weapons and was in reserve for the V1.

2.2 NORTHERN FRANCE – THE SITE AREA

Defeat of the French forces in June 1940 resulted in the partition of France into several distinct areas. The two largest were the area occupied by German forces and Marshal Petain's Vichy France. In addition, and of interest to the V-weapons offensive, there were two other areas. First, there was the 'forbidden zone', a 'closed' military area inside a line from the Belgian border and stretching about 20 miles from the coast, as far as the Spanish border on France's Atlantic coast. This line followed two major deviations. North of Abbeville it turned south, passing between Amiens and Arras before joining the Belgian border again near Hirson. Coming from the south and west, the line reached

Abbeville before turning south again, through Reims to join the Vichy boundary north-east of Vichy. The first deviation enclosed a large part of the industrial area of France and the second enclosed a huge area from the German border in the east, almost half-way to Paris.

The second area was enclosed by a line stretching from the Belgian border along the French coastline to St Valéry sur Somme, moving inland through Abbeville before rejoining the Belgian border at Hirson. This second area was administered from Brussels under direct German military control and hence became almost a foreign country within France. At the time this area was the industrial heartland of France, producing most of its coal, steel, chemicals and cement. The area is still littered with the remains of this industrial past, and although the coal and steel works may have gone the cement factories remain. Nevertheless, there are still many rusty, abandoned relics of the industry that produced millions of tons for the West Wall and the V-weapons sites.

These steel and cement works, up to the spring of 1940, had been producing material for the Maginot Line and the frantic scramble to extend the fortifications along the undefended Belgian border to the sea. They barely had time to cool down before they were producing material for their new masters. In fact, this area of France was particularly harshly treated during the war and it has been estimated that over half of the industrial and agricultural production of the area was either used directly by the Germans or transported back to Germany. However, with France neatly parcelled up into areas that could be controlled directly or indirectly from Berlin, the stage was set for the preparation of the V-weapons offensive. Initially work started on the sites in four main areas, each within a maximum distance of about 40 miles from the coast, and slightly overlapping the 'forbidden zone' in places. From east to west, these areas were (i) just north of Calais to the River Somme; (ii) the River Somme to the Seine; (iii) the Seine to the beginning of the Cherbourg Peninsula; and (iv) the Cherbourg Peninsula itself. Because the Cherbourg Peninsula could easily be cut off from the rest of France, the whole area became part of the 'forbidden zone', producing the ideal security situation for the weapons sites. In these four areas a vast system of over 400 sites was eventually built within a period of only 18 months, starting in the middle of 1943. The majority were intended originally for the V1.

Cormette V1 ski site, château Ducamp. A well preserved site, although the ramp has been demolished. Not annotated is the 100ft reception building alongside the top access road the château farm. Note also the Flak site, lower centre. (PRO)

The V1, simple to produce and requiring in the main only semi-skilled labour for assembly, was ideal as a weapon of mass-destruction. It may not have had the prestige associated with the V2 but it was efficient at what it did and originally the main effort of the site building programme was directed towards getting the V1 operational.

2.3 V1 Sites – Original Organisation

As originally envisaged in 1941–2, the V1 site organisation in France was to comprise the following:

(i)   Five bunker sites capable of storing, servicing and launching V1s equipped with conventional and unconventional warheads, from a secure environment, able to withstand the heaviest bombs available. Two of these sites, Siracourt and Lottinghen, were located in the Calais–Somme area, with three on the Cherbourg Peninsula, at Couville, Tamerville and Brécourt. All were originally 'green-field' sites except Brécourt which used an existing French underground oil storage depot.

(ii) Eight above-ground storage sites. There were four in the Calais–Somme area, at Renescure, Sautricourt, Beauvoir and Domléger; three in the Somme–Seine area, at Neuville au Bois, St Martin l'Hortier and Biennais; and one on the Cherbourg Peninsula, at Valognes.

(iii) One hundred launching sites, distributed with the main group in the area from Calais to the Seine and the remainder on the Cherbourg Peninsula. These original launch sites were called 'ski' sites by Allied Intelligence because the V1 storage buildings at the sites resembled giant skis laid on their sides. The first ski site to be identified was Bois Carré, near Yvrench, NE of Abbeville.

The figure of 100 is only approximate since it is known that some sites were built as decoys and some were never completed. The basic layout included three skis; compass alignment building; assembly and test workshop; storage for HTP, vehicles and trolleys; reception; personnel accommodation; water reservoir and the launch ramp and firing bunker, but there were variations.

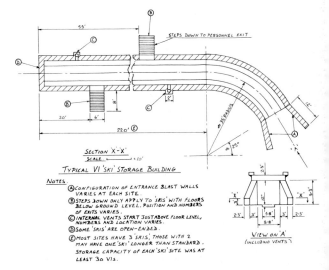

Detail of the distinctive storage building at a V1 ski site.

2.4 VI SITES – THE NEW ORGANISATION

On 5 December 1943 the first Allied bombing raid was carried out against twenty-three of the original ski sites. This relatively light attack was followed on 24 December by a raid on twenty-four more sites by 672 B-17 Flying Fortresses of the US 8th Air Force. These first raids were really only shots in the dark, since Allied Intelligence was not really sure what the Germans were planning, despite photographic evidence from Peenemünde of a small winged object at the base of a ramp and reports from French agents. Although only about seven ski sites were destroyed in these first air-raids, many were damaged and it was obvious to the Germans that the sites were too conspicuous and took too long to build (almost three months), and in many cases security was lax because of the use of French contractors. With the Allied bombing campaign against every type of suspicious new construction in northern France gaining momentum, a completely new generation of launch sites was designed and construction started in late 1943.

These new sites had only one permanent building, similar to a garage, sometimes with an extension, and the launch ramp was intended to be a temporary feature that could be erected and dismantled in a matter of hours. A small launch bunker was also provided and a water tank, access roads being concrete. The first of these new sites to be identified was near the village of Bel Hamelin on the Cherbourg Peninsula and Allied Intelligence consequently referred to such sites as Bel Hamelin or 'modified' sites. The buildings, pads and other features of the 'modified' sites are shown in several figures.

One other main factor was that the SS was now taking control of the V-weapons programme and initially this included the building work. French labour was no longer used as PoWs took over the construction work. Under General Kammler's supervision, urgency was the byword.

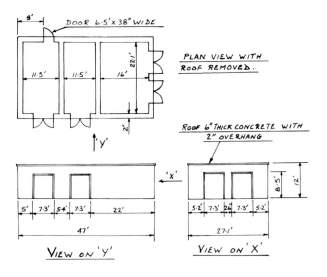

2.4.1 VI Bunkers

Of the four bunker sites that started from a 'green-field' site, at the commencement of the Allied bombing campaign only Siracourt was roofed over with the main structural work complete. Lottinghen and Couville were under construction but not very far advanced and Tamerville had only reached the site clearance stage and the laying of a rail link. In these circumstances work at Lottinghen, Couville and Tamerville was abandoned and any

The garage workshop building at a VI ski site.

work that did continue was as a decoy to divert Allied bombs from more important targets. Work at Siracourt proceeded but its use as a V1 site was abandoned and modifications were started to adapt the bunker for the launch of V2s. The ex-oil storage depot at Brécourt was virtually complete as a V1 launch site, with only the steel launch ramp structure missing from between the blast walls.

2.4.2 V1 Storage Sites

The eight original storage sites were problematical for both the Germans and the Allies. The Germans knew that the Allied bombers would soon turn their attention to these sites, which had been more or less ignored during the ski site bombing. Therefore new storage arrangements were required quickly, and these had to be bomb-proof, well concealed and further inland. The result was three new storage sites using existing caves and tunnels, all of which were at least 100 miles from the coast. These sites were at Rilly la Montagne, in a railway tunnel near Reims, and in former mushroom-growing caves at St Leu d'Esserent and Nucourt, to the north-east and north-west of Paris respectively. For the Allies, the purpose of the original storage sites had not been established although raids were carried out eventually against all of the sites, the German response was a limited programme of repair work at certain sites, adding to the problems of Allied Intelligence. In addition to the three new underground storage sites, another variation on the original scheme was also built, although there is only one known example, at Bricquebec on the Cherbourg Peninsula. Here, six of the 100ft long original storage buildings were built, plus a modified HDP storage building. Unlike the original sites where all the buildings were within a relatively small area, at Bricquebec they were distributed along existing country lanes over a considerably larger area, and from the air the site must have looked like a random collection of unconnected buildings.

The effect of the virtual take over by the SS and General Kammler of the V-weapons programme by late 1943, also had major changes for the VI. The bombing of the three new underground sites early in 1944, resulted in them being replaced by Ytres near Cambrai for Rilly la Montagne, and Bouvines and Renaix near Lille replaced Nucourt and St Leu d'Esserent, respectively. But even this was only an intermediate measure and by the middle of 1944, Allied Intelligence had identified over 50 possible V-weapons sites, most of which were new

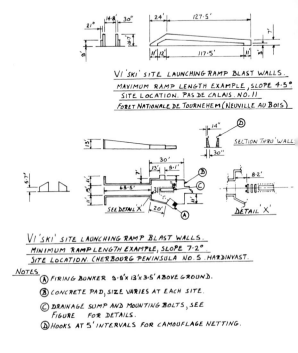

Ramp blast-wall details at a VI ski site for short and long ramps.

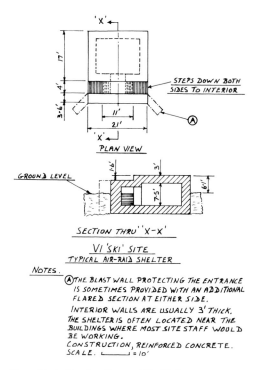

Air-raid shelter details at a V1 ski site.

locations. This final organisation was divided into 'Forward' and 'Rear' sites, the 'Rear' sites acting as supply depots for the 'Forward' sites, which in turn supplied the launch sites. Nearly all these sites were underground, the exception being those for the V2 where three above-ground 'Forward' storage sites were included. The complex nature of this organisation and the fact that some of the new sites may now have had a dual role, an idea that was already being developed for the launch sites, means that this final organisation is now discussed in Section 2.8.

2.4.3 Launch Sites

Not all the ski launch sites were abandoned. Some were repaired and some had suffered very little damage, hence probably around 20 to 30 of these sites were still available. The new generation of 'modified' sites numbered about 210 although not all were completed. The distribution of the new sites now produced a complete change to that previously used. Before, where around double the number of ski sites had been in the Pas de Calais, compared to the Somme-Seine area, with the modified sites this was now reserved, the actual numbers being 61 versus 29 (ski) and 58 verus 102 modified, respectively. In addition there were now 20 launch sites in the area from the Seine to the Cherbourg Peninsula, where before there had been none, and on the Cherbourg Peninsula there were now 30 modified sites compared to originally 8 ski sites.

As has been mentioned, the only building at the new sites was a garage type of structure and a small launch bunker. In addition there were two concrete pads, concrete access roads and a series of small concrete blocks intended as supports for the ramp structure, which was designed to be erected and dismantled in a few hours. The new concrete pads comprised a compass alignment pad with identical grooves to those found on the floor of the compass building at the 'ski' sites, this provided the facility for adjusting the magnetic compass onto the correct bearing of the target and, like the 'ski' sites, it was always on the same alignment as the ramp but being easily concealed, the detection problem was reduced considerably, the second pad being directly in front of the ramp.

The pad contained a roofed-over washdown sump to get rid of traces of HTP from the catapult and also, two rows of 0.8in diameter bolts, set in the concrete. At all the 'modified' sites seen by the author, there are twelve bolts, either side of the sump. These bolts were used for the attachment of two rails which were used to guide the V1 trolley

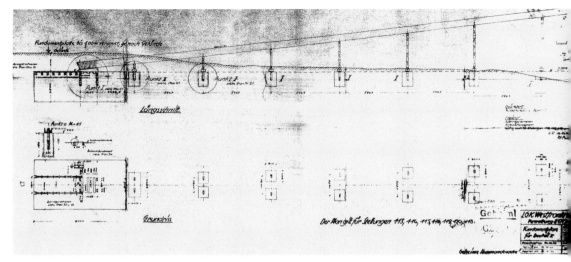

A German drawing of modified site launch ramps for different sites.

on to the base of the ramp and the rails ensured that this operation could be carried out as accurately and as quickly as possible. The V1 was at its most vulnerable from air attack when being transferred from the compass and onto the ramp. Once launched, the V1 was no longer the concern of the site launch team. The drawing above, apart from showing the bolts and rails, raises some interesting questions. It refers to the layout as being applicable to seven numbered types of firing points, Stellungen 113, 114, 115, 116, 119, 120, 118, and the Title block states they are for western France. The author has never

seen any variation in the layout of the 'modified' V1 launch sites so why was there a variation in the type of 'modified' site and when and where were they intended to be used? There is a total of 18 rail mounting bolts, compared to the usual 24, and the pad is approximately half the size of those at the normal 'modified' sites. However, the massive ramp blast walls of the ski sites have gone, as have the ski buildings themselves, both items had been almost impossible to conceal from the air. The single other feature of the original ski sites which had alerted the attention of Allied Intelligence had been the V1's compass alignment building, a large square structure

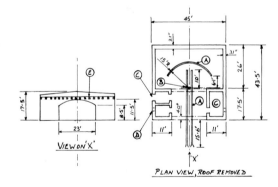

VI 'SKI' SITE, COMPASS ALIGNMENT BUILDING.

NOTES.
(A) THE PARALLEL AND CURVED FLOOR RECESSES ARE FOR THE VI TROLLEY AND COMPASS SWINGING EQUIPMENT. THE PARALLEL RECESSES ARE 42' LONG x 10" WIDE x 4'-6" DEEP
(B) THE 23" SQUARE RECESS IS THE PIVOT POINT FOR THE COMPASS ALIGNMENT OPERATION.
(C) AT SOME SITES THESE ROOMS ARE TRANSPOSED TO THE OPPOSITE SIDE OF THE BUILDING, DEPENDING ON THE LOCATION OF THE RAMP.
(D) WINDOWS, ONE EITHER SIDE, 23"x 30" DEEP.
(E) 6"x 8"x 17-OFF, RECTANGULAR RECESS FOR SUPPORTS FOR 2 SLIDING DOORS WHICH COULD BE USED TO CLOSE-OFF THE INTERIOR OF THE BUILDING.
BUILDING CONSTRUCTION IS EITHER RED BRICK OR CONCRETE BLOCKS.
SCALE. ⊢——┘ = 10'

The 'Richthaus' or compass alignment building at a V1 site. The structure contained no ferrous material.

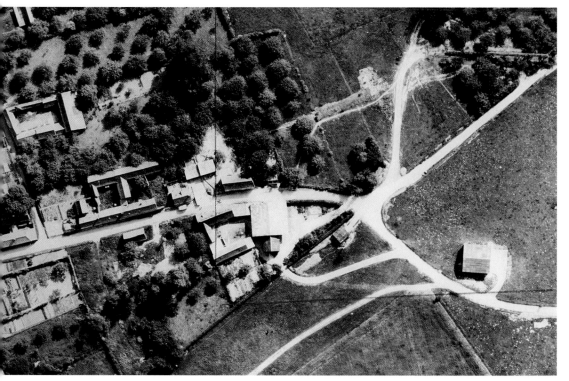

The V1 modified site at Vignacourt, Pas de Calais. The ramp is at top right. The compass alignment pad is under its removable weatherproof cover, centre right. Farm buildings have also been utilised.

that was always on the same alignment as the launch ramp. This had now been replaced with a concrete pad. Although the Bel Hamelin site was the first of this new generation of launch sites to be identified within a matter of days, many more had been photographed from the air, the modified sites were easy to conceal, especially in wooded areas and only a fraction of the total number were actually identified.

When the V1 offensive finally began in June 1944, virtually all the V1s launched came from 'modified' sites with seven of the ski sites being operational. By early September 1944, Kammler and the V-weapons organisation had moved to Holland and on 3 March 1945 a four-week offensive started against London and cities such as Antwerp and Brussels, the last V1 from Holland being shot down in Kent on 29 March after a total of over 300 successful ramp launches. ACIU records show that 22 launching sites were built in Holland and 14 in Germany, west of Koblenz (see Table 7).

2.5 SPECIAL SITES

Although all the original bunker sites could have serviced and launched V1s with unconventional warheads, by the end of 1943, all these sites except Brécourt on the Cherbourg Peninsula, had been abandoned or were being modified for the V2. From existing drawings we know that a version of the V1 was designed for use with an alternative warhead and from the date of the relevant drawing it is clear that the option for this use was still being considered.

But where was such a weapon to be prepared? There is one underground site where the Germans ensured that no signs remained of the excavations. Every piece of rock and debris was transported at night and dumped miles away. A similar site was started two miles away but progress was slower. Allied Intelligence only became aware of these sites after the German retreat. The main site near Monterolier, south of Dieppe is known locally as La Grotte de Clairfeuille or Beaumont I to the ACIU. One warm summer's day in June 1994, nine people died, including three children and five firemen. The tunnels at Clairfeuille were used for V1s and their warheads in 1944, one or two of the villagers saw them arrive at night, but security was strict and nothing was talked about in the village. After the war the site was forgotten, it was always meant to be a well kept secret, but a time-bomb was waiting to release its deadly cargo.

2.6 V2 Sites – Original Organisation

The V2 was the 'flagship' of the V-weapons offensive. It had cost much more than the V1 to develop and offered the possibility of providing a family of even larger and more destruction weapons. All flagships require special treatment, and although the operational use of the V2 was similar to that of the V1, in that there were bunkers, field sites and storage/service depots of various types, some of the V2 sites were constructed on a far grander scale.

First there would be the bunkers, and these would comprise:

(i)   Two bunkers in the Pas de Calais, Watten and Wizernes, and two on the Cherbourg Peninsula, Sottevast and Brécourt. All were capable of storing, servicing and launching the V2 and larger developments.

(ii) Forty-five unprotected field launch sites, thirty-nine between Calais and the Somme, four between the Seine and Cherbourg Peninsula, and two on the Peninsula. These field sites were basically concrete pads with parking for the various vehicles involved with the launch, mainly fuel tankers.

(iii) Seven main storage depots, four forward field storage depots and six transit dumps, the latter being used for temporary storage en-route to the launch sites.

(iv) Two liquid oxygen stores, one in the Pas de Calais at Rinxent and one in Normandy at St Marc d'Ouilly. These storage depots would be supplied with liquid oxygen from seven main production centres in Germany. Liquid oxygen was widely used in many industrial processes.

(v)   Alcohol, being readily available from the usual industrial sources, and posing few transportation or storage problems, was to be stored at Tourcoing, an industrial centre in the Pas de Calais and would be distributed from four field depots in the area plus one in the Somme–Seine area and one in Normandy.

Like the V1 sites, the V2 sites were planned in the euphoric atmosphere of the Third Reich in 1941–2. The first of the bunker sites, Watten, which was to have been the ultimate rocket base of the future, was started early in 1943, the site having been inspected by Ministry, Organisation Todt and Peenemünde personnel in December 1942, only weeks after the first successful launch of the V2. The Organisation Todt, part of the empire that Albert Speer had inherited from the previous Armaments Minister Dr Fritz Todt, was the construction arm of the Armaments Ministry and, as well as the West Wall fortifications, it was also in overall control of the V-weapons site building programme.

Work at Wizernes started in July 1943, a few months later than Watten, but with Watten due for completion in October 1943 the OT had a very tight schedule to keep to and providing sufficient labour was going to be a problem. Work at Sottevast on the Cherbourg Peninsula started in March 1943, by which time the job of converting the ex-oil depot at Brécourt was already under way.

Plans for the bunker sites, especially Watten, appear to have been personally approved by Hitler and there is no doubt that these sites were intended to be showcase examples for the new revolutionary type of weapon created at Peenemünde. With regard to the more ordinary sites for the V2 offensive, Dornberger sent a group from Artillery Regiment 760, under Oberst Hohmann, to northern France in the late spring of 1943 to find suitable locations for the field launch sites, field stores, transit and main storage depots, and for fuel production and storage sites.

By late 1943 work had started on the non-bunker V2 sites. In particular the seven main storage depots were well advanced, as were three of the four field storage depots. As the transit sites consisted basically of camouflaged off-road parking, it appears that little work was done on them other than to establish suitable locations. This is confirmed by work on the Cherbourg Peninsula at La Croix Frimot.

However, the euphoria did not last very long and after the bombing of Peenemünde on 17 August 1943, it was Watten's turn a few days later on the 27th. These raid were only the start of a major bombing campaign against the V2 bunkers in particular which would eventually destroy any chances of them becoming operational. As a result of the bombing, by May 1944 the Watten site resembled the surface of the moon, with smashed construction equipment everywhere and all work and access severely disrupted. Although the main building had not been seriously damaged, it was obvious to Berlin that Watten could never be used as originally intended and the same assessment also applied to the other bunkers.

In addition, as for the V1 sites, the SS was now playing an ever more influential role in the V2 project and once again Kammler was involved in spelling out the changes that were needed in light of the Allied bombing campaign.

2.7 NEW V2 SITE ORGANISATION

With Kammler appointed by Hitler on 6 August 1943 to the post of General Commissioner for all aspects of the V-weapons offensive, and with the Allied bombing gaining momentum, the stage was set for some radical changes to the V2 site organisation. Kammler was not of course in charge of the whole V-weapons programme at this time; in theory at least, the Army's representatives, Generals Heinemann and Metz, were still to direct the V2 and V1 offensives respectively, during the operational use of the weapons. But it would have been a very brave Army officer, regardless of rank, who chose to disagree publicly with someone with the authority and connections of SS General Hans Kammler.

With reference to the new site organisation there is one original German document dated 4 November 1943; IWM file MI14/865(v) is probably not the final word, but certainly it shows how things were moving. The revised V2 site organisation can be summarised as follows:

1 **Artois Region** (that is, from Calais to the Somme). Two Companies (Motorised) each with three Batteries and each Batterie capable of manning a maximum of three launching platforms.

(i) Twenty-four field launch sites, of which five were to be equipped with Leitstrahl beam guidance equipment and six were to be capable of withstanding a 1,200lb bomb. (This compares with the thirty-nine field launch sites originally planned. Two of the bomb-proof sites were probably the converted V1 bunker at Siracourt and eventually the still unfinished V1 bunker at Lottinghen.)

(ii) Two sites for special tasks, between Sangatte and Rinxent. These were probably located in the quarries at Hydrequent, already used for the storage of railway guns.

(iii) One completely protected launch position to replace Watten. (This was definitely Wizernes.)

(iv) Field storage was to be provided for a total of 200 V2s, with test stands by 31.12.43. This field storage could be accommodated by the expansion of two existing sites in the Fôret de Nieppe, La Motte and Thiernes.

2 **Dieppe Region** (that is, the Somme–Seine area). Launch positions for one Company, Motorised. Originally there were to be no V2 sites in this area.

(i) Six field sites, of which two were to be equipped with Leitstrahl and three were to be capable of withstanding a 1,200lb bomb. Field storage was to be provided for a total of 160 V2s.

3. **Seine to Cherbourg Peninsula**. No sites were mentioned for this area, although there were three main storage depots, one transit dump, two sites for LOX and alcohol storage and four launch sites in the original organisation.

4. **Cherbourg Peninsula**. Launch positions for one Company, Motorised.

(i) Nine field sites, of which three would be equipped with Leitstrahl and three would be 1,200lb bomb-proof.

(ii) Sottevast, also to be used for temporary and permanent V2 storage, if possible.

(iii) Brécourt, to be used for Special Operations (Sondereinsatz), including the storage of 30 V2s with their personnel, fuel and vehicles.

V2 on Meillerwagen. British controlled V2 launches. Operation Backfire, October 1945. (PRO)

The original plan for this area was for two bunkers, Sottevast and Brécourt, two transit dumps and two field launch sites, and it appears that the increased storage and launch capability for the Cherbourg area was based on using equipment and personnel originally intended for the Calvados area of Normandy.

Obtaining the required number of fully trained personnel had always been a problem with the V2 owing to the complicated pre-launch servicing, fuelling and launch procedure. For the field sites, the actual launch pad was relatively simple – an area of hard standing, ideally concrete, at least 30ft by 50ft with parking for the support vehicles. The maximum number of launch/service groups available for the V2 was five, Abteilungen 444, 485, 836, 953 and SS Abt. 500. Each group was composed of three batteries capable of manning a total of nine launch pads (Zuge). By 1944 all the Abteilungen were mobile, whereas originally Abt. 953 was to have been based at a bunker, but even the use of Brécourt on the Cherbourg Peninsula, untouched by bombing, was changed from a static launch site to providing accommodation for a mobile Abteilung. The supply situation for the new sites was also radically altered. For V2 storage only the Méry-sur-Oise site was retained with a new site at Bar le Duc, 150 miles further south, added to the list together with other sites still to be inspected. Méry-sur-Oise, and its associated forest areas, which had suffered little bomb damage, was also to be used for the storage of supplies, especially batteries. Each V2 used two 50v, one 36v and two 27v batteries. LOX production and storage in France was based on two new sites, Caumont and Canteleu-Dieppedalle, near Rouen. Rinxent was retained and Watten was still on the list, although it was probably not seriously considered. Also Sottevast was to be used for production and storage with Brécourt for storage only. The alcohol supply was not mentioned, presumably because it was readily available and storage only complicated matters since it could be moved around in ordinary road tankers.

This was the V2 site situation envisaged in late 1943, for an offensive due to start in the summer of 1944. It was reasonably realistic at the time in that, although Watten had been virtually written off, other sites were still untouched by Allied bombing. Wizernes was eventually bombed on 11 March 1944, Sottevast on 26 November 1943 and Siracourt on 31 January 1944, while Brécourt and Méry-sur-Oise suffered little or no bomb damage. Some of the original protected storage sites, such as Bergueneuse in the Pas de Calais, were also undamaged and capable of being used in the new organisation.

The field sites were almost impossible to detect and therefore, given the ability to supply the LOX (11,000lb) and alcohol (8,750lb) required at launch, plus the rockets themselves, the SS and Army must have considered that there was a good chance of the offensive starting as planned. But the sudden concentration of Allied bombing on

V2 armoured launch control vehicle (Feuerleitpanzer) towing the launch table (Bodenplatte); British controlled V2 launches, Operation Backfire, October 1945. (IWM)

the bunkers and other sites had put these plans in doubt by the spring of 1944, and when the Allied forces landed in Normandy on 6 June 1944 the whole V2 offensive from France was in jeopardy. The Cherbourg sites were lost almost immediately and those sites from the original organisation in Normandy and Calvados were also soon to be lost.

Despite a hold-up in front of Caen, the Allied advances after D-Day moved rapidly, reaching the River Seine by 20 August, and on 24 August the first Allied troops reached Paris. By 9 September all of the Pas de Calais had been cleared of German forces and Brussels was in Allied hands by 3 September. General Kammler, by now in charge of all the V-weapons, had retreated from Belgium to Holland in early September and, as the front-line stabilised in Holland, batteries from Abt. 485, 836 and 444 found suitable launch sites for the V2 on either side of the Hague and Walcheren Island, near Flushing. The sites were not purpose-built but simply areas that provided the necessary hard-standing for the launch table and camouflage for the launch team and their vehicles. One of the more exposed sites was near the racecourse at Haagsche Bosch. The first V2 was fired at London from Holland on 8 September 1944 and the last on 27 March 1945.

2.8 THE FINAL VI/V2 STORAGE ORGANISATION

For the V1 we have already seen how Ytres, Renaix and Bouvines were intended to replace Rilly la Montagne, St Leu d'Esserent and Nucourt. For the V2, field storage was to be provided for 440 V2s plus underground 'rear' storage for a total of 1,000 V2s at the Méry-sur-Oise sites and Bar le Duc. Storage existed at unnamed similar sites for further 500 V2s plus sites for spare parts and the overhaul of vehicles. By the spring of 1944, Allied Intelligence had identified a total of 58 possible storage sites, mainly underground, including those already bombed, such as Nucourt, which, although badly damaged, still had underground sections that were serviceable. The 'final' storage sites were intended in some cases to serve a dual purpose for both the V1 and V2, evident from the differing dimensions of the tunnels provided.

Table 5 lists the sites of the 'Final Rear Storage' organisation, all the locations are shown on Map 5. As the Germans retreated towards Belgium, some of the sites were inspected by RAF Intelligence Officers and their findings are included in the site descriptions in Chapters 4 and 5.

2.9 THE A9/A10 AMERICA ROCKET SITES

With time running out and sites capable of handling the 86ft A9/A10, such as Watten, no longer able to function as planned, suitable V2 sites had to be modified quickly. Based on archive information, it appears that only two sites were adapted for the new rocket. These were Haut Mesnil, south of Caen and La Meauffe, north of St Lô, both in Normandy.

These two sites were part of the original V2 storage organisation and, after a certain amount of work had started in 1943, their role was changed from purely storage, to storage and launch, using the Regenwurm system described in 5.5.5. Neither site had been bombed by early 1944 although they had been photographed and the ACIU were aware of their connection with the V-weapons campaign. The modifications to the two sites for the A9/A10 consisted of enlarged tunnels with curve radius in the looped galleries increased from the standard V2 dimension of 50ft (15m) to 100ft (30m) and provision of different roof-mounted lifting gear for the heavier, larger rocket.

2.10 RHEINBÖTE SITES

With the Rheinböte being held in reserve in case of the failure of the V1, it was always struggling for recognition and the resources necessary for it to be considered as a weapon in its own right. The bombing of the V1 ski launching sites, and the realisation that the V1 offensive could only take place if an alternative type of launching site could be provided, may have given the Rh a boost in late 1943. The 'modified' V1 launch sites were a gamble and if they too had been rendered unusable by Allied bombing then the Rh would have replaced the V1 immediately. Unlike the V1, the Rh

A Rheinböte on a modified V2 Meillerwagen, being prepared for launch. (PRO)

A Rheinböte dismantled for transporting to the launch test site. The first-stage motor casing appears to be non-standard. (Author)

did not need a ramp for launch, requiring only a concrete pad; moreover, as a solid-fuel rocket with no guidance and control system, it needed the absolute minimum of launch personnel and vehicles.

At the 'modified' V1 launch sites, the concrete pad immediately in front of the launch ramp was fitted with 0.8in (20mm) diameter bolts for the attachment of rails to enable the V1 to be pushed on its special trolley on to the base of the ramp as quickly as possible. These guide rails were essential when speed was the main criterion but these rails could also have been used by the Rheinböte. The Rh's mobile launcher could have been bolted to these rails, which are far stronger and more substantial than those provided at the ski sites, and this would have provided the rigid base necessary for an accurate Rh launch.

In addition, there are two other sites which may have been intended for the Rheinböte. Brécourt near Cherbourg is described in the V2 section (above) while the 'silo' site also near Cherbourg is described in detail later. The silo site was originally intended for two turret-mounted naval guns as part of the French pre-war coastal defence system for Cherbourg. Work at the site was incomplete, with the guns still in storage when the Germans arrived in 1940 and the author believes that one of the two silos was modified by the Germans for launching the Rheinböte vertically.

2.11 HOCHDRUCKPUMPE (HDP) SITE

Only one site was chosen for the HDP. Hitler may have approved and believed that Rochling could make the idea work, but he was certainly not going to make this weapon the mainstay of the V-weapons offensive. It was after all a very strange concept for a long-range weapon.

Ideally the site had to be as close as possible to the coast, to reduce the distance to London as much as possible but without making the HDP vulnerable to surprise attacks from the sea. The location finally chosen was a hill, 518ft in height, a few miles inland between Calais and Boulogne, near the village hamlet of Mimoyecques. The main railway line passes nearby. In April 1943 work started on the site, tunnelling into the hillside from both sides, with lateral tunnels and inclined tunnels built inside the hill. With a planned length of 450ft, the gun barrels had to be buried underground and only the exit nozzles for the shells would appear at the surface, protected by a massive concrete slab. Unfortunately for the HDP, the surface slab for the nozzles was one of the first items on the site to be completed and from the air it was soon noticed that the three openings for the nozzles were aligned exactly on London. In 1943 French agents reported that Germany was planning an offensive against the UK and London in particular using new secret weapons that would be served by new rail links and resembled giant mortars sunk in the ground. The fate of Mimoyecques and the HDP was almost a foregone conclusion. By the end of August 1943 some 4,100 tons of bombs had been dropped on the site – the heaviest bomb-load dropped on *any* of the V-weapons sites, including Watten. Although the HDP never fired a shot from Mimoyecques, the remains of the barrels and other items were moved to Germany before the Allied troops arrived at the site on 27 September 1944. Under Kammler's direction, two shortened barrels were erected on the banks of the River Ruwer, near Trier, just across the German border from Luxembourg. During a short campaign lasting from 30 December 1944 to 12 February 1945, approximately 200 shells were fired towards Luxembourg and the advancing Allied troops, apparently with little military effect. The barrels were then dismantled and probably melted down as scrap, the HDP concept, in a modified form, not emerging as a weapon for another forty years.

HDP barrel, less the breech, at the launch test site. The side branches contained the additional charges which were arranged to fire in sequence, increasing the acceleration of the shell as it passed along the barrel. (Author)

CHAPTER 3

The Allied Intelligence War and Bombing Campaign Against the Sites

In November 1939 a document was delivered to the British Embassy in Oslo. Sweden remained neutral throughout the war and hence travel was possible from Germany without arousing suspicion. The author of the so-called Oslo Report was anonymous, and to this day it is still a mystery as to who provided the information it contained. The report said that Germany was working on several highly secret military projects. Peenemünde was mentioned as being the centre of work on rockets and pilotless aircraft, and reference was also made to new types of radar being developed. The report was sent to London but in 1939 there were more important things to attend to and it was filed. For the next two or three years the file slowly grew as reports were received from agents in the occupied countries but everything was still speculative. However, one name that kept cropping up was Peenemünde, and so it became a target for the Allied photo-reconnaissance aircraft covering northern Germany.

On 15 May 1942 a PRU Spitfire flown by Flt Lt D.W. Steventon was on its way back from Kiel with orders to photograph the naval base of Swinemünde. Flying over the island of Usedom, Steventon noticed construction work, a new airfield and some strange looking 'rings' among the trees, so he took a few shots of the area. Back at Medmenham House, in southern England, home of the Allied Central Interpretation Unit (AICU), the photos of Peenemünde were studied and the prints filed. The mysterious 'rings' at Peenemünde, although the ACIU did not know it at the time, were Dornberger's new rocket launch pads and test stands, soon to be used for the V2. From 1942 onwards the expansion of Peenemünde meant that technical and skilled workers were brought in from the occupied countries as well as PoWs for the manual work, the two groups being housed in separate camps further along the coast from the main staff accommodation. This vast influx of foreign workers, nearly 20,000 of them in all, meant that security problems were inevitable. By the end of 1942 there was a regular flow of reports from agents into London and Peenemünde was frequently mentioned. By this time regular launches were taking place of the V2 and, from December, of the V1, both activities being difficult to keep hidden from view as the rockets fell into the Baltic Sea. By January 1943 the reports from agents had reached such proportions that they could no longer be ignored and General Nye, Vice-Chief of the General Staff, arranged for the circulation of an up-to-date report on German rocket and secret weapon work, based on all the available information. Government ministers were included on the circulation list and on 12 April 1943 Prime Minister Winston Churchill was informed of the investigation.

All the evidence pointed to some sort of long-distance bombardment threat. Churchill took the advice of the Chiefs of Staff to appoint a coordinator to take charge of the investigation, and the following week he gave the task to his son-in-law Duncan Sandys. An Army colonel with some experience of artillery and ballistics, Sandys had been declared unfit for active military service following a motoring accident. He had returned to Parliament as an MP and Churchill had given him a job in the wartime Ministry of Supply, involving research, development and production of new weapons. Therefore Sandys was ideally placed to be put in charge of the new investigation. From the very start, however, clashes of personality developed and these very nearly ensured that the German V-weapons threat was never taken seriously. From the political wilderness of the 1930s, Churchill had brought with him into power when he became Prime Minister in 1940 a number of friends and associates who had remained loyal and supported him during those despondent times. Some of these old colleagues now resented the personal confidences he shared with his 35-year-old son-in-law and when Sandys started putting together his first report on the possibility of a long-range bombardment it provided ample ammunition for those interested in discrediting him.

Secret agents are rarely technically trained to make objective reports, and the size and scale of the rockets and other weapons they referred to often varied according to their imagination. Another problem of credibility was that military rocket development in the UK and USA had not progressed much beyond small, solid-fuel, unguided anti-aircraft rockets. But now Sandys was faced with including in his first report the launch from Peenemünde of 100ft rockets weighing 60 tons – and clearly the established scientific advisers to Churchill and the Government would be likely to describe such information as rubbish. On 29 April Sandys was shown photographic evidence of the activities at Peenemünde which included not only the strange-looking elliptical and circular concrete 'rings', but also such details as the new power station with power lines running to the many new buildings. On 9 May Sandys visited Medmenham to see all the photographs of Peenemünde taken so far and to discuss what the evidence might mean in terms of rockets and pilotless aircraft. In June 1943 Peenemünde was visited four times by PRU aircraft, specifically to photograph the new Luftwaffe base and Dornberger's rocket facilities, and on 23 June the photographs clearly showed two white-painted rocket-like objects lying horizontally on trailers within the elliptical construction.

At the Air Ministry Intelligence branch of MI6, the task of collating and analysing the various agents' reports and other evidence was given to a young scientist, Dr R.V. Jones. This turned out to be a very fortunate choice. Dr Jones had already established his reputation in 1940 for his work on the Luftwaffe's use of radio beams. His insistence, against overwhelming scientific opinion, that the use of radio beams over the long distances between Germany and England was possible as a means of guiding bombers to their target had resulted in the resignation of Sir Henry Tizard, Chief Scientific Adviser to the Air Ministry, who had led the opposition to Dr Jones's theory.

Sandys' first generally circulated report was issued on 14 May 1943 and was based on agents' reports, information from Dr Jones and the Peenemünde photographs. It concluded that a large rocket existed, although no evidence had been found for pilotless aircraft. After further photographic coverage of Peenemünde, Sandys issued another report which included the rocket-like photos and related the evidence of the bugged conversations of several captured high-ranking German officers who had referred to the new rocket weapons.

Now that Sandys believed the rocket threat was all too real, he requested that PRU flights should include the whole of northern France, from Cherbourg to the Belgium border, within a 150-mile radius of London. In particular, any new large buildings, especially if they were served by a rail link, were to receive special attention from the ACIU. As early as May some suspicious new activity had been photographed in a forest area near the town of Watten, not far inland from Calais, and now the work at Watten was revisited. By the beginning of July it was clear that a very large concrete structure was being built here, and in addition two other large sites were also being cleared within the 150 mile radius.

Sandys' report of 28 June was discussed by Churchill and the Defence Committee (Operations) on 29 June. Among those present at the meeting were Sandys, Dr Jones, Lord Cherwell, Churchill's Chief Scientific Adviser, and Dr A.D. Crow, Director General of Projectiles at the Ministry of Supply. Lord Cherwell played an important part in trying to discredit the rocket theory. Born in 1886 at Baden-Baden in Germany, and educated at Berlin University and the Sorbonne in Paris, his work on the thermal effects in the new science of nuclear reactions won him worldwide recognition. In 1914 he became Director of the Royal Aircraft Establishment's Physical Laboratory at Farnborough and in 1919 he was made Professor of Experimental Philosophy at Oxford. As Professor Lindemann, he made the Clarendon Laboratory the centre for low temperature research in the UK and during the 1930s he became a close friend of Churchill during his 'wilderness' years. Professor Lindemann obviously enjoyed the political 'fringe' and aristocratic circles that Churchill moved in during this time and Churchill was impressed by his ability to describe complicated scientific ideas in simple terms and relate them to the everyday facts of life. Lindemann benefited from Churchill's appointment as Prime Minister in 1940; he was created a baron in 1941 and was Paymaster-General from 1942 to 1945, a government post of considerable power and influence in the armed forces.

From his own knowledge of rockets, Cherwell regarded Sandys' evidence in his report as extremely dubious and did not accept that the Germans were working on large rockets. In this respect he was supported by Dr Crow, whose experience was limited to relatively small solid-fuel missiles. The belief that the rockets, if they existed, would have to be powered by solid-fuel was responsible for most of Cherwell's and Crow's scepticism. They argued that a rocket of 60 to 100 tons would require huge launching installations in northern France, resembling a giant mortar buried in the ground and served by numerous rail-links. Nothing like this had been discovered in France despite the massive coverage by PRU aircraft. The white rocket-like objects at Peenemünde were judged by Cherwell and Crow to be a massive hoax, a 'mare's nest' and even possibly barrage balloons. Even Dr Jones's information that Peenemünde now had the highest priority rating for resources was dismissed as being related to some type of radio-controlled bomb and research on jet aircraft.

Despite the scepticism of the experts, the meeting agreed to take several actions, and these included an attack by RAF Bomber Command on Peenemünde as soon as possible. Further, more detailed PRU coverage should be made of northern France within a 150 mile radius of London. On the night of 17 August 1943 597 aircraft of Bomber Command attacked Peenemünde, of which 40 failed to return. On 27 August 185 B-17 Flying Fortresses of the US 8th Air Force carried out a high-level daylight raid on the large concrete structure near Watten. Both these raids were to some extent 'shots in the dark', as there was no firm evidence that large rockets existed and no one was sure what the true purpose of Watten was and if there was a link between the two sites. The damage caused by both raids was relatively minor. Due to an aiming error, virtually none of the rocket workshops at Peenemünde were affected, most of the bombs falling on civilian accommodation. At Watten the damage looked worse than it actually was, as none of the main buildings was seriously damaged although the surrounding area was pitted with craters and some construction equipment was destroyed. If the material damage resulting from the raids was not important, the psychological damage was much more serious. A large proportion of the testing and launch work for the V1 and the V2 was transferred to Blizna, the first stage in the take-over of all V-weapons work by the SS. Secondly, the vulnerability of sites like Watten was revealed and it suddenly put a large question mark against the original site plans for both the V1 and V2 where bunkers were involved.

By September 1943 the War Cabinet Defence Committee (DCO) was labouring under the advice from two different camps. One side was supported by the huge file of evidence from prisoners' statements and agents' reports, together with photographs and their interpretation by the ACIU, plus the opinions of Sandys and Dr Jones. On the other side was the advice from the extremely influential Lord Cherwell and Dr Crow that a rocket of even 40 tons would have to be at least 100ft long and would have to be launched like a giant mortar, buried in the ground.

Sandys was still convinced that the objects at Peenemünde were rockets and he organised an investigation to determine if it was possible to power a large rocket by any means other than solid fuel. Experiments were being carried out on small liquid-fuelled rockets and a Shell engineer, Isaac Lubbock, was ordered back to the UK to report on trials using liquid oxygen and petrol as fuel. In the meantime, on 21 October, Sandys requested another PRU survey of northern France, involving about a hundred sorties, searching for the elusive rail-link to the giant mortars. At another meeting of the DCO on 25 October, with Lubbock present, he was asked about the experimental work in the US on liquid-fuelled rocket motors. The meeting agreed that for a very large rocket, more than 40 tons and 45ft long, liquid fuel was possible but it would require a power unit capable of producing several thousand horsepower in order to provide the very high fuel flow rates necessary. This power unit would have to fit inside the body of the 'rockets' photographed at Peenemünde and Cherwell estimated that such a fuel pump would have to be about 20in in diameter, which, he said, was clearly impossible. (The actual diameter of the blades of the V2's HTP fuel-pump turbine was 18.5in.)

Once again it was suggested that the objects at Peenemünde were barrage balloons. Nevertheless the evidence that the Germans were planning some form of long-range bombardment of the UK from northern France was becoming difficult to ignore. A multiplicity of new concrete installations was appearing within a 130- to 200-mile radius of London and this included the HDP site at Mimoyecques. In addition, Dr Jones had been following the activities via agents and intercepted radio traffic of a German signals organisation that specialised in radio and radar tracking. It was eventually established that the 14th Company of the Luftnachrichten Versuchs Regiment had moved to the radar tracking stations along the coast from Peenemünde, providing more evidence of the existence of a rocket.

The V1 ski site at Yvrench/Bois Carré, 6 July 1944. Bois Carré was the first ski site to be identified. The three ski V1 storage buildings are clearly visible; lower left is the ramp and above that the compass alignment building. The blast walls of the launch ramp are still standing (inset). (PRO)

On 28 October 1943 Churchill, tired of the bickering, convened a meeting at which Cabinet Ministers, Chiefs of Staff, Cherwell, Crow, Sandys, Jones and Lubbock were present, in an attempt to determine the truth about the threat from long-range weapons. Cherwell again tried to convince everyone that the rocket threat was a myth. He still believed that solid fuel was the answer and that it would be impossible to design a small device capable of pumping the huge amount of fuel required per second for a large liquid-fuelled rocket. Lubbock and other engineers had re-examined the problem a few days earlier in the light of the release of some details of Frank Whittle's work on gas turbines. The point was made at the meeting that the Germans might have perfected some form of gas-turbine-driven pump. Once the meeting accepted that such a device was possible, the main foundation of Cherwell's argument vanished and he abruptly left the meeting after refusing Churchill's offer to head a committee to advise the War Cabinet of the progress of the missile threat. In his place Sir Stafford Cripps accepted the job and a few days later, after studying all the available evidence, he told Churchill that the threat of an attack by long-range missiles definitely existed.

As early as 29 September 1943 the German propaganda machine had been promising retaliation for the mass bombing of its cities. Speer had publicly stated that retribution for the Allied bombing would be carried out using secret weapons. Together with similar threats from other German leaders, this was now a threat that could not be ignored. At the beginning of November 1943 a report reached London from an agent in France. It said that he was working for a French construction company building some new structures at eight sites near Abbeville in the Pas de Calais. None of the construction workers knew what they were for but the agent suspected they were for a secret weapon. On 3 November all eight sites were photographed by PRU aircraft and the results studied at Medmenham. There were no railway lines to the sites and the buildings looked innocent enough, and certainly there was no obvious connection with large rockets. At the most advanced site, in a wood called Bois Carré near Yvrench, three of the buildings were almost identical, although one was longer than the other two, and to the ACIU interpreter they resembled giant skis laid on their sides.

This was, of course, the first of the original V1 launching sites, although their purpose was not yet understood in Britain, and from that time they became known as ski sites. The significance of the alignment of the ramp foundations with another square building nearby was not immediately appreciated, as the overriding concern was the search for sites connected with a large rocket and the ski sites seemed not to be involved with such a weapon. On 8 November Cripps held a high-level meeting at which the Chiefs of Staff, scientific experts and ACIU interpreters were present. Despite overwhelming circumstantial evidence, there was still no definite proof that rockets or other types of missile existed. Towards the end of the meeting the ACIU representatives were asked if they had any new information possibly related to the missile threat. By this time nineteen ski sites had been discovered and when this was mentioned, together with the alignment of some of the structures on London, whose significance had already been recognised as most likely being connected with a magnetic compass device, the meeting was quickly adjourned for two days, while a search for other similar sites was carried out and the information fully analysed. By 10 November twenty-six ski sites had been discovered, all with the same type of buildings.

At the meeting on 10 November the 'Bodyline' investigation, as it had been called, was reorganised, since it was obvious now that at least two different weapons had to be considered. Sandys' own inquiry came to an end, although he was still retained as an adviser on the rocket threat, and the investigation became the responsibility of the Air Ministry. By 24 November ninety-six ski sites had been identified between Calais and Cherbourg, but in addition there was a new site being developed at Mimoyecques which now had three dummy haystacks on a new concrete slab above the rail tunnel workings. Construction work was also being carried out at Siracourt, Lottinghen, and on the Cherbourg Peninsula. On 28 November a Mosquito piloted by Sq Ldr John Merrifield was returning from an abortive attempt to photograph Berlin; as one of his secondary 'targets' was the island of Usedom, he finished off his film above Peenemünde. Back at Medmenham House a photograph of a previously noted ramp-like structure at Peenemünde showed a tiny, winged object at the base of the ramp. This was the first time that the ramps and the V1 had been identified together. A rapid search of earlier photographs of the whole area revealed two more ramps near Zempin. The codename 'Bodyline' was replaced by 'Crossbow' for the campaign against the threat from all V-weapons, and the rocket investigation was put to one side for the time being. Eventually the codename 'Diver' was used for the V1, 'Big Ben' for the V2 and 'No Ball' for the operational use of any V-weapon.

Once the connection had been established between the ski sites in France and the new weapon, the Allied air forces started a bombing campaign against the French sites. This campaign included not only the ski sites but also any sites that were thought to be connected with the pilotless aircraft. This involved exploratory raids against some of the original V1 storage sites, such as Domléger. The damage at Domléger was not repaired and this caused a problem, because Allied Intelligence was always working a few steps behind the Germans planning the next move in the V-weapons offensive. In fact the original V1 storage sites had been written out of the organisation, as had many badly damaged ski sites.

The decision was made that any parts of the original organisation that could take part in the V1 offensive due to start in early 1944 would be used, and some ski sites would be repaired if it served a useful purpose, such as a hoax. In fact, despite the bombing campaign, which included many daylight raids using Flying Fortresses, very few of the ski sites were totally destroyed: as few as seven of the original ninety-six had been written off, while others were to be repaired and used later in 1944. Although the rocket threat appeared to have diminished, bombing raids against the bunker sites, which were believed to have some connection with either the V1 or the V2, were intensified in early 1944.

Watten had been bombed repeatedly from August until September 1943, but then the attacks lapsed. On 2 February 1944 they started again and continued until May, by which time the site was in a chaotic state, although the main building had escaped virtually undamaged. Attacks against the other bunker sites followed a similar pattern. The main campaign against Wizernes started on 11 March 1944, that against Siracourt on 31 January, Mimoyecques on 19 March, Lottinghen on 24 February, Sottevast on 8 February and Couville on 7 January. Heavy daylight raids took place against two of the new V1 storage sites, St Leu d'Esserent and Nucourt, which evidence from agents linked with the V1.

The problem for the Allies was that all German V1 transport movements were now taking place at night, with vehicles parked during daylight hours in specially camouflaged areas, forests, etc. During the bombing campaign in early 1944 the weapons threat appeared to have gone quiet, and in fact technical problems with the V1, compounded by the site damage, led Colonel Wachtel to estimate that the offensive would actually start some time in May or June 1944 instead of the original start date in February.

During this quiet period PRU coverage of northern France continued and on 25 April a new type of construction was identified near the village of Bel Hamelin, near Cherbourg. A new type of ramp was spotted in a farm courtyard at La Granchette. The ACIU interpreters noticed the tell-tale alignment of the row of foundation blocks for the ramp

This massive tunnel at Haut-Mesnil was used for the V2 and probably also the A9/A10 American rocket, shown here together for comparison. This is the only image known to exist of the A9/A10. (Author)

and the identical alignment of a concrete pad in a nearby field, the site being aligned on Bristol. Once again the 'Crossbow' alarm sounded and by May 1944 sixty-eight of the 'modified' Bel Hamelin-type sites had been discovered between Cherbourg and Calais. The most puzzling aspect of the new sites was the lack of an actual launching ramp. Once access roads, a garage-type building and other road improvements were completed, the construction activity stopped. The answer finally came from Zinnowitz, where one of the new sites was being built for training purposes. Within a day prefabricated ramp sections had been brought up and the ramp assembled ready for use, with the concrete blocks as supports. It was an ominous development.

Unfortunately for Allied Intelligence the apparent lull in the V-weapons threat appeared to be a good opportunity to change 'Crossbow' staff and Air Commodore Pelly, who had been advising the DCO on the flying bomb threat, was replaced by Air Commodore Grierson, a newcomer to intelligence work. By the end of May 1944 over 23,000 tons of bombs had been dropped on the original V1 sites and some effort was made to bomb the 'modified' sites, but the lack of a ramp and other aiming points, and the fact that such sites were well camouflaged, meant that only low-level attacks were of any use, and these were inconclusive.

On 11 June, only six days after D-Day, PRU coverage of the V1 sites revealed frantic new activity with numerous personnel and vehicles in evidence. On 13 June Colonel Wachtel had assembled 2,000 V1s ready for use and about a hundred launch sites were operational, mainly 'modified' sites but also a few ski sites. Of the ten V1s launched that day, only four reached southern England, resulting in six people killed. Despite the fact that the start of the offensive had taken Allied Intelligence by surprise, the scale of the attack was regarded as rather an anticlimax. Three days later, on the 16th, Wachtel's men had solved most of their teething troubles and up to 5 September, when the last of the French sites was captured, over 9,000 ramp launches took place at an average launch rate of 100 per day. The apparent Allied failure to appreciate the scale of the threat from the 'modified' sites was only one of the reasons why the V1 offensive came as a surprise. FlakRegiment 155(W) and its commander Colonel Wachtel had been playing a deadly game of hide-and-seek with Allied agents since the end of December 1943. Their original headquarters at Saleux near Amiens was vacated before Christmas and the HQ staff moved to a château near Creil, 30 miles north of Paris. Wachtel dyed his hair and changed his name to Wolfe, while the whole regiment changed vehicles and uniforms, emerging as LuftwaffeFlakGruppe Creil.

The German counter-intelligence branch of the SS, the Sicherheitsdienst (SD), under Sturmbannfuhrer (Major) Kieffer, operating from the infamous Avenue Foch in Paris, was experiencing a remarkable run of success against agents specifically gathering information about the V-weapons threat. The agents' job had been made more difficult by the fact that security at the launch sites was now much stricter. Construction of the 'modified' sites was under overall SS control using PoWs, mainly Russian, and with the threat of an Allied invasion somewhere in northern France all the German forces were on heightened alert.

The fate of many Special Operations Executive (SOE) operatives and their contacts in France also contributed to the Allied problems. Despite orders to the contrary, recently arrived SOE agents who were stopped at roadblocks and the more frequent spot-checks were often found to be carrying lists of passwords, contacts and safe addresses. This resulted in whole networks being eliminated. Some were reorganised under German control, supervised by SD officer Bleicher, who specialised in the operation of fake networks from Avenue Foch.

By mid-July, with Wachtel launching over 100 V1s a day, the V1 offensive was no longer secret and Allied Intelligence switched its emphasis to the original problem of large rockets, even though there was still no definite proof that they existed. The only evidence was still agents' reports and a few photographs. On 15 April and 5 May 1944 Mosquitos flying from San Severo in Italy photographed Blizna, and once again the elusive rocket was identified on a trailer. Further investigation of the Peenemünde coverage produced more evidence of the rocket but the situation changed dramatically at the end of September 1944 when a complete V2 was reconstructed from parts of three rockets. The first came from a V2 being used as a test vehicle for the guidance system of the Wasserfall anti-aircraft rocket. Launched from Peenemünde, the rocket suffered a control failure and landed in Sweden, 200 miles away. Its remains were shipped to Britain after clandestine negotiations with the Swedish Government, which was concerned about offending the Germans. The remains of two other V2s were recovered by Polish resistance workers from marshy ground near the River Bug. These rockets had been launched from Blizna and the remains were concealed until they could be handed over to the Allies. London was duly informed and on 26 July 1944 a Dakota made the perilous trip to Poland and airlifted the V2 parts back to the UK. It was an extraordinary mission. The reconstruction, however, provided the answers to all the most important questions concerning the V2, its size, weight of warhead, type of fuel and range.

The French V1 sites had been overrun by September 1944 but, as the Allied advance into Holland began to slow down, a small group of new V1 sites became operational in Holland, possibly six in total. Great emphasis was placed on camouflage and these new sites were usually built in the grounds of existing industrial premises. Known locations were the oil refinery at Rotterdam-Pernis, the sugar refinery at Puttershoek, the Lever Brothers' soap factory near Rotterdam and a glue works south of Delft.

Launches against the UK using a lighter and faster version of the V1 started on 3 March 1945 and lasted for four weeks, during which time 275 V1s were launched, the last ramp-launched V1 being shot down by anti-aircraft guns as it approached the Essex coast at midday on 28 March 1945. Operational air-launches of the V1 had started on 16 September 1944, KG3 having available an initial total of seventy-five He 111s, and a sporadic air-launched offensive started from Dutch airfields and lasted until January 1945. Allied Intelligence was aware of the airfields being used but, as very little preparation was required to load up a He 111 with a V1, pinpointing which airfields were being used at any particular time proved difficult. A total of 1,300 V1s were air-launched but action by Allied fighters and other problems resulted in total German aircraft losses of seventy-seven. Worse, they lost valuable, specially trained crews. In a typical attack, on Christmas Eve 1944, fifty He 111s launched their V1s against Manchester from the

North Sea. Only thirty-one V1s actually crossed the English coastline and only one came down within the city boundaries, the remainder falling between 10 and 20 miles from the target. Sadly the single V1 that did reach Manchester struck a row of small terraced houses in the suburb of Bury, killing a number of people, who were no doubt looking forward to a happy Christmas and the end of the war.

With all the French sites overrun by 5 September, Allied Intelligence advised the 'Crossbow' Committee that it was extremely unlikely that a V2 rocket attack would develop. However, a few days later, on 8 September 1944, the first V2 launched from Holland landed at Chiswick, London, killing three people and severely injuring another ten. Between then and 27 March 1945 Kammler and three launching batteries fired 1,346 V2s at UK targets, of which 1,115 were launched successfully. The initial problems experienced by the launch teams included the effects of the reduced check-out time before each launch, aggravated by the fact that many rockets, owing to poor storage, had suffered from deterioration of electrical and delicate mechanical components. Eventually a system known as 'Warme Semmel' (hot cakes) was implemented whereby rockets were transported direct from Nordhausen to the launch area.

Despite total air superiority during the V2 offensive, it proved impossible for the Allies to detect the location of the launch sites, the main suspected areas being on either side of the Hague in residential suburbs and on Walcheren Island. For some strange reason, known only to German Intelligence and General Kammler, thirty-two V2s were aimed at Norwich and Ipswich between 25 September and 12 October, from Staveren in Friesland, north of the Zuider Zee. All of these impacted on land, killing no one and injuring very few. The problems in taking effective measures against the V-weapons offensive from Holland were hindered by the infiltration of the Dutch Resistance by the German counter-intelligence service, the Dutch SOE being labelled 'Der Englandspiel' by the Germans. As a result agents sent out from the UK were quickly arrested. In the case of Huub Lauwers, who was tricked into sending false messages to England, this led to the capture of many RAF crews taking part in the campaign.

The V2 offensive finally ended on 28 March 1945 when the launch batteries were withdrawn to Germany and the remnants surrendered to US forces on 9 May. Allied Intelligence was always at least one step behind the V-weapons threat, which is not really surprising because the weapons themselves were so new and innovative in their conception and use. Many people believed that the whole affair was a gigantic hoax, despite the overwhelming evidence to the contrary. Stories of secret weapons are part of the folklore of war and the Second World War was no exception. It was fortunate that common sense finally prevailed in the face of a great deal of expert opinion which eventually was shown to be based only on limited experience, knowledge and arrogance.

CHAPTER 4

V1 Site Descriptions
and Locations

ORIGINAL V1 STORAGE SITES

Eight V1 storage sites were planned to supply the original ski launch sites and the
author has visited all eight. In the area from Calais to the Somme there were four
sites. From E to W, these sites were Renescure, Sautricourt, Beauvoir and Domléger.

(i) Renescure *Map 1: site 16. Michelin map No. 51; IGN map No. 2304 Est.*

Location: starting from the large town of St
Omer, take the N42 in the direction of
Hazebrouck and Renesecure is about 4
miles distant. Just before leaving
Renescure, turn left on to the D406, over
the level-crossing, and the site starts in the
fields on either side of the road after a few
hundred yards. The buildings are still more
or less complete although they have
deteriorated in the last few years. The site
was obvious-ly convenient for rail access,
as all V1s arrived from Germany by rail,
and the Luftwaffe had several airfields in
the St Omer–Calais area, so, as originally
envis-aged, air cover would have not been
a problem. There is some bomb damage
around the site but it amounts to only three
or four craters, one of which is still in use
as a duck pond, so the air-raids must have
been of a minor nature. Surprisingly,
although the V1 was one of Germany's
most closely guarded secret weapons, this
storage site was built in open farmland,
virtually without cover of any sort, and

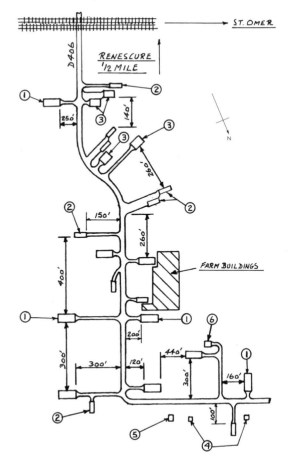

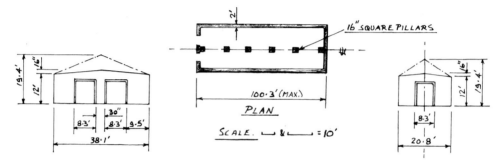

THERE ARE 4 STANDARD BUILDING SIZES USED AT THE V1 STORAGE SITES:-
DOUBLE WIDTH IN OVERALL LENGTHS OF 100·3'; 69' AND 30'.
SINGLE WIDTH WITH OVERALL LENGTH OF 69'.
STORAGE/WORKSHOPS ARE PROVIDED WITH WINDOWS ON ONE SIDE, EITHER 3 OR 7,
DEPENDING ON BUILDING LENGTH. SOME BUILDINGS HAVE THE WORKSHOP ADDED
TO ONE SIDE OF THE STORAGE, USUALLY WITH 7 WINDOWS.

V1 storage/workshops at a V1 original storage site.

only one or two of the buildings were built close to farm buildings. This area of the Pas de Calais as far as Abbeville was a special department administered by the military authorities in Brussels and was therefore like one gigantic armed camp, but even so the lack of any attempt to hide the buildings, and hence their purpose, from the local farming community does seem strange. It reinforces the impression that in 1942 the planners in Berlin were working in a fantasy world, convinced that nothing was going to disturb their military supremacy in Europe.

The total number of storage buildings at Renescure is twenty-three, of which nine are 100ft long double-width, four are 69ft long double-width, and ten are 69ft long single-width. The V1 had an overall length of just over 25ft and with a handling trolley width of about 5ft (the wings were only fitted shortly before launch), this gives a storage capacity at Renescure of around 270 V1s. In addition, there is an air-raid shelter, with the front disguised to look like a house, and three workshops/garages. Most of the buildings are connected to the D406 via concrete access roads. Each V1 arrived at the launch sites with at least 150 gallons of petrol and this was provided at the storage sites, either from underground tanks or from mobile tankers. There is no sign of accommodation for site personnel and it is likely that they were billeted in Renescure and local farms. One item missing from Renescure is a storage building for the HTP used with the launch catapult. Each launch required approximately 25 gallons of HTP and half a gallon of potassium or calcium permanganate catalyst. Some sites did have HTP storage, and it seems likely that the supply of HTP to the launch site depended on the site's proximity to a local HTP production centre; given the vast amount of industrial activity in the St Omer area this is probably the reason for the lack of HTP storage at Renescure.

If all eight storage sites had been completed to the same extent as Renescure, the total storage capacity would have been just over 2,000 V1s. This figure is consistent with the original target figure of 2,000 launches per week.

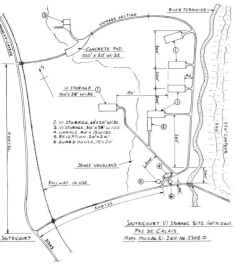

SAUTRICOURT. VI STORAGE SITE (not to scale)
PAS DE CALAIS
MAPS MICH.No.51. IGN No.2305 O

(ii) Sautricourt, Pas de Calais *Map 1: site No. 55. Michelin map No. 51; IGN map No. 2305 O.*

Starting from St Pol, take the D343 towards Anvin. Sautricourt village is about half a mile beyond St Martin and about 4 miles from St Pol. Turn right in the centre of Sautricourt, over the level crossing and 300yd further on is a well-concealed entrance on the left. The concrete access road has almost vanished. In comparison to Renescure, Sautricourt is very well hidden from view and it is clear that some effort was made to conceal the site from the air. The River Ternoise has carved a valley through the area, along which the D343 and the railway now run, and the site has taken advantage of this natural feature. One bank of the Ternoise is flat while the other rises vertically 250ft to a wooded area, and it is on the flat, lower bank that the site is located. With most of the buildings built in the shadow of the opposite river bank, the site would have been very difficult to detect from the air and there are no signs of bomb damage although the site was on the 'Crossbow' target list. This description is based on a visit in the 1970s. The area is much more overgrown than it was, and the remains of the site's narrow gauge railway have disappeared.

At the site entrance were the remains of a light railway, 24-in gauge, the standard Decauville track used at most sites during construction. The first two buildings on the left and right are 20ft square and were probably used for reception purposes and offices. The right-hand one still has its heavy steel door with small barred windows, while the other has a counter-like opening along one side and is filled with water to an unknown depth. The third building near the entrance, again on the left, is 40ft long and 15ft wide, with full-width doors at either end; it appears to be a garage for site vehicles. The main site concrete road runs alongside the river and side branches taken off it lead to the storage buildings. In total

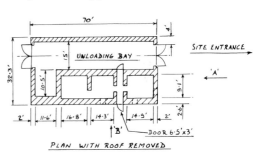

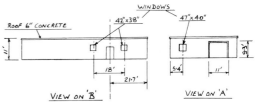

VI RECEPTION, UNLOADING AND ADMINISTRATION.
SCALE ⊢——⊣ = 10'

NOTES.

THIS BUILDING IS NOT PROVIDED AT EVERY 'SKI' LAUNCH SITE.
THERE ARE DETAIL VARIATIONS BETWEEN BUILDINGS. THE UNLOADING BAY CONTAINS LIFTING POINTS IN THE CEILING.
CONSTRUCTION IS USUALLY LARGE RED BRICK, SKIMMED WITH CONCRETE.
WALL THICKNESS IS A MINIMUM OF 2'.

The reception, unloading and administration offices at a VI ski site.

there are five of the standard buildings at 100ft x 38ft wide, and one at 69ft x 20ft wide. They are still in good condition, and the furthest one has been partially converted into a holiday home.

Beyond the last 100ft storage building, the road curves round to the left away from the river and after 100yd the concrete ends, restarting just before the road splits into two. The right-hand section curves round to the right and gives access to a standard unit 38ft wide x 30ft long and a few yards beyond that the concrete road ends in a mass of dense undergrowth. The left-hand fork of the road leads almost immediately to a concrete pad, 100ft long x 50ft wide, beyond which the road is no longer accessible. This branch may originally have joined up with the other access road for the site. About 400yd further along the D343, heading towards Monchy Cayeux, another concrete road goes off to the right, over the railway, and now provides access to some relatively new buildings. It is likely that originally there was an almost circular route around the site. Sautricourt appears finished but the total storage capacity of the site was only about 100 V1s – less than half of that at the other two sites visited in the area. The 100ft concrete pad is an unusual feature at Sautricourt and may have provided an alternative use for the site. It is certainly large enough to provide a firing point for the V2.

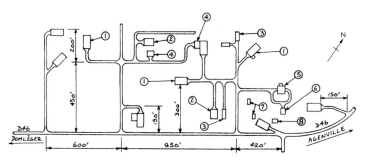

(iii) Domléger *Map 1: site 95. Michelin map No. 52.*

Location: from Abbeville travel north-east through St Riquier on the N25 for 8 miles, then at Longvillers turn left on to the D46 and the Domléger site is outside the village, going towards Conteville. Railway access was provided by a spur off the main line NE of Conteville station and the route of this line can still be traced across the fields. The site is in open farmland on one side of the road and in the 1970s it was clear that the farm buildings on the opposite side of the road were also made of concrete, probably constructed by the OT for use by the site staff. The site was bombed eight times from 14 June 1944 and approximately 15 per cent of the buildings were damaged (in the 1970s the craters and damage could still be seen), but the site could have remained operational if required.

There are seventeen of the standard storage units, nine of 100ft x 38ft, two of 69ft x 38ft, three of 69ft x 20ft and three of 30ft x 38ft, some units being connected together. Total storage capacity was about 200 V1s. At the top of the site is a 450ft length of concrete, 12ft wide, and there are remains of concrete foundations on either side of this roadway. These foundations may have been for further storage buildings destroyed in the air-raid.

Also included at Domléger is an HTP storage building, opposite. This two-storey building housed two large, vertical aluminium vessels (HTP reacts violently with anything ferrous), with a capacity of 3,750 gallons each – enough for about 300 launches. The vessels sat in saucers, with troughs below that took any surplus outside to

The HTP storage building at Domléger V1 storage site. This building contained two aluminium vessels holding a total of 7,500 gallons of HTP for the V1 launch catapult. (Author)

a water tank along the full length of the building, HTP being soluble in water. Adjacent to the HTP storage is a garage-like building, 30ft x 20ft x 13ft high, probably intended for the handling/pumping equipment associated with the filling/emptying of the vessels. Also on the site are two air-raid shelters, 30ft x 15ft with 2ft thick roofs, partially sunk into the ground, and a 20ft square sunken boiler room, still with the remains of some of the equipment. All three V1 storage sites in the Pas de Calais are in remarkable condition.

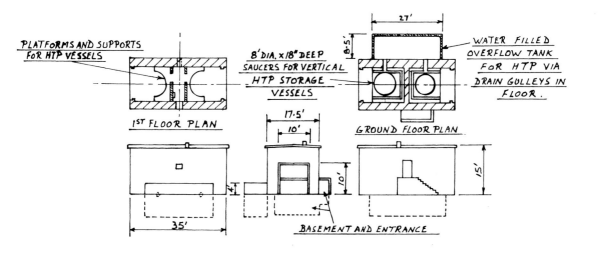

HTP storage at the Domléger V1 original storage site.

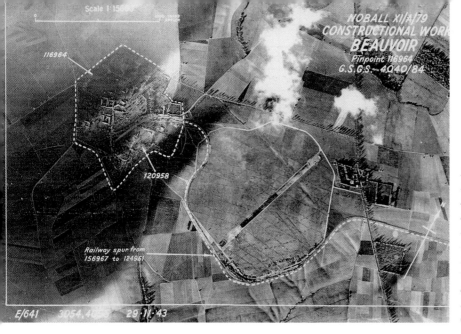

Beauvoir V1 ski
launch and storage
site. 120958 is the
ski site, 11694 is
the storage site.
The mock 'airfield'
runway is clearly
visible. This is the
only combined V1
launch/storage site.
(PRO)

(iv) Beauvoir, *Map 1: site No. 83. Michelin map No. 52.*

Location: Beauvoir lies midway between Doullens and Frevent. From Doullens go north on N16, then turn left on to the D115 and Beauvoir village is on the left before Bonnieres. The Beauvoir site is unique in that it started off as a ski site and late 1943 or early 1944 storage buildings were added adjacent to the launch site. The whole complex was served by a railway spur, taken off the Doullens–Frevent branch line, over 1.5 miles away. In addition, a 'dummy' airfield was built next to the site and this must have added to the confusion of the ACIU interpreters.

It seems that the ski site came first, as this was reported as being under construction in December 1943. The site was bombed later in the month but further attacks were suspended while the situation was reviewed. By February 1944 it was realised that an airfield had appeared next to the ski site, the main 'runway' of which can clearly be seen in the PRU photograph, along with other new buildings. The new buildings were thought to be part of the airfield complex and only when it was discovered that the airfield was a dummy was the true reason for the additional buildings realised.

Perhaps the storage site was not part of the original planning. The Domléger storage site is only 5 miles to the south-west, and the storage buildings at Beauvoir may have followed a similar policy to that of Bricquebec on the Cherbourg Peninsula, which is a storage site built months after the nearby Valognes site, as part of a new variation on the V1 storage theme. Many of the storage buildings are destroyed and badly damaged, but total storage capacity was about 200 V1s.

Moving to the south-west, the next three storage sites are in the Somme–Seine area and once again there is a distinct variation in the layout of the sites. The first site, closest to the Somme, is Neuville au Bois.

(v) Neuville au Bois, *Map 2: site No. 4. Michelin map No. 52.*

Location: from Abbeville take the N28 south-west towards Blangy-sur-Bresle. After 12 miles turn left off the N28 at St Maxent on to the D29 and Neuville au Bois can be reached across country via Fresnes-Tilloloy. Alternatively, follow the D29 to Oisemont and then take the D53 north-east to Neuville. From Oisemont, the site starts on the right before the church on the left and the main collection of site buildings lies in a wooded area about a mile further on the right. Both sections of the site were served by a spur taken off the main railway line at Oisemont. Unfortunately, owing to Allied bombing very little now remains of the storage buildings at Neuville, perhaps the best example being a 100ft x 38ft unit with attached workshop. Between 23 April and 2 July 1944 ten raids were carried out here, initially by Spitfires and Typhoons and later by Liberators, Fortresses and Lancasters, with almost 300 tons of bombs being dropped on the site. As Allied Intelligence had not established the true purpose of the storage sites, Neuville may have been used as a test case to determine the German reaction to the bombing.

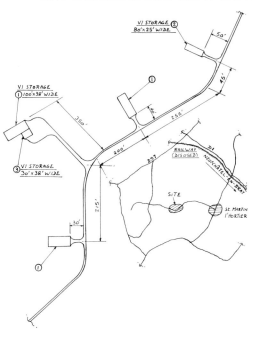

(vi) St Martin l'Hortier *Map 2: site No. 126. Michelin map No. 52; IGN map No. 2009 OT.*

Location: some 22 miles directly inland from Dieppe is Neufchâtel-en-Bray. Take the D1 out of Neufchatel towards Dieppe and 1 mile out of the town turn left over the abandoned railway for Aulage and St Martin l'Hortier. In the centre of St Martin turn right and the site is about 1.5 miles further on the right. The road is single track and very twisty and it is surprising that the site was built so far along this narrow road when, there were many other more suitable locations nearer the village and the railway. In addition, the site is in open grazing land with no cover whatsoever. There are only five buildings, comprising four 100ft x 38ft units, one 38ft x 30ft unit and one 80ft x 24ft wide single-door unit. The latter is a non-standard size. Total storage was 80 V1s. As there are several ski sites in the area, it is likely that work at St Martin was abandoned before completion. There is no evidence of bomb damage around the site even though St Martin was on the 'Crossbow' target list and between 24.3.44 and 6.7.44, it was bombed twelve times. Between the 1970s and 2001 nothing has changed at St Martin apart from the abandonment of the railway, although the rusty track is still in place. The buildings are used by the local farmer as cattle shelters and today it is difficult to imagine the original purpose of the site.

Unused V1 storage buildings at the original storage site at St Martin l'Hortier, Neufchâtel-en-Bray. (Author)

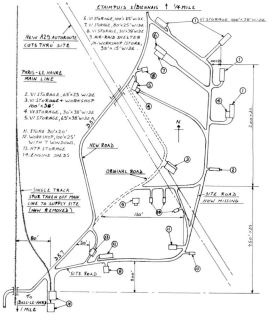

(vii) Biennais, Somme–Seine *Map 2: site No. 127. Michelin map No. 52.*

Location: from Neufchatel-en-Bray follow the N28 south-west towards Rouen. From St Saens take the N29 towards Totes and after 5 miles turn left on to the D151 to Bosc le Hard. From here take the D57 towards Etaimpuis. Unfortunately, the new A29 motorway now cuts across the area and this has disrupted some of the original road layouts, producing diversions. In fact the site, which lies on the D57, is now cut in half by the A29 and some of the site buildings have been destroyed during the road building. Luckily, the most interesting parts of the site have survived and the new bridge over the motorway provides a panoramic view of the site's layout, in open grazing land with few trees. A spur was taken off the adjacent main line and although this spur has not survived, the two site engine sheds are still in place. Despite the large area covered by the site, there are not many standard storage units, and much of the work appears to have involved repair, refurbishment and maintenance. Only eleven of the buildings are storage-only buildings; the remainder are equipped with windows or have an attached workshop, identical to the single building at Neuville. There is an HTP storage building, identical to that at Domléger, but there is no adjacent garage. Eight of the buildings are workshop/stores or have a workshop attached; unfortunately, the largest of these, item 3 on the site plan, has now vanished in the road alterations. It was a 100ft x 38ft wide storage unit with the addition of a full-length workshop with seven windows along the right-hand side. The original storage would have accommodated 110 V1s, plus another 46 in the workshops, giving a total of around 160 V1s on the site. In addition, there are four small store/workshops and an air-raid shelter designed to look like a house from the front. The buildings that remain are in good condition and one of the 100ft units has been converted into living accommodation, the rest being used for agricultural storage. Biennais was on the 'Crossbow' target list but although one of the buildings, item 7, has some damage, and the site was bombed five times, the attacks do not appear to have been accurate. As at four of the other storage sites, no attempt was made to conceal the site from the air and the effort made to construct an air-raid shelter that looks like the front of a house seems all the more odd given that it was surrounded by buildings intended for the top-secret V1.

The V1 original storage site at Biennais, The air-raid shelter here was designed to resemble the front of a house. (Author)

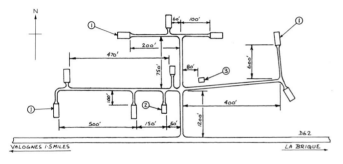

(viii) Valognes *Map 2: site No. 43. Michelin map No. 54; IGN map No. 1210 E.*

Valognes is the only original V1 storage site on the Cherbourg Peninsula and unfortunately it has suffered the most from developments in the area. From Valognes on the N13, about 13 miles south of Cherbourg, follow the D62 out of Valognes west, in the direction of La Brique. The N13 now takes a wide detour west of Valognes and this new section of road has affected the site area. In the 1980s it could be reached from the D62, on the left-hand side of the road about 500yd from the new N13 intersection point for Valognes. At the first visit in the 1970s some of the buildings had already vanished as a result of the construction of a new industrial estate, and since the N13 changes this industrial area has now expanded, probably affecting even more site buildings. The destroyed buildings, the remains of which could still be seen under mounds of rubble, were in the eastern sector of the site, towards Valognes. The storage at this time comprised eight 100ft x 38ft units, two 69ft x 38ft units and a 28ft x 20ft x 11.7ft high administration building divided into rooms with windows and a fireplace. This gave a total storage of about 130 V1s, but it is known from an American report written, after the D-Day landings in 1944 that the site also included HTP storage. Judging by the concrete access roads still visible in the 1970s, the author estimates that originally there were three more storage units giving a total capacity for the site of just under 200 V1s. One of the unusual details still visible in the 1980s were the German fence posts running alongside the concrete access roads. Made of galvanised steel and about 4ft high, they had an 8in square flat plate on top, on

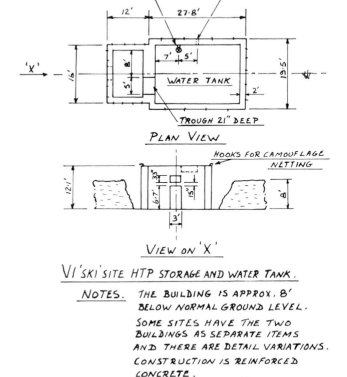

V1 'SKI' SITE HTP STORAGE AND WATER TANK.

NOTES. THE BUILDING IS APPROX. 8' BELOW NORMAL GROUND LEVEL. SOME SITES HAVE THE TWO BUILDINGS AS SEPARATE ITEMS AND THERE ARE DETAIL VARIATIONS. CONSTRUCTION IS REINFORCED CONCRETE. SCALE, ⊢——⊣ = 10'

Standard HTP storage and water tank at a V1 ski site.

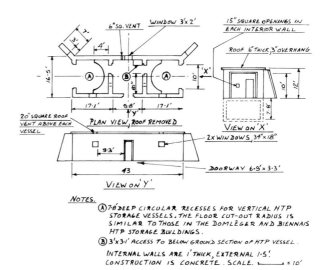

HTP storage at a VI 'new' storage, site, Bricquebec.

to which a lamp was attached, and these acted as markers for site operations at night. The construction materials at Valognes were unusual – mainly large, red, ventilated bricks with a honeycomb interior, skimmed over with concrete. They were very light in weight and provided virtually no protection from air-raids; at the other sites concrete blocks were used.

The total storage capacity of these eight sites, as built, allowing an additional 200 for Beauvoir, gives a figure of 1,200 V1s. The original launching figure for the ski sites was 2,000 per week and FlakRegiment 155(W) had enough personnel to operate 64 launch sites simultaneously, giving a frequency of 31 V1s per launch site or just over four per day. Each ski site with three skis had storage for at least 25 V1s, equivalent to four or five days' operations, and therefore it would have been well within the capabilities of the original storage sites to provide the launch sites with a continuous top-up of V1s to achieve the 2,000 launches per week target figure. During the most active period of the V1 offensive, from 12 June to 15 June 1944, FlakRegiment 155(W) launched an average of 140 V1s per day, or just over two V1s per operational site per day. One further type of site was incorporated into the original V1 storage organisation, holding spare parts for both the V1s and launch site equipment. Of the three examples identified by the ACIU, Conteville, Cramont and Parmain, both Conteville and Cramont are adjacent to the Domléger storage site. ACIU reports in November 1943 identified new building work adjacent to Conteville station, south of the village. By March 1944, reports stated that a road was being built from the new buildings to Domléger, although the purpose of the Conteville work was uncertain. Also in November 1943, building work was reported north of Cramont, near the ruins of Château Le Ménage and once again the purpose of the work could not be identified, but in both cases it was thought to be in connection with V1 spares. An inspection of the Conteville/Cramont area in 2002 produced some interesting results. The new road from Conteville does not go to Domléger, but instead joins a concrete access road around a dummy runway, approximately ½ mile long. A concrete access road from the Cramont site served several parking areas inside the Bois de Ménage and later joined the new Conteville road. Despite the overgrown state of the access roads, it is estimated that at least five concrete parking areas were provided, extending at least 200yd into the forest in each acase. Since Domléger was not bombed until June 1944, we can assume that the Conteville/Cramont work had no connection with V1 storage of any description. The width and curvature of all the access roads from Conteville and Cramont plus those into the forest, give the impression that the site was intended for the V2. Since work had started before November 1943, it is likely that the site was intended to replace the nearby Fransu V2 storage site which was part of the original organisation and where no evidence of building work was found.

Parmain comprises three separate sites and is located almost directly across the River Oise from the V2 site at Méry-sur-Oise. From Parmain, take the D64 towards Nesles-la-Valée, and the first site is on the right in the wooded grounds of a château, with at least two tunnel entrances among the trees. The second site is in a wooded quarry area, also on the right, about a mile further along the D64 and comprises at least three more tunnel entrances. The third site is at Jouy-le-Comte, about 2 miles north of Parmain along the D4. A new access road was taken off the unmarked Jouy road, the single tunnel entrance ending between tree-covered banks on the left. US forces discovered V1 unloading equipment at Parmain and hence the railway station may have served as one of the many V1 unloading depots. Aerial coverage of Parmain convinced Allied Intelligence that the three storage areas were not being developed after March 1944 and the sites were not bombed.

4.2 NEW V1 STORAGE SITES

(i) Nucourt, Somme–Seine *Map 5: site 1. Michelin map No. 55 or 97.*

Location: Nucourt is almost midway between Paris and Rouen. From Paris take the N14 towards Rouen. Some 5 miles before Magny-en-Vexin, turn right on to the D206 and the village of Nucourt is 2 miles distant. Carry on along the railway line and the storage caves are adjacent to the track. A site plan has not been included because the railway line is within 200yd of the two site entrances into the former mushroom-growing caves, but the photograph shows one of the entrances and the proximity of the track. The railway is a cul-de-sac, ending at Magny-en-Vexin, but is connected to one of the main lines into Paris. The site was last visited by the author in the 1980s and the track may since have been removed, but the V1 entrances will still be in place. At the end of June 1944 Nucourt was bombed by B-17s of the US 8th Air Force. This raid and others in July using RAF bombers resulted in rock-falls within the tunnel system and when the author visited the site there were still at least 200 V1s trapped in the damaged sections. The overall storage capacity was 3,000 V1s. It is not known if these V1s were ever removed.

V1 'new' storage site at Nucourt. This is the first entrance to the storage caves. (Author)

Compass alignment building at La Flague V1 ski launch site, Cherbourg Peninsula. (Author)

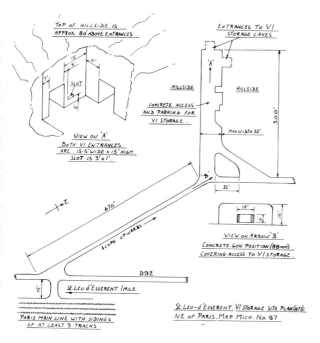

Top of hillside is
approx. 80' above entrances

Slot

VIEW ON 'A'
BOTH VI ENTRANCES
ARE 15.5' WIDE x 15' HIGH.
SLOT IS 3'x 1'.

HILLSIDE

CONCRETE ACCESS
AND PARKING FOR
VI STORAGE.

ENTRANCES TO VI
STORAGE CAVES

'A'

HILLSIDE

300'

MAX WIDTH 32'

'B'

32'

14'

VIEW ON ARROW 'B'
CONCRETE GUN POSITION (88MM)
COVERING ACCESS TO VI STORAGE.

670'

SLOPE UPWARDS

D92

St.Leu d'Esserent. 1 MILE

St.Leu-d'Esserent. VI STORAGE SITE PLAN(NTS)
NE of PARIS. MAP MICH. No.97

PARIS MAIN LINE WITH SIDINGS
OF AT LEAST 9 TRACKS

(ii) St Leu d'Esserent, north-east of Paris *Map 5: site No. 2. Michelin map No. 56 or 97.*

Location: from Paris follow the N16 north, and beyond Chantilly turn left on to the D44 for St Leu d'Esserent. In St Leu turn right on to the D92 for Montataire and Nogent-sur-Oise. The site entrance is only one mile out of St Leu and is on the left-hand side of the road by a restaurant. The original concrete access road is easily missed as it climbs away from the D92 at an acute angle. St Leu was bombed at the same time as Nucourt but the raids at St Leu carried on into July with increasing severity, the town itself being badly damaged. This was probably due to the fact that of the three new sites, St Leu had the largest storage capacity – perhaps as many as 10,000 plus. On the other side of the D92 are multi-track railway sidings, with at least nine tracks. The site lies on one of the main lines from Paris to the north-east and hence rail communications from Germany were excellent. The site access road climbs up for a

The gun emplacement at St Leu d' Esserent, September 2000. Note its undamaged condition. (Author)

St Leu d'Esserent V1 storage site, 15 August 1944. There is bomb damage to the main tunnel entrance. Note the concrete gun emplacement protecting the site access road, at lower left. (PRO)

*St Leu d'Esserent, V1 'new' storage site.
This plaque on one entrance to the caves
commemorates the courage of the townspeople and
the award of the Croix de Guerre. Most of the town
was destroyed by Allied bombers. (Author)*

few hundred yards and at the top is a large concrete gun emplacement covering the entrance; the road then turns left, the concrete widening out, and the two cave entrances are directly ahead. Both entrances are open, and to judge by the draught of fresh air coming out of them, other entrances must exist. On one of the entrance walls is a marble plaque commemorating the courage of the townspeople during the Allied bombing of the site, which lasted from 17 March to 28 August 1944. The heaviest raids were on the 7 and 8 July and 5 August 1944, and resulted in 85 per cent of the town being destroyed. There were large numbers of civilian casualties. As the plaque says, the town was awarded the Croix de Guerre for its courage. The entrance with the plaque is now used as a tip and is piled up with household rubbish.

(iii) Rilly la Montagne *Map 5: site No. 3. Michelin map No. 97 or 56.*

Location: Rilly la Montagne is the most southerly of the three new V1 storage sites and lies about 10 miles south-west of Reims. A railway line from Reims passes through Rilly immediately before it goes through a tunnel some 1.5 miles long, and it was this single-track railway tunnel that was used as the V1 storage site. Nothing now remains of its wartime use, and only the large area covered by what were sidings, at one side of the station, give any indication of how busy it originally was in 1944. Rilly was bombed several times in 1944, the heaviest series of raids occurring between 17 July and 2 August, causing extensive damage to the track, to both north and south tunnel entrances and to houses in the village itself. The railway is now double-track and electrified but through the tunnel it is still single-track.

DATE	TIME	FORCE	CLAIMED	EXCENT	LINES	PRELIMINARY RESULTS	ENEMY REACTION	P.R.U. ASSESSMENTS.

TARGET RILLY LA MONTAGNE.

NO. XI/D/12.

TYPE D.I.P.

Immediate Interpretation Report K.S.1394 d/d 2 August, 1944.

Report on damage between 1400B hours on 17th July, 1944 and 1905B hours on 1 August, 1944.

Many craters are seen in and near target areas.

A direct hit was made on the edge of the roof of the Northern tunnel entrance, breaking off the edge. Some rubble has fallen into mouth of tunnel. Other craters farther North are seen on embankments and tracks, completely blocking and severing railway lines.

Numerous hits on the embankments and railway tracks leading to Southern tunnel entrance have completely blocked and severed the railway line in many places.

Other craters are seen East and West of both tunnel entrances with extensive damage occurring to village buildings about Northern tunnel entrance and more in open fields.

Report of the bombing raids between 17 July 1944 and 1 August 1944 on Rilly la Montagne V1 storage site.(PRO)

Despite the lack of wartime remains, a visit to Rilly la Montagne is well worth while for those interested in motor racing and champagne. In the 1950s and 1960s Reims hosted the Grand Prix and other sports car racing events and the remains of the old Reims-Gueux circuit can be found on one of the routes to Rilly (see over). If you follow the new N31 out of Reims towards Soissons and turn left on to the D26 after about 2 miles, this road eventually forms part of what was the old Grand Prix circuit. The last race was in 1966. Remarkably the pits and stands are still there, intact, and with the remains of the old advertising boards everywhere. It is all very evocative and the whole area can be explored. Reims was a high-speed road circuit, but modern safety concerns meant the circuit became outdated.

To reach Rilly from Gueux, the D26 follows the 'Champagne Route' towards Epernay, passing through villages like Sacy and Ecueil, each with their own champagne 'houses', and the vines are everywhere. It provides a superb diversion from the V-weapons of the Second World War and one cannot but admire the German planners who suggested that the railway tunnel at Rilly la Montagne would make a good V1 storage site. Rilly is quite a small town – you can walk round it in 15 minutes – but it is one of the centres of the champagne industry and within the town there are forty-seven champagne houses. September is the best time to visit, during the picking and pressing of the grapes: the aroma alone is intoxicating, as the vats are open to the air. Each 'house' has its own cellar and visitors are welcome to inspect and taste the final product. It is estimated that if you have a quarter of a glass at each 'house', you would consume around two bottles of champagne during a complete tour of all forty-seven cellars, which would be a remarkable achievement!

Rilly la Montagne new V1 storage site, using a railway tunnel. (Author)

The Reims motor-racing circuit grandstand and pits are en route to Rilly la Montagne. (Author)

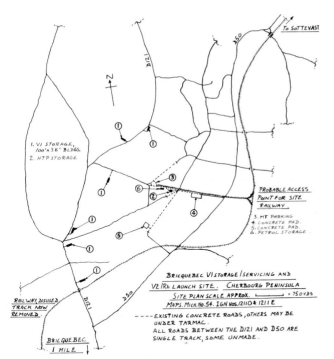

1. VI STORAGE,
100'x38' BLDGS.
2. HTP STORAGE

PROBABLE ACCESS
POINT FOR SITE
RAILWAY

3. MT PARKING
4. CONCRETE PAD.
5. CONCRETE PAD.
6. PETROL STORAGE.

RAILWAY DISUSED,
TRACK NOW
REMOVED.

BRICQUEBEC
1 MILE

BRICQUEBEC VI STORAGE/SERVICING AND
V2 IRh LAUNCH SITE. CHERBOURG PENINSULA
SITE PLAN SCALE APPROX. ⊢———————⊣ = 750 YDS
MAPS. MICH. No. 54. IGN Nos. 1211O & 1211 E

– – – – EXISTING CONCRETE ROADS, OTHERS MAY BE
UNDER TARMAC.
ALL ROADS BETWEEN THE D121 AND D50 ARE
SINGLE TRACK, SOME UNMADE.

(iv) Bricquebec *Map 4: site No. 44. Michelin map No. 54; IGN maps No. 1211 O and 1211 E.*

Location: Bricquebec is on the Cherbourg Peninsula. Follow the N13 from Cherbourg to Valognes, then take the D902 west for Bricquebec, about 8 miles from Valognes. Just before the centre of the town, turn right on to the D121 and after ¾ mile the road passes over the remains of a level crossing, although the railway track has now gone. This is the start of the storage site. The single-track line once joined the main Paris–Cherbourg line at Sottevast. The line was used to serve many sites in the area, including Bricquebec.

In the new V1 organisation, a new storage site was also required to serve the 'modified' launch sites and ski sites on the Cherbourg Peninsula, to replace the original storage site at Valognes. But unlike the Pas de Calais and Somme–Seine areas, there were no convenient caves or tunnels on the Peninsula – nothing like Nucourt or Rilly la Montagne. If the original storage sites consisted of a group of standard buildings within a relatively small area, making them easy to spot from the air and thus vulnerable to bombing, the only alternative on the Peninsula was to use the same buildings but space them out over a much wider area and integrate them into the countryside.

The resulting storage site at Bricquebec is a most interesting development. The first storage building is 200yd from the level crossing and 80yd from the road, on the right. The remaining five storage units are all in similar positions on either side of the D121, with one exception which is down a single-track lane leading to the D50. All six are the standard 100ft x 38ft wide units, giving a total storage capacity of 110 V1s. In addition to the V1 storage, HTP and petrol storage was also provided and here again there was a modification. Unlike the two-storey buildings at Domléger and Biennais, Bricquebec has a single-storey building with the vertical HTP vessels sunk into the ground. However, to judge by the internal dimensions of the building, it provided the same capacity as the others. This resulted in a building that was much easier to conceal. Instead of the external water tank for the overflow, as before, there was a drain at the base of the vessel supports. Adjacent to the HTP storage, four petrol tanks were sunk into the ground, giving a total storage capacity of 26,400 gallons, enough for nearly 200 V1s. A spur was taken off the single-track line into the site and ran past both the HTP and petrol storage positions. Great care was taken to conceal this track: it was built level with the concrete road and brushwood was scattered over it when it was not in use. It has now disappeared, but it probably entered the site close to the D50. Also on the site near the HTP storage was a pumphouse containing two electric pumps and two galvanised water tanks. Electric power was distributed around the site via a Swiss-manufactured Brown-Boveri 50kV transformer. From the HTP storage, concrete roads radiate in at least three directions, two of them ending in a large concrete area, the original usage of which cannot be determined. Item 4 on the plan is now occupied by a scrap metal firm but originally it appears to have included a pad at least 100ft x 50ft. Item 5 is also a concrete pad but it is now occupied by a rubbish disposal plant and access is not possible. There are no signs of bomb damage at Bricquebec and all the original storage buildings are in good condition, most still being used for workshops or storage. The site did not appear on the 'Crossbow' target list and its presence was only discovered when US forces landed nearby after D-Day. Valognes was on the 'Crossbow' list, and hence the strategy of concealment using dispersal as the main factor definitely appears to have been effective. Bricquebec could have been used in the new V2 organisation as a temporary storage depot and the large concrete areas used as launch platforms.

Of the three 'new' site replacements, Ytres, Renaix and Bouvines, the picture is incomplete. Renaix and Bouvines were located near Lille, now a very large and much expanded major industrial city, and as no ACIU interpretation report exists for these sites it is not known how far work there had proceeded. At Ytres it is a different story. Although the site has not been visited by the author, it is likely that a considerable amount of the original construction work still exists. South-west of Cambrai in the Pas de Calais, the Canal du Nord enters a tunnel, north of the A2 autoroute, and exits south of the village of Ytres. Originally a single-track railway line, now removed, passed near Ytres, and a spur was taken off this line to serve both ends of the canal tunnel, which was drained by the Germans.The new line actually passed through the tunnel with two lines emerging from the northern end. Several narrow-gauge lines were built for construction purposes and the ACIU photo coverage reported intensive activity around the site in July and August 1944. With a total tunnel length of over 3 miles and double-track, Ytres could have provided storage for nearly 1,500 V1s and hence this may be the reason why little work was carried out at Renaix and Bouvines.

Like Parmain, the new V1 storage organisation appears to have had at least one example of a spare parts site. At the southern end of the Forêt du Helle(t), Allied Intelligence identified a number of sunken concrete buildings, 65ft x 56ft, their roofs level with the ground, and a large number of wooden huts, 100ft x 50ft or 145ft x 50ft, actually in the forest, were built early in 1944. The site is in the Somme–Seine area, Michelin map No. 52 and IGN map 2009 OT. From Neufchâtel-en-Bray take the D1314 north and the southern end of the forest starts about 3 miles from Neufchatel. The site was attacked by Mosquitos five times between 2 and 30 March 1944 and after this Allied Intelligence appears to have lost interest in the site, preferring the numerous V1 'modified' sites in the area.

As referred to in Chapter 2.8, Allied Intelligence had identified 58 possible V1/V2 storage sites, mainly underground and divided between 'Forward' and 'Rear' locations.

Of the 'rear' storage depots on List/Map 5, the actual V1 sites can be listed as St Leu d'Esserent, Rilly la Montagne, Ytres, Renaix, Bouvines, Thiverny and Parmain, the only new site being Thiverny, NE of Paris. For the 'Forward' sites and based on ACIU reports plus inspections of some sites by Allied Intelligence soon after the Germans retreated, it is likely that the following were intended as V1 sites: Auchey les Hesdin; Rollencourt; Beaumont I and II, Authieux-Ratierville; Conde sur Risle; Authou. One determining factor is the tunnel width, which had to be at least 10ft (3m) to provide clearance over the fins of the V2. After the German retreat, the above sites were measured at less than this figure, 8.25ft (2.5m) and below. Rollencourt has been visited and from St Pol, Michelin map No. 51, take the N39 for Hesdin and after 6 miles turn right onto the D104 for Blangy sur Ternoise. In Blangy, turn left onto the D94 for Rollencourt, 3 miles, and then turn right onto the D107. The first site access road starts on the right about 250yd from the junction, parallel to the railway, leading to a stores area, and at least two more access roads are on the right, a further ½ mile along the D107. The site covers an area of about ½ square mile and it was also served by a spur line taken off the main line on the Blangy side of the village. By 17.7.44, at least five tunnel entrances had been identified at the northern, wooded part of the site, although this area is now part of a private estate and could not be inspected. Authieux-Ratierville, Michelin map No. 52 or 55, has also been visited. From Clères, north of Rouen, take the N6 in the Buchy direction and after about two miles the road dips into a wooded valley. The site entrance is on the left as the road climbs out of the hollow. Four L-shaped galleries, driven into the hillside, were inspected by Allied Intelligence but now the entrances are obscured by 50 years' growth of trees and brambles.

4.3 THE V1 LAUNCH SITES, ORIGINAL AND MODIFIED

ACIU map 6 on page 192, dated 30 August 1944, was used to indicate the location of all types of V-weapon sites identified up to that time in northern France. It is far from complete in that many sites are not identified, especially the later 'modified' V1 launch sites. The author has produced maps, which show the locations of all the known sites in northern France based on postwar information and these total over 450, compared to the ACIU map total of 180 sites. The main problem is that, although in 1944/5 surveys were carried out by the Allies on the large bunker sites such as Watten and Wizerns and reports produced on their findings, the Sanders report is the best known British example, no survey was carried out on the launch and storage sites of the V1 and V2. For the V1, this means that we do not always know precisely what type of site exists at a particular location, if it is a 'ski' site or 'modified' site, unless the site has been visited. There is one exception, the Cherbourg Peninsula, a relatively compact area and one where based on German and Allied records and visits to each site, it has been possible to state exactly what type of site is at a specific location.

The lists included with the author's site maps give an indication, where it is known, of the type of site at that location. Not all the sites have been visited, possibly a third of the total, and where nothing was found or where there are few remains, the site is not described in the following pages. One point regarding the Calais-Somme area, the German military regime here was particularly harsh, especially regarding the appropriation of agricultural and industrial products. When the German forces finally retreated from the area, many of the V1 ski sites and especially the ramps, were destroyed to prevent any possible future use. Site material was used to repair bomb-damaged farm buildings and hence, at some of the sites, only parts of the ramp blast walls, isolated buildings, of use to the farmers, plus the concrete access roads remain.

4.3.1 Calais–Somme Area (Map 1)
Site No. 11: Forêt Nationale de Tournehem *Michelin map No. 51; IGN map No. 2204 E.*

Location: this 'ski' site is between the village of Neuville and the edge of the trees, a large, State-owned forest between St Omer and Boulogne, clearly marked on the maps. In 1980, only the blast walls of the launch ramp remained, all other buildings had been destroyed, leaving only foundations in some cases. The blast walls are unusual in that they are an early example of the longest ramp used for the V1, over 150ft. Later sites used ramps of less than 70ft with much lighter construction to shorten the time needed to build the ramp.

Site No. 12: Cormette *Michelin map No. 51.*

Location: take the N43 out of St Omer towards Calais and after 4 miles turn left onto the D214; the village of Cormette is 2 miles along the D214. The 'ski' site is located in the grounds of the Chateau Ducamp and the attached farm and although access is restricted, most of the site can be seen from the adjacent roads and the entrance to the farm. From the location of the compass building, not in good condition, the launch ramp would have been on what is now a ploughed field, but all traces have now disappeared. The photo on page 26 is an excellent ACIU low-level photo of the site, complete with launch ramp. The 100ft reception/pre-launch storage building is hidden in the trees along the access road to the farm, beyond the driveway to the Château. During this visit, sites numbers 13 and 15, ski sites Zudausques and Wisques were also visited but no remains were found although there are PRU photographs of the sites in the archives.

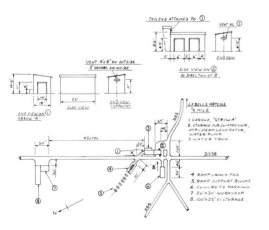

Site No. 23: La Belle-Hôtesse *Michelin map No. 51; IGN map No. 2304 E.*

Location: take the N42 out of St Omer towards Hazebrouck, through Renescure and turn right after 1.3 miles on to the D238. Follow the D238 for a mile and the site is actually at the crossroads with the D55. The garage/storage buildings for the V1 handling trolley, launch catapult HTP steam generator and air compressor are in good condition. The remains of the concrete blocks for the launch

The garage at La Belle-Hôtesse modified V1 launch site. The extension housed the V1 steam generator, air compressor and site trolley. (Author)

ramp are in the field on the opposite side of the road, although the compass alignment pad could not be found. About 450 yards along the D238 on the left-hand side in the Sercus direction are two buildings that are now used as part of a farm. Although they have been modified, they look like two standard V1 buildings. Item 7 on the site plan looks like a garage/workshop and Item 8 a 100ft x 38ft V1 storage building. La Belle-Hôtesse is one of the very few 'modified' sites in the Pas de Calais which is more or less complete, and the addition of the storage/workshop buildings is an unusual feature.

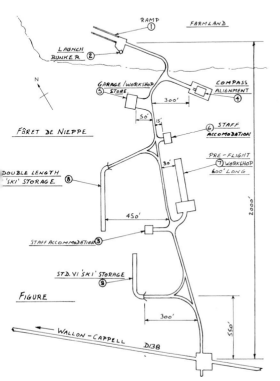

Site No. 24: Bois des Huit Rues *Michelin map No. 51; IGN map No. 2304 E.*

Location: follow the N42 from St Omer and take the D238 turning as for site 23 but after only 400 yards turn left on to the D138 and the Forêt Domaniale de Nieppe is a mile along this road. There is a large parking area by the D138 at the site entrance, which is on the left-hand side of the road. The forest is State owned and popular for picnics. Perhaps because it is State owned, this ski site has survived in remarkable condition. According to local information, it was one of the very few operational ski sites in the Pas de Calais,

Les Huit Rues V1 ski site. This photograph was taken between the launch ramp blast-walls of one of the few ski sites to fire V1s in 1944. (Author)

despite being bombed, and it continued to fire V1s at London until the German retreat. Although the main site entrance is on the D138, the best view of the ramp can be obtained from the D106: turn left on to this road just before the start of the forest, and after about half a mile the blast walls can be seen on the right on the edge of the trees. A farm track leads from the D106 giving access to the ramp walls, which are in very good condition.

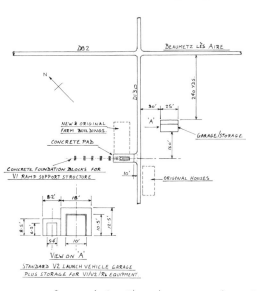

Site No. 38: Beaumetz-lès-Aire *Michelin map No. 51; IGN map No. 2305 O.*

Location: from the Beaumetz-lès-Aire crossroads, south of Thérouanne, take the D130 towards Lugy and this 'modified' site is 250 yards from the crossroads. On the left-hand side is the small garage/storage building and immediately opposite are the remains of the ramp launch pad; in the field are the concrete blocks that supported the ramp structure. The compass alignment pad could not be found, but some new farm buildings a few yards away were probably built over it. The site was not operational but one of the local residents remembers very clearly what happened in 1944. He was fourteen at the time and when the Germans arrived to build the site early in 1944, his whole family was moved out of their house at a moment's notice and given lodgings in nearby St Pol. Fortunately the site was not bombed and they were able to return to an almost intact house after the arrival of the Allied forces.

Site No. 122: Le Groseillier *Michelin map No. 51; IGN map No. 2305 O.*

Location: leave the Beaumetz site on the D130 for Lugy, at the first junction 250 yards from the site. Carry straight on, leaving the D130 for Le Grosseillier. Turn right in the centre of the village (crossroads) and the site starts about 400 yards along this road. Le Grosseillier is a 'ski' site but it was never completed. The site had two skis, only the foundations for the third were finished and the compass alignment building was also incomplete. Other buildings at the site include combined garage/workshop, two air-raid shelters and the launch ramp. All the buildings are in good condition except for the ramp blast walls, which are missing, apart from the foundations. There is no natural camouflage at the site, it is open farmland, although it is close to the village, and this lack of cover many been the reason why work was abandoned before it was finished. The larger of the two air-raid shelters, 40ft x 12ft and with its roof almost at ground level, may have been used as a workshop and its size means that it could have accommodated the whole staff of the site, around 30 men.

Site No. 112: Bois Carré, Yvrench *Michelin map No. 52.*

Location: From Abbeville take the N25 for St Riquier, then the N41 towards Auxi-le-Château. 1½ miles beyond the D108 cross-roads turn left onto a minor road for Yvrench, and Bois Carré is about a mile on the right. The site gave its name to all 'ski' sites as it was the first one identified by Allied Intelligence, the others being known as 'Bois Carré' type sites. Heavily bombed, it has survived remarkably well, and is well worth a visit. In particular the compass building and ramp blast walls are virtually intact, but the site was never operational. Photographs on page 46 show the site on 6 July 1944, after bombing, and a damaged 'ski' and ramp blast walls in 2002.

Site No. 56: Eclimeux *Michelin map No. 51.*

Location: from St Pol take the N39 towards Hesdin for 10 miles, turn right on to the D105 and Eclimeux is a mile along this road. It was perhaps the most unusual site in the area. In 1943 the village was completely cleared of inhabitants and the village itself became the site. It was a typical French village of the time, with a single main street and houses on either side, and all the V1 buildings were built into what had been the original single-storey houses. The ramp started in the churchyard and finished in the cemetery. Nevertheless the site was identified and was included on the ACIU list of sites. In 1972, when the author first visited Eclimeux, it was abandoned almost as the Germans had left it in 1944, a very strange and sad place. In 2001 it was unrecognisable. Eclimeux had been completely rebuilt and the church, like everything else was new. The cemetery was still there but there were no traces of the V1 ramp. It is now an attractive modern village.

If Eclimeux were the ultimate in camouflage, then site number 75, Vacquerie-le-Boucq, was the other extreme. Located to the south-west of Frevent, just above Auxi le Château and to the right of Buire-au-Bois, on the unmarked road to the D116, this ski site was built on the only piece of high ground in the area with no natural camouflage. The battered remains of the buildings stand out like a monument to one of the more bizarre aspects of the V-weapons organisation.

4.3.2 The Somme to the River Seine (Map 2)

There are 130 known launching sites in the area and much of the recent site location work has been carried out by a local group of French enthusiasts who are interested in the history of the V-weapons. At the Val Ygot ski site the group has cleared access roads and buildings of debris and undergrowth and part of a ramp has been installed complete with a V1, making this site a unique glimpse of history. The only information not

The abandoned railway at Neufchâtel-en-Bray, south of Dieppe, in 2000. This railway was used by many operational modified V1 sites in the area of the Forêt d'Eawy. (Author)

Abandoned V1 'modified' site, unknown French location. In the foreground are the remains of the handling trolley for general site movements of the V1. (IWM)

available on the 130 sites is the type of launch site, ski or 'modified'. As in the Pas de Calais, many sites have been visited and included here are those sites which have actually been found and where a large number of the buildings remain, or where there are features of special interest.

Much of the central area from Aumale and St Saëns to the coast 25 miles away is densely wooded, mainly with pine trees, and this provided the ideal location for building the later generation of 'modified' sites. The author estimates that out of the 133 total, 46 are ski sites and 77 are 'modified' sites. There are two 'hot-spots' of sites in these forest areas. North of Aumale in the Forêt d'Eu there are 23 sites, and north of St Saëns and Neufchâtel-en-Bray in the Forêt d'Eawy there are 24 sites. In both cases the majority are 'modified' sites and were operational. The author has concentrated mainly in the Forêt d'Eawy area, where the Val Ygot restored site is located, using Neufchâtel-en-Bray as a base. The abandoned railway that served many of the sites in the area, including the St Martin l'Hortier storage site, passes through Neufchâtel. This part of France is renowned for its food and cider and towns like Neufchâtel, St Saëns and Aumale make ideal touring locations. The ski sites in the area appeared to have suffered a similar fate to those in the Pas de Calais and of those visited, with the exception of Val Ygot, most have only a couple of buildings remaining. Typical are Les Petits Moraux (39), La Chenie (41) and Les Hayons, Le Logis de Hayons (48).

VI 'modified' site ramp, destroyed by bombing, unknown French location. (IWM)

Six 'modified' sites are grouped together in the Forêt d'Eawy. All were operational and La Mare du Four is one of the best examples. La Laie Madame 'modified' site is also worth visiting, situated as it is in another branch of the forest, Les Nappes, on the other side of the D915.

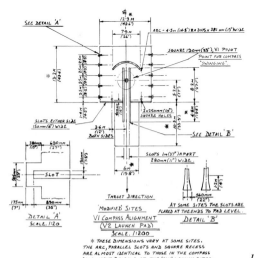

(i) La Mare du Four: site No. 55 *Michelin map No. 52; IGN map No. 2009 OT.*

From Pommerval, north of St Saens, take the D915 towards Dieppe. About a mile after Les Petits Moraux, with its ski site remains on the right-hand side of the road, turn left on to the D77. After a mile turn left on to the D22 and continue through Le Hoquet for about ¾ mile into the forest. The site starts on the D22 just after the second turning on the left (the first is an unmade

Details of the compass alignment pad at modified launch sites.

track). On the left, a few yards from the junction, are the remains of the garage and 100 yards beyond, on the left, is a short concrete access road. This leads to the compass alignment pad with its curved trough and parallel slots for the wheels of the V1 trolley. In the centre is the rectangular recess above which the V1 was suspended from a portable hoist while its compass was adjusted to the correct target bearing. In this central recess, even after nearly sixty years, is the aluminium socket into which the V1's pivot post fitted, allowing the missile, which weighed nearly 2 tons, to rotate about its centre of gravity during the compass adjustment. Across the road another short concrete access road leads to the launch pad; here the V1 was pushed on to the base of the ramp prior to launch. The ramp and its concrete support blocks have vanished but the wide trench in the ground can still be

La Mare du Four, Forêt d'Eawy, operational modified V1 site. The umbrella is in the socket that was used as a pivot point to 'swing' the V1 for compass alignment checks before it was transferred across the road to the launch ramp. (Author)

seen. The ramp ended at the edge of the forest, giving a clear path for the V1 to leave the end of the ramp. A few yards to the left of the base of the ramp are the remains of the small launch bunker, partially buried in the ground. Looking around, it is not difficult to see how this site, like many others in the forest, managed to escape detection from Allied aircraft, launching their V1s up to the very last minute.

(ii) La Laie Madame: site No. 56 *Michelin map No. 52; IGN map No. 2009 OT.*

Location: retrace your route along the D77 back to the D915 is reached, then carry on straight across the D915. After ½ mile the D77 enters the forest and almost immediately on the right are the remains of a concrete road, disappearing into the trees. A few yards along on the left is a concrete apron with some modern garages plus the remains of some small storage buildings for the site. Follow the concrete road into the forest, and 200 yards further on the concrete ends and among the trees on the right, only a few yards from the road, are the remains of the launch bunker, pads and ramp. This site was also operational, launching its V1s towards London, and it too appears to have escaped detection.

The launch bunker of the modified V1 launch site at La Laie Madame in the Forêt d'Eawy, Somme–Seine. This site was operational in 1944. (Author)

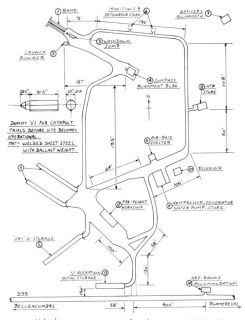

VI 'SKI' LAUNCHING SITE PLAN. SCALE/DIMENSIONS ARE APPROXIMATE.
POMMEREVAL – VAL YGOT – FORÊT D'EAWY.
SOMME – SEINE. MAPS MICH. NO. 52. IGN NO. 2009 OT

(iii) Val Ygot, Ardouval (La Grande Volée): site No. 39 *Michelin map No. 52; IGN map No. 2009 OT.*

Val Ygot came as something as a surprise to the author, after years of looking for site remains where, in many cases, not only had the Germans made every attempt to hide the location from prying eyes but the results of many years of natural growth had resulted in superb camouflage. The surprise came a couple of years ago, while exploring the Forêt d'Eawy. At one road junction there was a signpost to the 'V1 Site' – the first and only time that the existence of a site had been made so obvious.

Location: probably the most convenient way to reach Val Ygot is from Pommerval, north of St Saëns. Take the D99 out of

The launch bunker at Val Ygot ski site. (Author)

Dummy V1s like this one at Val Ygot ski site, were used to test the launch catapult before a site became operational. (Author)

The 'Richthaus' compass alignment building, Val Ygot ski site. The parallel slots for the V1 trolley can still be seen, as can the 'arc' for 'swinging' the V1's compass. (Author)

Pommerval towards Bellencombre. The road soon runs alongside the forest and the site entrance is on the right a few yards after the road enters the forest proper. There is a large parking area off the road, and immediately on the left as you enter the site are the remains of the V1 reception building, badly damaged by bombing. Val Ygot was never operational, possibly due to the bombing. All three ski storage buildings have disappeared, although their access roads and foundations are still in place. Altogether nine buildings have survived in good condition, including the main workshop for fitting out the V1 prior to launch. The non-magnetic compass alignment building also has provision for heating the concrete pad immediately underneath the V1 pivot point. This underground, coal-fired heating system appears to have been used only where damp was a problem, usually in a forest location. As with the V2s, the operation of some of the more delicate parts of the V1 was adversely affected by moisture. It is only a short distance from here to the launch point and the fact that part of the steel ramp structure is in position, complete with a V1, gives a completely different atmosphere to the site. The launch bunker can be entered and the viewing slot provides a good picture of the launch point, although the ramp has been positioned about 15ft too close to the concrete launch pad. The viewing slot now looks out at part of the ramp instead of the start of it, where the V1 would have been sitting, waiting for the final injection of steam into the launch ramp tube, accelerating the V1 from 0 to 250mph by the time it reached the end of the ramp, less than 100ft away. Near the launch ramp pad is one of the test weapons, a welded steel cylinder filled with concrete and weighing 3 tons. It was used before the first live launch of a V1 to check that the ramp was functioning correctly. This is a very rare item and may even be the only one in existence.

All the buildings have noticeboards describing (in English) what they were used for and this helps to understand how the site functioned. At a ski site like Val Ygot, the V1 arrived by road fully fuelled and armed and it was put into ski storage on a simple trolley. Before launch, the V1 was transferred into the main workshop where the tailplane, fin and rudder were fitted, and fuel system, auto-pilot and control system checked out. If a radio transmitter was fitted for flight corrections and target impact information, this was also checked, together with its 50ft trailing aerial in the tail. The V1 was then lifted on to a special double trolley, the 'Zubringerwagen', with the top part resting on springs and locked to the lower section. It was then moved to the 'Richthaus' or 'Einstellhaus', the non-

The ramp catapult piston, Val Ygot ski site. It was fitted into the tube below and the 'fin' on top engaged in the underside of the V1. The 'Dampferzeuger' HTP steam generator was bolted on to the end of the tube and steam forced the piston and V1 along the ramp. (Author)

magnetic building, aligned in the same direction as the ramp. In the Richthaus the wings were fitted on to the single wooden spar and locked in position. The auto-pilot compass was then adjusted on to the correct target bearing, with the V1 swinging freely above the

A V1 on the ramp at Val Ygot ski site. The ramp should actually be moved forward to the start of the concrete pad. (Author)

grooved arc on the floor. Other checks were carried out on the gyros and the rate of turn clock, if fitted. At the ramp the gas seal was fitted into the ramp tube, followed by the 300lb piston which was pushed 6–8ft along the tube; then the gas seal behind the piston was checked with compressed air, brought up in cylinders on another trolley. When the V1 arrived from the Richthaus, final checks were carried out on the weapon's compressed air supply that powered the control surface servo-motors and it was topped up if necessary. Final arming of the warhead was completed and the V1 was pushed on to the base of the ramp with the top part of the trolley, which then disengaged and moved backwards when the V1 was in its correct position at the base of the ramp and engaged into the top of the piston. The HTP steam generator or 'Dampferzeuger', already filled with 26 gallons of HTP and half a gallon of catalyst (calcium or potassium permanganate), was then bolted on to the end of the ramp tube. Electrical connections were made between the Argus ram jet's sparkplug and other launch systems and the launch bunker via an extendable arm near the end of the ramp. Final checks and launch procedure were completed, which took about 30 seconds as the motor ran up to full power and the steam pressure built up to a maximum of 1,000lb psi, shearing off a ¼in pin holding the V1 stationary on the ramp. The V1 then accelerated along the ramp, reaching a free air speed of 250mph. Final operations as it left the ramp included activation of the weapon's electrical system, including the three fuses for the warhead, and the uncaging of the gyros from their stops. The tube piston and launch cradle, the top part of the Zubringerwagen, went their own separate ways after launch; the heavier piston would fly about 250 yards and the cradle about half this distance and both were recovered and used again if possible. After each launch the pad behind the ramp was hosed down to remove all traces of the volatile HTP, a drainage sump being provided for this.

The total number of personnel at a ski launch site was about fifty, of whom twenty were solely involved with moving the weapons around the site; the remainder were assembly, systems and servicing staff. The operational use of 'modified' sites such as La Mare du Four was probably very similar to the ski sites, the main difference being the lack of covered facilities for the personnel fitting equipment and carrying out checks.

4.3.3 River Seine to Cherbourg Peninsula (Map 3)

This area is unique as there are only twenty-three V1 sites in an area that is almost as large as the Somme–Seine region and there is not a single ski or storage site. All the sites are the 'modified' type. The area's location put the target cities – London, Portsmouth, Southampton, Plymouth and Bristol – at the extreme end of the V1's range. The gradual improvement in the V1's performance, achieved from 1943 onwards, meant that eventually their range increased and the situation changed to the extent that the area featured in the revised plans for the V1 offensive. Once again the bulk of the sites occur in two 'hot-spots'. Moving west from Rouen, the first group of eight is within a 15-mile radius of Brionne, and the second group of nine is within a 10-mile radius of St Pierre sur Dives, between Lisieux and Falaise.

The variable survival of the 'modified' sites is clearly shown in this area. If the site is in a rural area, still devoid of modern building projects, especially new roads, then the only building above ground, the dual garage, as at La Belle-Hôtesse in the Pas de Calais, is likely to have survived intact as agricultural storage. If there are new roads in the area, nothing will be left. Typical of this is the Vimont site (20) near Caen, which has been lost to new road developments. The remainder of the V1 sites are well scattered and in isolated positions to the west of Caen, and their location seems illogical bearing in mind the security and supply needs of each site.

(i) Le Petit Boisney: site No. 5 *Michelin map No. 54 or 55.*

West of Rouen is now a maze of motorways, but head for Caen on the A13 motorway and take the N138 towards Bourgtheroulde, passing through Brionne to the large roundabout at the junction with the N13. Turn right on to the N13 for Lisieux and right again after a few hundred yards for Petit Boisney. Follow the road to the right, heading back towards the roundabout, parallel to the N13, and the site buildings are on the left, opposite open fields and adjacent to a farm. The buildings were used for storage of the V1 towing vehicle and

The modified V1 site at Le Petit Boisney. In the extension to the garage the metal troughs for the HTP steam generator are still in place after fifty-five years. (Author)

trolley, and the small extensions for storing the HTP steam generator, air compressor and cylinders. What is remarkable about the site is that the raised metal troughs used as guides for the wheels of the steam generator are still in situ in the side extensions to the garage. In fact it looks almost as if the site was in use only a short time ago. Non-ferrous containers were probably placed between the troughs to catch any HTP overflow and this is the reason why they were raised off the floor as HTP reacts violently with concrete. Similar troughs or rails were installed on the concrete pad in front of the ramp so that both the V1 trolley and the steam trolley could be pushed up to the ramp in exactly the right position. In particular, the steam trolley bolted on to the front of the launch tube by mating with four 1in diameter studs projecting from the ramp tube front plate, a gas-tight seal being essential between the tube and steam generator. The rails ensured that these studs were aligned correctly with the holes in the steam trolley flange.

It is remarkable that in the year 2001 these fittings were still in place. The whereabouts of the compass alignment pad, launch pad and ramp blocks could not be determined.

4.3.4 Cherbourg Peninsula (Map 4)

For the Germans the whole Cherbourg Peninsula was part of the 'forbidden zone' and was easily isolated from the rest of France. For this reason, and also perhaps because none of the sites became operational, both 'ski' and 'modified' sites have survived in better condition here than in any other site area. Because of its relatively small area, we know precisely how many sites were built, and the author has visited each one of them. Eight 'ski' sites and thirty 'modified' sites were built; some were bombed but the greatest damage has been done by new housing developments spreading out from Cherbourg.

(i) Hardinvast (Bristellerie): site No. 5
IGN map No. 1210 E.

From Cherbourg take the D3/D904 for Les Pieux. (Alternatively, take the N13 and before leaving Cherbourg take the D900 turning to the right. The D900 joins the D3/D904 and then branches off to the left after ¼ mile.) Follow the D900 for 1.5 miles and then turn right on to the D152 for Hardinvast. After 300 yards turn left on to a concrete and tarmac road and the site is among some new detached houses, on either side of the road. This ski site was the first one discovered by the author

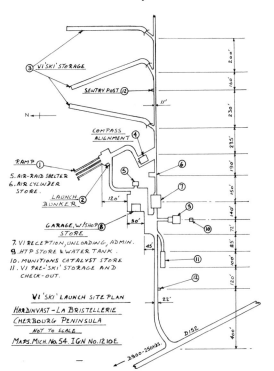

in 1970 and at that time the area around Cherbourg was very little different from what it must have been like in 1944. The site itself was absolutely untouched, and once we were among the buildings there was an intense atmosphere that was difficult to describe, but we would not have been surprised to suddenly have been challenged by some grey-uniformed soldiers. There were no signs of bomb damage and all three skis were intact, as were the ramp blast walls, the Richthaus, the V1 reception and the pre-flight check-out. Nothing had been touched or damaged, in fact inside the first ski near the entrance was stencilled 'MAX SPEED 30 MPH' – a relic from the US occupation of 1944. The skis themselves were almost completely earthed over and had the appearance of tunnels. The ramp blast walls are 69ft 6in long, the shortest ramp length used for the V1, and they are aligned on Bristol.

Thirty years later things have changed at Hardinvast. Developers have built a number of new houses on the site. The pre-flight check-out building remains, as do the blast walls and the skis, but the reception building has gone and the workshop/garages are now in someone's garden. However, there is plenty of space to park a car on the site and for the more adventurous the adjacent site of La Motterie (6) is within walking distance. Along the site road, past the skis on the left, a track leads off to the right and crosses the D119. After 300 yards take the left-hand fork on to the Chemin du Poirier, one of the 'Chemin Rurals'. (Some of these are paved and some are 'green lanes' but there are lots of them in northern France and they are ideal for walking.) The site starts ½ mile on the right with the first of the three skis, and the road is now concrete. The second ski is a few yards further on the right and then the track joins a wider track. The magnetic building, ramp and workshops were on the left and the reception and pre-flight check-out on the right. Some of the buildings have been converted: the magnetic building in particular has been turned into a very attractive house. La Motterie does not have the simplicity of layout of Hardinvast and access is not as convenient but it does show two widely differing approaches to site layout.

West of Cherbourg there are two more ski sites, both aligned on Bristol, as are all the sites in the northern sector of the Peninsula. Both these sites were given names by the ACIU that provided very little help in the task of locating them, years later. The ACIU list describes them as X1/A/10 Flottemanville-Hague I and 10B Flottemanville-Hague II. Like many sites, these were built overlapping several local boundaries and hence I is between Le Pivot and La Moulinnerie and II is near La Roussellerie, at the La Croix Rouge crossroads.

(ii) Flottemanville–Hague I, Le Pivot–La Moulinnerie: site No. 7 *IGN map No. 1210E and 1110 E.*

Location: take the coast road west from Cherbourg, towards Equeurdreville. At the Equeurdreville roundabout, take the D901 exit for Beaumont and La Hague. Turn left on to the D16 at Le Manoir and turn right at the first crossroads on to the D152. After a mile there is a pylon and small football stadium on the right and the site is in the fields on the opposite side of the road. The site is surrounded by green lanes and access is possible to all the surviving buildings. The lack of concrete access roads gives the site the appearance of having been built at random in the fields. This isn't helped by the fact that the compass building and the skis have disappeared. Only two skis were built and these were located alongside the D123. Park by the access road to the football stadium and the V1 pre-flight storage is across the road against the hedge, looking slightly the worse for wear. Follow the track opposite the stadium and this leads to the ramp, now overgrown; the blast walls are more or less complete. Uniquely at this site additional ramp support blocks were added at the end of the blast walls. The original ramp length was similar to that at Hardinvast, about 70ft, but it was subsequently decided to extend the ramp length by some 50ft, resulting in a total of 120ft. Bristol was at the extreme limit of the original V1's range and increasing the ramp length meant that a heavier V1 with more fuel or heavier payload (or both) could be used. Why was this modification only made at this site? There may have been a programme under way to extend all eight sites on the Peninsula, but events overtook these plans. When US forces landed at Utah Beach in June 1944 the Peninsula itself was very quickly cut off, leaving only air and sea routes open, and all major construction work by the Germans here would have stopped immediately.

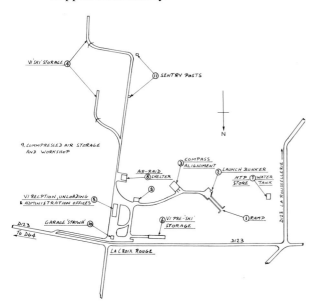

(iii) Flottemanville-Hague II, La Croix Rouge: site No. 8 *IGN map No. 1210E.*

Take the D123 from Flottemanville-Hague I in the Cherbourg direction and La Croix Rouge is at the junction with the D406. Turn right at the junction and the site is on the right in the fields. It has suffered from bomb damage, with the ramp blast walls and compass building in a poor state but there are still enough remains with access roads to inspect the layout. One unique feature at this site is the presence of a garage, as found at the 'modified' sites. Only the foundations remain but it appears to have been of about the same size, and its location at the site entrance and close to the main areas of concrete may be significant. Garages at the 'modified' sites were also suitable for the V2's armoured half-track launch control vehicle, and hence Flottemanville-Hague II may have been modified to function as a V2 launch site. This is covered in more detail in the later V2 section.

The remaining four ski sites are all to the east of Cherbourg and form another 'hot-spot'. They are all within a short distance of one another and they are all relatively well preserved and accessible.

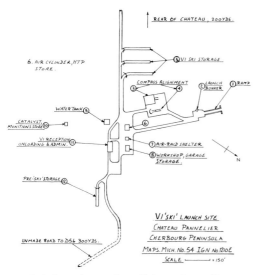

REAR OF CHATEAU, 200 YDS.

6. AIR CYLINDER, HTP STORE.

COMPASS ALIGNMENT ③

⑤ VI SKI STORAGE

④ LAUNCH BUNKER ① RAMP

WATER TANK ⑨

CATALYST, MUNITIONS STORE ⑩

VI RECEPTION UNLOADING & ADMIN. ⑪

⑥

⑦ AIR-RAID SHELTER

⑧ WORKSHOP, GARAGE STORAGE.

N

PRE-SKI STORAGE ⑫

UNMADE ROAD TO D56 300 YDS.

VI 'SKI' LAUNCH SITE
CHATEAU PANNELIER
CHERBOURG PENINSULA
MAPS. MICH. No. 54 IGN No 1210E
SCALE ⊢———⊣ ≈ 150'

V1 ski launch site plan: Château Pannelier.

(iv) Château Pannelier: site No. 10 *IGN map No. 1210 E.*

Location: take the N13 from Cherbourg and leave it at the second junction, for Delasse. Rejoin the N13 heading back towards Cherbourg and after only a few yards the Pannelier turning is on the right. The entrance to the château is on the right, 300 yards from the N13, but this is not the best way of entering the site. Turn left off the N13 on to the D56, which passes over the N13, and after ¾ mile on the left is a disused entrance to the château grounds, and in the distance some of the site buildings can be seen from here. The château at Pannelier has been empty for at least thirty years, possibly even since the Germans hurriedly left in 1944. Conversations with other local château owners with sites in the grounds elicited the information that part of the V1 launch team and all the Organisation Todt officers supervising the construction work were billeted at the house. Such cohabitation with the enemy sometimes led to a situation where the original owners were hardly the most popular people after the liberation. Whatever the reasons for its abandonment, the farmhouse adjoining the château is occupied and in 2001, the author was told that it had been sold. If this is so, and a lot of work needs doing to the house and grounds, the new owners may restrict access to the site.

The Pannelier site is very well laid out, in many ways resembling the symmetrical layout at Hardinvast, which would have made operational use of the site very easy. All the buildings are intact, including the three skis, V1 reception, pre-flight check-out, magnetic building and blast walls. The only missing item is a concrete access road from the D56. From the position of the V1 reception it seems likely that the D56 was intended to be the access point, and the final stretch of roadway would probably have been added just before the site became operational. The unique feature of Pannelier lies next to the Richthaus compass alignment building and consists of a concrete pad with a set of recesses in the concrete identical to those found in the building; this is the alignment arc, the square above which the V1 was swung, and the troughs for the V1's trolley. This pad is also identical to the pads at the 'modified' sites. This means that two V1s could have had their compasses checked and other pre-flight operations carried out, one under cover and the other in the open, at the same time. There are several possible explanations for this. First, two V1s could have been prepared for launching at the same time. It is unlikely that Pannelier was intended to have a faster launch rate than other sites in the area, but it is the only ski site in northern France with this feature. It is extremely unlikely that the open-air pad was built on the whim of the OT, just as a 'good idea'. But there is another, more sinister, possibility and one which is definitely based on fact. It is possible that some of the warheads at Pannelier were intended to be loaded not with high explosive but with something far more noxious: poison gas. In the Richthaus, with the doors closed and the V1 fuelled and virtually ready for launch, any problems with the warhead while it was swinging for its compass-target alignment would have been disastrous. With a conventional warhead, although not finally armed, it was a dangerous procedure, but with poison gas it was potentially lethal. The poison gases most easily manufactured and used in the First World War and still being produced in the Second were chlorine and phosgene. Both are heavier than air, chlorine 2.5 times and phosgene 3.5 times, and they would take effect very quickly, within seconds. The Richthaus had only two small windows and the heavy double doors were usually closed during the final checks, and thus if something went wrong everyone inside the building would have been doomed. Was this the reason for the open-air pad at Pannelier?

Another interesting point regarding these pads was that British Intelligence had noticed that if the compass building at a ski site was destroyed, it was not rebuilt but was replaced with one of the pads as at the 'modified' sites.

(v) La Sorellerie: site number 11 *IGN map No. 1210 E.*

Location: leave Pannelier on the D56, travelling away from the N13, and the next ski site is barely half a mile away on the left. It can be seen from the road, so there is little danger of it being missed, especially as it stands on the highest piece of ground south of Cherbourg, at 584ft above sea level. Nearby is the modern communications mast for the Cherbourg area. In 1943–4 the site must have been clearly visible from the air, with most of the buildings being in open farmland. Despite being heavily bombed, La Sorellerie has survived remarkably well and all the buildings can be inspected. (You may find the fields occupied by very large and inquisitive French cows.) Most easily accessible are the pre-flight check-out at the site entrance, the V1 reception and the first ski; one of the smaller workshops is actually built into the farmhouse. The layout at La Sorellerie is conventional, the only unusual feature being that one ski is separated from the other two by a few hundred yards, on the opposite side of the site.

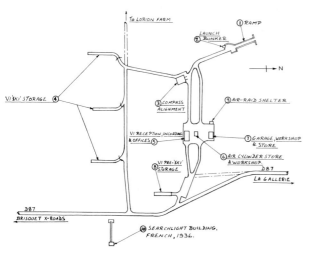

(vi) Lorion: site number 12 *IGN map No. 1210 E.*

Location: carry on along the D56 from La Sorellerie for a mile to the crossroads with the D87 and turn left on to the D87. This leads to the farm at Lorion and the site starts from here, on the left-hand side. The site entrance is on the left, but it is on a bend. Cars can be parked on the concrete access road or on the left by the gate, further around the bend. This other

The mysterious 'searchlight' building at the Lorion V1 ski site. (Author)

entrance is a green lane. The buildings at Lorion are in good condition although some of the concrete access roads are so overgrown with grass that it is difficult to see how the site was arranged. All three skis are on the left along the entrance road to the farm; the pre-flight check-out is immediately on the left at the main site entrance, and this leads to a large concrete pad which in turn leads on to the V1 reception, garages/workshops, compass alignment and ramp. It is quite clear from this site how far each V1 travelled during its preparations for flight. From the ski storage to the pre-flight check-out and the compass building is a considerable distance, and towing vehicles would have had to be used. In the final stages the V1 may have been manhandled on to the ramp but all other movements would have been motorised.

Lorion also has a strange feature. Almost opposite the farm entrance on the D56 is another building, standing by itself in the field. Given its location, it seemed logical to assume that it was connected with the site, but it is a type of building that the author had never seen before at a V1 launch site. It is about the size of a detached house, but with only one storey. From the large double front entrance, two rails, 57in apart and set in concrete, lead out into the field for 120ft towards the D56, ending in a concrete pad 12ft x 22ft and only a few feet from the road. The alignment of the rails is due west, so that probably ruled out anything launched towards England. If it was for mobile anti-aircraft guns, it seemed an unnecessarily complicated method of providing them. Inside the 'house', to the left of the double doors, was a large concrete plinth, obviously meant for a static power plant, and at the back of the building were some large concrete tanks, 8ft high, with slots in the concrete. The mystery wasn't solved until 2000, after another visit to Pannellier. Leaving by the front entrance, we turned right on to the D121. The road dips down and climbs back through some trees and just before the first bend is a newish house set back from the road. To the left of the house and 50ft from the road was another of the mystery buildings. The lady of the house was cutting the grass and we waited by the gate until she came across. We explained what we were doing and she went for her husband. He knew all about the mystery building in his garden. It was built in 1936 by the French for a searchlight, as part of the air defences of Cherbourg. The searchlight ran out on a trolley on the rails, and when not in use it was hidden from view in the 'house'. Power came from the mains, but a generator provided an emergency power supply and the concrete tanks were filled with water as a coolant supply. Did the Germans ever use the searchlight at Lorion? Probably not – the V1 sites were difficult targets and all the air-raids took place during the day. At least the mystery was solved!

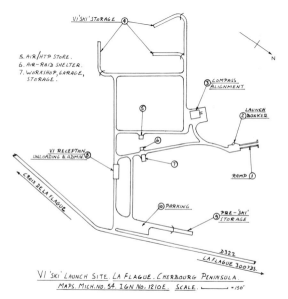

VI'SKI' LAUNCH SITE. LA FLAGUE. CHERBOURG PENINSULA.
MAPS. MICH.NO. 54. IGN No. 1210E. SCALE. •————• =150'

(vii) La Flague: site number 9 *IGN map No. 1210 E.*

Location: from Lorion carry on past the D87 and the first D413 junction, until the T-junction and turn left on to the D413. After ½ mile turn left on to the D322 and the site is ¾ mile on the right, in the fields close to the road. Once again, all the buildings except the ramp walls are in good condition. The blast walls are overgrown and barely visible under the brambles and the same applies to the skis which are at the rear of the site and partially buried. In exceptionally good condition is the V1 reception building, where the V1s were unloaded from the lorries and transferred to the general site movement trolley before being moved to the ski storage. The reception also contained the offices for the clerical staff and their paperwork. No fittings were ever left at the sites – the Germans removed everything before retreating – but it does not take much imagination to picture how it would have looked in 1944.

All these four sites are in superb walking country, undulating and wooded in places with numerous chemin rural. La Flague, Lorion and La Sorellerie are all connected by these tracks and a full day could easily be spent walking between the three. La Flague is the last of the ski sites on the Peninsula, and the next group of sites is in some ways even more impressive than the original V1 launch sites. The Cherbourg 'modified' V1 launch sites are different from those in the rest of northern France. The basic layout is similar, with two concrete pads. One contains the slots for compass alignment, as found on the floor of the Richthaus, and this pad is usually at least 50 yards from the ramp. The other pad leads directly on to the base of the ramp and it contains a large covered-over drainage sump, 18ft long x 30in wide and about 10ft deep. On either side of the sump is a row of twelve 0.8in (20mm) bolts, set in pockets. From German drawings it seems that these bolts were used to hold two rails on to which the V1's trolley was pushed, allowing it to be located in the correct position at the base of the ramp as quickly as possible. These rails and the bolts were far stronger than would have been required for this operation and it is likely that the Rheinböte's mobile launcher was intended to be clamped to the rails before firing. The main difference from other 'modified' sites is in the garage, the only building of any size at the sites. On the Peninsula it is always a single building with no extensions, whereas at the other site areas, such as La Belle-Hôtesse, attached to the garage is a substantial addition containing several entrances. Each garage, regardless of its location, usually had a small, sunken water tank, either attached to it or adjacent. (This tank might also be near the compass pad.) The tank, made of concrete, was about 12ft x 6ft and about 5ft deep and was used as an emergency water supply, for diluting HTP, and so on.

The ramp itself was intended to be erected and removed in a few hours. A pre-fabricated steel framework was bolted together at the site and the seven pairs of legs fastened into small, steel-framed, hardwood blocks recessed into concrete blocks sunk into the ground. Compared to the ski sites, which used a more substantial ramp structure, the ramp and fittings at the 'modified' sites may have been lightweight versions, especially the launch tube piston which normally weighed 300lb. During assembly of the ramp at the ski sites, rails were usually laid on the concrete inside the blast walls, and these were used by a portable crane that assisted with assembling the ramp structure. This was not possible at all the 'modified' sites because the concrete support blocks were usually laid on rough ground and in many cases there were no flat areas to provide access from the side; hence most of the ramp assembly work at these sites must have been done by manpower alone.

Thirty 'modified' sites were built on the Peninsula and they have all survived in remarkable condition with the garages and pads. One of the problems with the pads is that farmers use them as hard-standing for cattle feed – as shown in the photograph of the compass pad at the Cadets site. Not many of the launch ramp concrete blocks have survived; at many sites they have been dug up and disposed of or used to obstruct gaps in hedges. Where they have survived, they usually contain the hardwood blocks for the ramp support legs. It is clear from the method used to erect the ramp that these blocks were intended to be used only once and then replaced. As there are thirty sites they are not described individually, but, because many of the sites are very difficult to find, details are included of their location.

Note: the numbers on the V1 'modified' launch site plans refer to the following features (all access roads and pads are concrete): 1) V1 compass alignment pad, which replaced the Richthaus at ski sites. At some sites where access was possible for a Meillerwagen, this pad could be used as a V2 firing point; 2) V1 launch pad with HTP wash-down area and rail bolts. This pad was positioned immediately in front of the ramp; 3) Launch bunker. Two versions were used, a smaller bunker usually partially buried and an above-ground 'telephone-box' type. In both cases the viewing slot overlooked the base of the ramp; 4) The garage. For the V1 it housed the 'Dampferzeuger' steam generator, water pump, air compressor and site trolley. If the site was used for the V2 it housed the half-track launch control vehicle, and in this role it was referred to by the V2 mobile batteries as the 'Striwa'; 5) Concrete parking for weapons and service vehicles; 6) Additional parking or passing places; 7) Sentry post positions; 8) Launch ramp support blocks; 9) Water tank. The two most complete sites are described in detail below:

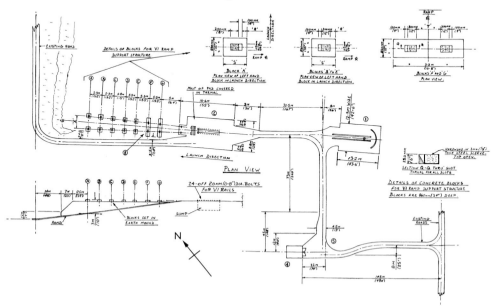

(i) Hameau de Haut: site No. 21 *IGN map No. 1210 E.*

Location: leave Cherbourg on the N13 and at the Delasse junction turn right on to the D56. After ½ mile turn right on to an unmarked road for Hameau de Haut. The garage is at the first bend, facing down the road; it has been re-roofed but there are still traces of camouflage paint on the side walls. The road is now concrete under the tarmac and a few yards further on the concrete widens, forming a parking/passing place. At the next bend the road turns sharply to the left and on the right-hand apex of the bend, which has been widened to improve access, is the short entrance to the compass alignment pad. Follow the road round to the left, and where the concrete widens the ramp pad and concrete blocks are on the right. The blocks are built into a slightly raised bank of earth, which runs alongside the original road, and this would have allowed a mobile crane to be used for erection of the ramp, if required. The firing bunker has disappeared but it was probably on the left, close to the hedge, with a good view of the start of the ramp. The outline of the 18ft drainage sump in the ramp pad can still be seen, together with the remains of the two rows of bolts that ran on either side of the sump. The ramp blocks are all complete and some of them still have the hardwood inserts complete with steel sleeves for the legs of the prefabricated ramp structure. From the undamaged state of these blocks it is clear that they were never used, but Hameau de Haut was certainly complete and ready for operations.

(ii) La Capitainerie: site No. 25 *IGN map No. 1210 E.*

Take the N13 from Cherbourg as far as the Valognes junction, and in the centre of Valognes turn left on to the D902 for Quettehou. After ½ mile turn left on to a single-track road for La Capitainerie. After about 250yd the site starts with the garage which is built into farm buildings on the left. The compass pad is 100yd further on in the field on the left and the ramp and pad are 70yd beyond this on the right. The firing bunker is right on the edge of the road and looks like a concrete phone box.

With the garage built into farm buildings, it seems that a serious attempt was made to make this site invisible from the air. The whole area in front of the farmhouse has been concreted over as parking, although the short section from the garage has been left as original. The concrete road, now under tarmac, continues to the compass pad, which is in good condition and opposite, against the hedge, is the concrete water tank. The launch pad is also well preserved and the outline of the sump can be seen, although the bolts were not fitted, and the pockets in the concrete are empty. The ramp blocks extend into the trees, with only one pair missing, and many of them have the hardwood blocks for the ramp support legs. As already mentioned, the launch bunker is by the road and is of the above-ground telephone-box type. There were two distinct types of launch bunker at 'modified' sites: the telephone-box type and the below-ground type. These were like a smaller version of the original ski sites.

La Capitainerie also has another feature that appears at some 'modified' sites. This is the concrete sentry post, looking rather like a dog kennel. There were usually two, on the edge of the site road. At La Capitainerie they are a few yards past the launch pad, the first on the left and its companion further on the right. They are about 4ft high by 4ft square, and contain a recess with the remains of a door, large enough for supplies such as ammunition, food and drink. They were most probably intended for soldiers checking vehicles using the site road but, as at La Capitainerie, they are sometimes on one side of the site only or they are missing completely. At the Hardinvast ski site there are two larger versions, one at each end of the

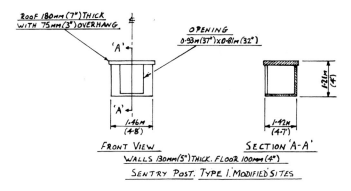

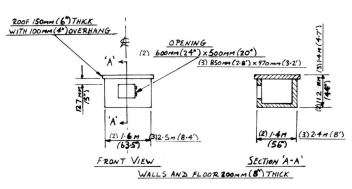

Details of two types of sentry post at modified sites. Scale 1:150

site entrance road, but generally they did not appear at ski sites. The author believes that their apparently random appearance relates to the amount of non-site traffic allowed at a particular site. Some roads were closed off to local vehicles and sentry posts would only then be installed where access to the fields was still allowed and so occasional farm traffic required checking. At other sites, depending on the risk, it was considered that the level of security could be reduced.

La Capitainerie is a well-concealed site. The ramp extends under the cover of mature beech trees and would have been invisible from the air. The farmhouse has always been empty during the author's several visits to the site, and it would have been used by site personnel during and after construction. Some sites were still occupied by German troops when US airborne forces arrived early in the morning of 6 June 1944. Conversations with people who witnessed these events as children indicate that at some sites the Germans were killed in the buildings they were occupying. This may explain why the farmhouse is maintained, but remains empty. Following are the locations of the remaining 28 'modified' sites on the Peninsula, starting with those to the west of Cherbourg and continuing with those to the E or S.

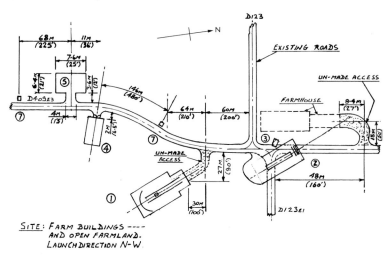

SITE: FARM BUILDINGS ----
AND OPEN FARMLAND.
LAUNCH DIRECTION N-W.

Site No. 13: Bel Hamelin, La Granchette *IGN map No. 1210 E.*

Location: this site, also known as La Granchette after the farm where it was built, was the first 'modified' site to be identified by the ACIU at the end of April 1944. Subsequently the ACIU often referred to modified sites as Bel Hamelin-type sites, after the nearby village. From Octeville, one of the south-western suburbs of Cherbourg, take the D123 for a mile and the farmhouse La Granchette is at a staggered crossroads where the D123 and D409 meet. The ramp pad and ramp were built at the end of the farmhouse; the pad is now covered by a barn and the ramp extended on to the crossroads. The compass alignment pad is in the field across the road, in the Octeville direction, and the garage is on the left, further on towards Octeville. There are two sentry posts on either side of the garage, which has a concrete parking area opposite.

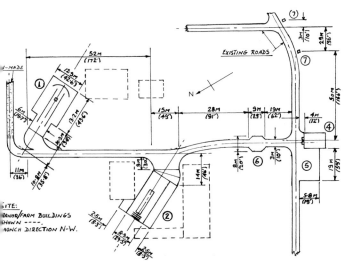

Site No. 14: Tonneville Le Manoir *IGN map No. 1110 E.*

Take the D901 from Cherbourg, Hameau de la Mer, towards Beaumont. After the Tonneville junction (D152), take the next turning on the left and the site is among the farm buildings on the left. Opposite the site entrance is the garage, with parking on either side. The farm buildings have recently been modernised but access is still possible. The ramp pad and ramp were squeezed between two farmhouses and the outline of the sump and remains of the two rows of bolts are still visible, although the ramp blocks have vanished. The compass pad, further along on the right, was in perfect condition, but recent building work may have taken its toll.

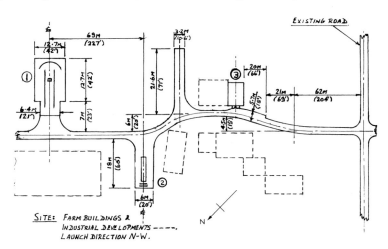

Site No. 15: L'Epinay Ferme *IGN map No. 1110 E.*

Rejoin the D901 in the Beaumont direction and take the third turning on the left for the DIY/builders' centre. The compass pad is almost directly opposite the DIY entrance and can be used as a parking place. Walk on towards the farmhouse. The ramp pad and ramp were built on the right, just before the first house, but new concrete and other buildings have hidden these from view. The garage is on the left, opposite the main farmhouse, and is built into the end of a barn: it is very well disguised. New industrial developments have affected the atmosphere of the site but the present farmers remember very well the German occupation and their sudden departure to Cherbourg after the D-Day landings, taking with them some items of furniture which were later returned.

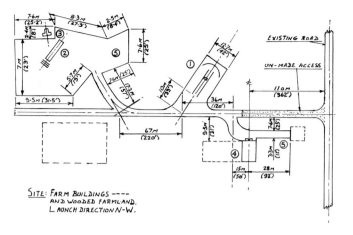

SITE: FARM BUILDINGS ----
AND WOODED FARMLAND.
LAUNCH DIRECTION N-W.

Site No. 16: Lillerie Ferme *IGN map No. 1110 E.*

Return to the D901 and head towards Beaumont. Leave the D901 at Delasse, on the D404E, and continue along the old section of the D901 parallel to the new road. Lillerie Ferme site is ¼ mile along the old road on the right. As the name indicates, it is built on a farm and a car can be left opposite the farm entrance on the left. The farm entrance is about ¼ mile long and the site starts where the road surface changes to concrete. Half-way down on the left is an access road to the garage, now incorporated into some new barns. Some 50 yards further on the compass pad is on the right, close to the road, and the ramp pad and ramp were actually built in the farm courtyard. Nothing remains of the ramp blocks but the outline of the pad can still be seen.

Site No. 17: La Vaquerie, also known as L'Epinette *IGN map No. 1110 E.*

Location: from Lillerie, return to the D901, still heading towards Beaumont, and at the large junction take the D37 for Vasteville. After a mile turn right on to the D237 and after a further mile there is a staggered crossroads. Across the road on the right is the site garage and the concrete road continues along the D237. About 100yd on the right is a new house, in the grounds of which the ramp pad and ramp were built. Nothing now remains. A further 100 yd on the left, in the field, is the compass alignment pad, much overgrown. From the site, the D237 and D318 make their way down to the sea, past the old wartime grass airfield at Vauville. The bay is a vast expanse of sand and sand dunes, ideal for a picnic.

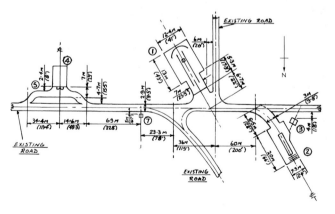

Site No. 18: Montaigu la Brisette, also known as Hameau des Blonds *IGN map No. 1310 O.*

Location: take the N13 from Cherbourg and leave at the Valognes turning, in Valognes take the D902 for Quettehou. After 5 miles turn left on to the D63 for Montaigu, following the road round to the left to bypass Montaigu, and the site starts just before the staggered crossroads. There is ample parking in the grounds of the village hall. The garage is before the crossroads, set well back with a double-access concrete road. The compass pad is alongside the crossroads, by the hall, and the ramp pad and ramp are further along, about 100yd on the right. Nothing remains of the ramp blocks but the pad can be seen, together with the small, almost buried, launch bunker on the left of the pad. Two sentry posts are positioned on either side of the road, between the garage and the compass pad, inside the site boundary.

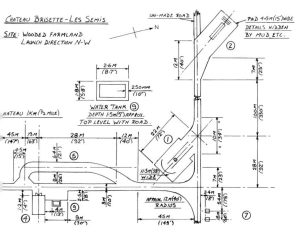

Site No. 19: Les Semis, Château Brisette *IGN map No. 1310 O.*

Location: return along the D63 and cross the D901. Staying on the D63, after a mile turn right for Les Semis and Château de la Brisette. The site starts at the T-junction, 250 yards from the turning. The garage is along the D216, on the left, complete with water tank, and opposite is a large double access parking area. The compass pad is at the T-junction and the ramp pad and ramp are along the other branch of the 'T', on the edge of the trees on the right. Nothing remains of the ramp but the pad is in good condition. Just before the T-junction are two sentry posts.

The garage at the modified V1 site at Château Brisette/Les Semis. None of the Peninsula garages has an extension. Across the road is a loop of concrete similar to that found at the V2 launch site on page 157. These buildings could also house an armoured half-track V2 launch control vehicle, and in this role they were referred to as 'Striwa' by the German V2 troops. (Author)

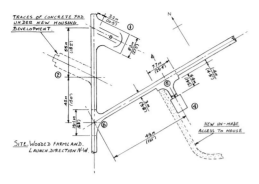

Site No. 20: Le Bécot, also known as L'Arbre-Tison *IGN map No. 1210 E.*

Leave Cherbourg on the N13 and take the D119 turning for Brix, doubling back over the N13 towards Rufosse. The site starts at a Y-junction ½ mile from the N13, with the garage on the right. The other pads are along the D119. The ramp pad and ramp have disappeared under some modern houses on the left, although the occupants are aware of the site's history. The compass pad is still intact, on the right, about 200 yards further along the D119.

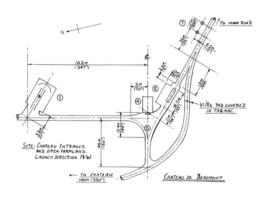

Site No. 22: Château de Beaumont *IGN map No. 1210 E.*

Location: return to the N13, taking the Valognes direction, and leave it at the Valognes turning. Cross over the N13 and turn left to return to Cherbourg and take the small side road off to the right before you rejoin the N13. This is the access to the château. The remains of the concrete road go off to the left towards the house and then disappear and it is likely that this road led to the ramp but nothing now remains. If, like some others, it had been built in front of the house, then it would be the first thing demolished after the war. Follow the concrete road round to the right for 200 yards; this leads to the compass pad on the right, which is in good condition.

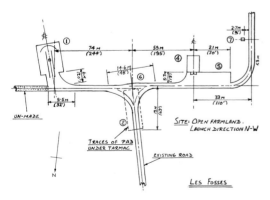

Site No. 23: Les Fosses *IGN map No. 1210 E.*

Location: from Cherbourg take the N13 and at the Delasse junction turn left on to the D56, over the N13, and continue on this road for 2 miles and then turn right on to the D87. After ½ mile turn left for Les Fosses and after 300 yards turn left on to a narrow single-track road. Follow this road round the right-hand bend and the garage is on the right, at the side of an old cottage. The ramp pad and ramp were built into the sharp left-hand bend a few yards beyond the garage. The remains of the pad can be seen in the tarmac, together with the widened sweep of the bend at this point. A concrete access road continues at right angles to the road and 100yd on the right, in the field, is the compass pad. Just before the bend and the garage is a single sentry post on the right, in the hedge. V1 transporter access to the site would have been via the D256 from the D56.

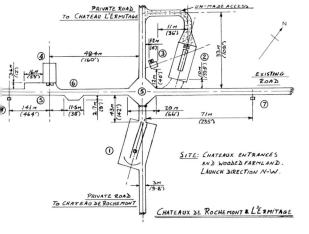

Site No. 24: Château L'Hermitage and Château Rochement *IGN map No. 1210 O.*

Of the thirty modified sites on the Peninsula six were built into farms, ten in château grounds and No. 24 was shared between the grounds of two châteaux.

Location: on the N13 from Cherbourg, leave at the Brix junction, turning left on to the D119. This takes you over the N13, past Le Bécot. Continue on the D119 for 1½ miles, through the wooded section, and where the trees end there are two driveways on the right and left. Right is Château Rochement and left Château L'Hermitage, and this crossroads is the centre of the site. Immediately on the right, almost buried, is the small launch bunker, still accessible and in good condition. Following the line of sight from the viewing slot, you can see that the ramp was located in the adjacent field. Access was from the road but a ditch now cuts through what was the access road. The ramp pad is still in the field although the ramp blocks have vanished. The compass pad is across the road along the L'Hermitage drive, set at an angle across the concrete. The garage is further along the D119 on the right and there is a sentry post beyond this on the left with another in a similar position on the opposite side of the crossroads. The locations of these two posts indicate that the D119 was open to local traffic while the site was active.

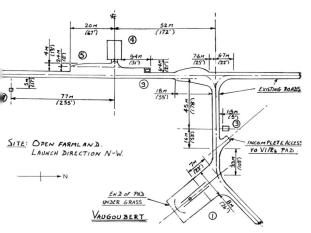

Site No. 26: Vaugoubert, also known as Saussemesnil II *IGN map No. 1210 E.*

From Valognes take the D902 towards Quettehou but before leaving Valognes turn left on to the D224. After 300 yards turn left for Hameau les Longs and the site garage is 150 yd on the left, with ample concrete parking. The concrete road, continues to the right, the bend having been widened to allow V1 access, and 100yd further along on the left, in the hedge, is the telephone-box type launch bunker. From the line of sight the ramp should be in the adjoining field but nothing now remains. The compass pad is 100 yards further on, recessed into the bend, on the right.

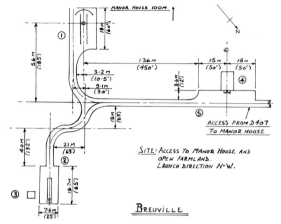

BREUVILLE

Site No. 27: Breuville *IGN map No. 1210 E.*

Location: leave Cherbourg on the N13 but turn right on to the D900 before leaving the town. After 1½ miles turn left on to the D3/D904 and ½ mile further on turn right, back on to the D900. In Breuville turn left on to the D407 and after ½ mile turn left into the driveway for the manor house. The site garage is on the right, 300 yd along the drive, access continues to the right-hand bend, where it splits, the left-hand section leading to the ramp pad and former ramp. The right-hand section leads to the compass pad, neatly recessed into the right of the drive, just before the actual entrance to the house. The occupants were very friendly and helpful, and the St Bernard dog that came out to investigate was a big softy and we left him sitting by the compass pad with strict instructions not to move. He may still be there!

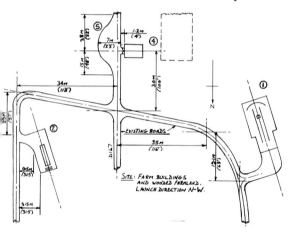

Site 28: Rauville la Bigot I, (Vauvicard) *IGN map No. 1210 E.*

The village of Rauville la Bigot has three 'modified' sites within its boundaries, and one of the reasons for this was that a large Russian PoW camp lay just outside the village. The PoWs were transported in groups of 50 or so to construct the new V1 sites on the Peninsula and it made sense to save time and fuel by building as many sites as possible within walking distance of the camp. Location: from the previous site, Breuville, rejoin the D900, turning left for Rauville la Bigot. Continue through Rauville for a mile and then turn right on to the D367. After 500 yards the D367 turns sharply left but carry straight on, taking the D167 towards La Lande. The site starts just before the crossroads with the garage on the left, among the farm buildings, with parking opposite. The flat roof has been replaced with a pitched roof and the farmer was certain that this modification had been done by the Germans. Turn left at the crossroads and the compass pad is 100 yards along on the left, at an acute angle to the road. The pad has been partially broken up. For the ramp pad and ramp, turn right at the crossroads and the access road is 150 yards on the left. The pad is overgrown and the ramp blocks are missing.

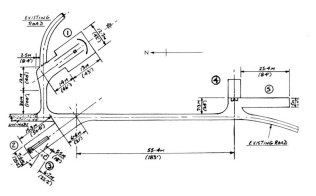

Site No. 29: Rauville la Bigot II, (La Hectonnerie) *IGN map No. as 1210 E.*

Take the D167 away from La Lande and in ¾ mile it joins the D62. Turn right on to the D62 and almost immediately turn left down a single-track road. The garage is 250 yards along on the right, with parking alongside. The two other pads are straight ahead. Gaps in the hedge on the left have been plugged with some of the ramp concrete blocks. The ramp pad and ramp are at the T-junction, in the field on the left. The launch bunker, of the buried type, is to the left of the pad, surrounded by several of the ramp support blocks. The compass pad is also at the T-junction, in the field on the right.

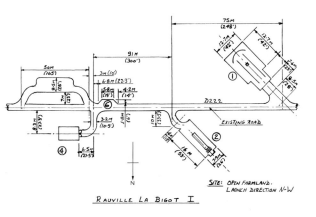

RAUVILLE LA BIGOT I

Site No. 30: Rauville la Bigot III *IGN map No. 1210 E.*

Location: return to Rauville via the D62 and turn left on to the D900, heading towards Cherbourg. After 300 yards turn left on to the D122 and the garage is ½ mile on the right with a large double access parking area opposite. The ramp pad is 150 yards further along on the right, but the pad blocks are missing. The compass pad is a further 150 yards on the left, at a sharp angle to the road. Despite the lack of camouflage, Rauville III is a very well laid out site with the minimum amount of movement required for the V1 between the two pads.

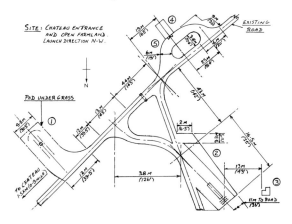

Site No. 31: Bricquebosq, (La Grande Maison) *IGN map No. 1110 E.*

Location: take the D900/D904 out of Cherbourg for Les Pieux and after 12 miles turn left on to the D222 for St Christophe du Foc. Pass through the village on the D222 and after 1½ miles turn right on to the D56 for Bricquebosq. Go through the village and after 300 yards turn right on to the D204. The garage is 250yd further along on the right, just before the entrance to La Maison. The compass pad is 200yd along on the right, with access now hidden by the hedge. The route to the ramp pad and ramp cuts across the corner, rejoining the D204, and the pad is now in the driveway of a postwar house. The ramp itself was where the house now stands. There is usually an American flag flying and both the house owner and his son are aware of the site's history. The launch bunker, to the left of the pad, is in very good condition and is now a garden store. The owner remembers the site being built in great urgency by the PoWs under Organisation Todt supervision.

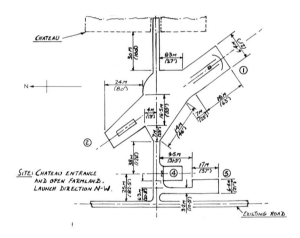

Site No. 32: Bonnetot, (Grosville) *IGN map No. 1110 E.*

Location: as for Bricquebosq, take the D900/D904 from Cherbourg, continuing almost to Les Pieux, but turn left just before the town on to the D23 for Grosville. Follow the D23, which passes to the right of Grosville, and turn right on to the D331 for Bonnetot. The garage is ½ mile on the left at the farm and château entrance. Both pads are on the driveway to the farm and house, but new concrete has obscured the original layout. The outline and features of the ramp pad can just about be made out, on the left, 100yd from the garage and the compass pad was almost opposite, among the new farm buildings.

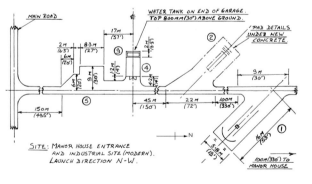

Site No. 33: La Haulle (La Lande) *IGN map No. 1210 E.*

Location: take the N13 for Valognes and in the centre of the town turn right on to the D902 for Bricquebec. After 1½ miles (about ¼ mile past the D87 turning on the left) turn right on to an unmade driveway. The road changes to concrete after 100yd and the garage is on the left with a large concrete parking area alongside. At the back of the garage is the water tank. A further 100yd on the left is the access road to the ramp pad and ramp but new industrial developments have obscured the details. A further 250yd on the right, towards the house called La Haulle, is the compass pad, set at an acute angle to the road.

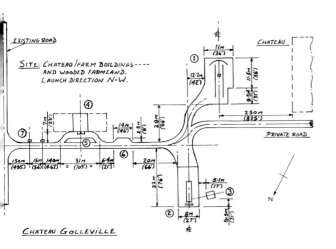

EXISTING ROAD

SITE: CHÂTEAU/FARM BUILDINGS----
       AND WOODED FARMLAND.
       LAUNCH DIRECTION N-W.

CHÂTEAU

PRIVATE ROAD

CHÂTEAU GOLLEVILLE

Site No. 34: Château Golleville
IGN map No. 1211 E.

Location: from Valognes take the D2 south towards St Sauveur le Vicomte and after passing through Colomby turn right a mile later on to the D126. After ¼ mile turn left on to an unmade road for the farm and château and the garage is among the farm buildings on the left. In the driveway before the garage are two sentry posts by the hedge. The ramp pad and ramp are 80yd down the concrete road on the right. The launch bunker on the left is in good condition although the ramp blocks have vanished. The compass pad is round to the left in a wide curve, and the farmer has placed a large cattle feeding trough on the centre of the pad, which is otherwise undamaged.

Site No. 35: Le Quesnoy IGN map No. 1211 E.

As for site 34, take the D2 but stay on it until Les Hauts Vents and then turn right in the village on to the D42. After ¾ mile, at a crossroads, the D42 turns left for St Colombe but go straight on and continue along this single-track road, ignoring the branch to the right for La Campionnerie. After 250yd the road makes a sharp left turn and the site concrete starts after a few yards. On either side are two sentry posts and the garage is on the left, 200yd from the bend. About 100yd further on an access road goes to the farm and at this point the ramp pad is built into the junction with the launch bunker on the left, still in excellent condition. A further 100yd towards the château the compass pad is on the left, surrounded by trees. Le Quesnoy was a well-concealed site. When the ornamental lake was drained and cleaned out in the hot summer of 1998 the residents found a large quantity of pistols, rifles and live ammunition, dumped there by the site troops after news of the Allied landings on D-Day.

Site No. 36: Château St Colombe *IGN map No. 1211 E.*

Returning from Le Quesnoy, at the first crossroads head for St Colombe, turning right on to the D42. Just before the right-hand bend take the unmade road for the farm and château and after ½ mile the site concrete starts and the garage is on the right. The site road bends round to the right and the compass pad is on the left, partially hidden by a tennis court. The ramp pad and ramp were right in front of the château, were removed very quickly after the war. Part of the house was occupied by the Organisation Todt and other military personnel during the site construction in February 1944, and the daughter of the wartime owner of the house remembers the Russian PoWs and the harsh conditions they worked under.

Site No. 37: Le Hameau Margot *IGN map No. 1211 E.*

Location: from site 36, return to the D42 and turn left for Nehou. In the centre of Nehou turn right and after 100 yards take the right fork at the Y-junction. After ½ mile turn right for Margot, carry on through the village and the site is on the left at the sharp right-hand bend. The compass pad is in the field on the left before the bend. The ramp pad and ramp are also on the left at the apex of the curve. The ramp blocks are missing. The launch bunker used to be accessible but recently it has been covered with soil. The garage is a further 250 yards on the right and is now part of some farm buildings.

Site No. 38: Hameau Piquet *IGN map No. 1211 E.*

Location: from site 37 return to Nehou and rejoin the D42, heading towards St Jaques de Nehou. Carry on across the D900 and after a mile turn right for Hameau Piquet, on an unmarked single-track road. Drive through Piquet, following the road round to the left at the sharp bend. The garage is on the left a few yards before the T-junction with the D187. For the ramp pad, turn left on to the D187 and the pad is down an unmade track about 50 yards along the road. It is overgrown but visible, although there is no sign of the ramp blocks The compass pad has never been found at Piquet although it cannot be far from the ramp pad and must be buried under grass somewhere close by.

Site No. 39: Bois de Denneville *IGN map No. 1211 E.*

Location: from site 38 return along the D42 to the D900 crossroads and turn right on to the D900 for a mile. Some 200 yards past the turning for Hameau Mangan, turn right

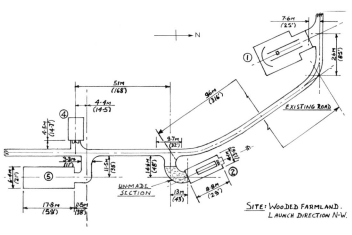

for La Rue de Denneville. The garage is 500 yards on the left. Opposite is a concrete parking area which has been converted for other uses and the ramp pad is 100 yards on the right in the field. Nothing remains of the blocks. The compass pad is 200 yards round the bend to the left and is in the drive of a modern house. It is set at an acute angle to the road.

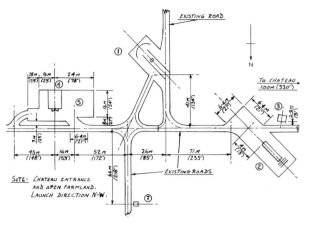

Site No. 40: Château Crossville *IGN map No. 1211 E.*

Location: from site 39 return to the D900 and take the St Sauveur le Vicomte road. In St Sauveur, a medieval walled town well worth a day's visit itself, turn left on to the D2 for Valognes and after ½ mile, at Le Mont, turn right on to the D15 for Crossville sur Douve. After 1¼ miles turn right on to the D130E2 and go through the village of Crossville, and 300 yards further on is a minor crossroads. Turn left here and the garage is 100yd on the right, connected to the road by a concrete loop and a massive parking area. Follow the concrete road across the junction and on the left the concrete branches off to the left, eventually connecting to the compass pad set at an angle across the road. The ramp pad and ramp are straight ahead on the entrance road, and before the main entrance the launch bunker is on the left and the pad on the right. Some of the ramp support blocks are still visible as grass-covered humps; the ramp actually passed between two château buildings. There is a single sentry post in the hedge before the crossroads on the D130E2. The parking area by the garage is considerably larger than normal and it is connected to the road by two loops, giving excellent access for long loads.

Site No. 41: Hautmesnil *IGN map No. 1211 E.*

Location: Hautmesnil is the most southerly V1 site on the Peninsula, and because of the distance to targets in the UK all nine sites around St Sauveur were aligned on Plymouth instead of Bristol. From site 40 return to the D900 and head south through St Sauveur in the direction of La Haye du Puits. After 1½ miles turn right for Les Hameaux and continue on this road until the junction with the D147 and then turn left on to the D147. The garage is on the right, built against an old cottage. The ramp pad and ramp were on the right, 100 yards further on at the Y-junction, but little now remains. Only the foundations of the launch bunker are still visible. The compass pad is 150 yards along the left-hand fork of the junction, in the field on the left.

Site No. 42: Cadets *IGN maps No. 1211 E and 1211 O.*

Location: using Map 1211 E return to St Sauveur and turn left on to the D15 in the St Lô d'Ourville direction. After ½ mile turn right on to the D130 for Portbail. Continue for 3½ miles and change to Map 1211 O. Shortly after passing the signs for Hameau Rouland on the left, the D130 makes a sharp right turn and the garage is on the left at this bend. Further along the D130, at the left-hand bend, a concrete access to the right leads to the compass pad, used as a storage base for cattle feed. The location of the pad was only

The compass alignment pad at the modified V1 launch site at Cadets. This heap of turnips shows why some remains are difficult to find! (Author)

discovered when some of this feed was removed. The ramp pad and ramp are missing but it is likely that these were located at the crossroads with the D127. No remains have been found. This is the last of the modified V1 launching sites on the Cherbourg Peninsula and the majority of them, like the ski sites, are located in areas which are ideal for sightseeing, walking and picnics. In addition, the D-Day beaches are not far away, especially Utah Beach – and wherever you are on the Peninsula you are never more than about 10 miles from the sea.

4.3.5 HOLLAND AND GERMANY

The ACIU identified 22 V1 launching sites in Holland and 14 in Germany, all aligned on either London and British south coast ports or cities such as Antwerp and Brussels. The site locations are shown on the ACIU Map 7 and Table 7. The ACIU interpreters noticed that many new concealment methods were used at the new sites in Holland. The ramps were no longer orientated on a specific target, deviations of up to 42 deg. were noted. Treetops were often tied together to conceal access roads, the 'garage' no longer appeared and the ramp was pre-fabricated for quicker assembly and removal. Around Rotterdam, industrial sites were used to disguise the ramp and launching activities, including scorch marks and scars from the piston and cradle as they hit the ground after launch. Sites included an oil refinery and the Lever Brothers' soap factory at Rotterdam, a sugar factory at Puttershoek and a glue works south of Delft. It is believed that only six of all the Dutch sites were operational and none of the German sites. At the top RH edge of Map 6, Altenwalde is marked, this was the launch point for the British controlled V2 launches in September/October 1945, Operation Backfire.

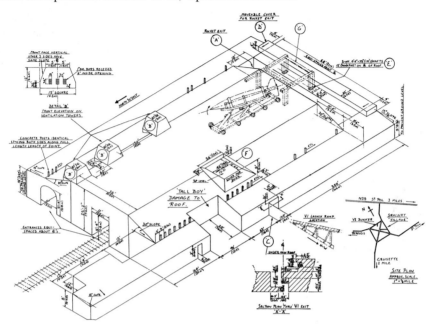

Siracourt, showing V2 on trolley. (PRO)

4.4 VI BUNKERS

In the Calais–Somme area there are two V1 bunkers, at Siracourt and Lottinghen.

(i) **Siracourt (Wasserwerk Saint Pol)** *Michelin map No. 51.*

Location: from St Pol, between Arras and the coast, take the D39 for Hesdin. After 3 miles turn left for Siracourt and the bunker lies at the northern edge of the village.

There is no natural camouflage at the site and the bunker itself is built on a slightly elevated position. Siracourt may have been intended to launch V1s equipped with unconventional warheads, but it could also be used for launching the normal V1, and a mile to the south in the village of Croisette are the remains of eight standard V1 storage buildings, of the double and single-width, 69ft-long type, giving a total capacity of 50 V1s. This site (60) was not part of the original organisation and was probably intended as a replenishment base for Siracourt once it became operational. The main railway line from St Pol to Doullens passes nearby and a spur was taken off this line to serve both Siracourt and La Croisette, the line actually entering the bunker at the north-east entrance. Work started at Siracourt in August 1943 using the 'Erdschalung' (earth shuttering) system developed by the Organisation Todt, in which the foundations and supporting walls were built first, leaving the ground in between to support the roof; after completion of the roof, the earth was removed. Constructed of reinforced concrete, the roof and walls have a maximum thickness of 16ft 6in and 21ft 11in respectively. Siracourt was originally intended for the V1 but it is a good example of German adaptability in the face of a changed military situation and with the V-weapons programme under 'new management', in the shape of the SS and General Kammler. The operation of the site can be explained using the site plan on the previous page. The V1s, fully armed and fuelled and ready for launch, were originally intended to emerge from exit 'C', which was 22ft wide, and the ramp was immediately outside this entrance. The remains of the ramp mounting blocks can still be seen. The increased thickness of the roof at 'F' was intended to accommodate the mechanism for a bomb-proof sliding door, moving in a slot 8ft wide and protecting the bunker interior. These features were abandoned, and exit 'C' was reduced in width to 13ft 6in with a dog-leg arrangement of concrete pillars added inside the entrance, providing simple but effective blast protection for the interior. These modifications meant that a V1, even without wings fitted (the wingspan varied from 16ft to 17ft 6in depending on model and range), could not use 'C' as an exit. At the south end of the bunker a new section was added, 48ft 6in long, for the full width of the roof. This was provided with an opening, 'A', 18ft wide and 68ft long, extending through the full depth of the extension roof to the interior. There are two smaller rectangular slots at

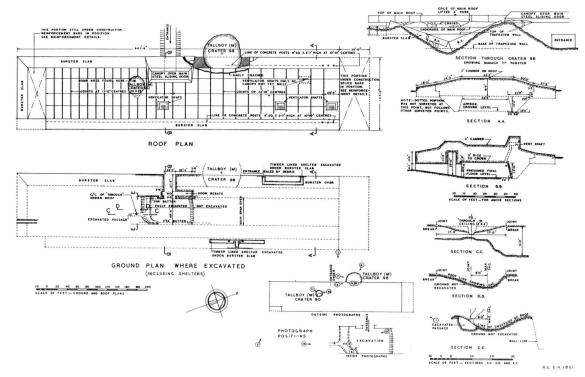

Siracourt V1 bunker. Details of the structure and bomb damage. (PRO)

Bomb damage at Siracourt V1 bunker, 7 July 1944. Centre left is the original exit for V1s and front centre under construction is the new exit point for rockets. (PRO)

'E', on either side of the roof centre line, intended for lifting gear 'G', of which a typical example is shown. Resting on the rear of the extension roof is a massive concrete block, 'D', 6ft thick x 22ft wide x 74ft long. This block is not a fixed part of the roof and it overlaps the slot by 4ft at either end and is 4ft wider; its original purpose was to act as a protective cover for the slot, sliding on concealed runners. The new slot was wide and long enough for a V2 (45ft long x 13ft wide with fins fitted) or a Rheinböte to be removed from the bunker interior and launched from the roof. There are concrete posts along the roof line for camouflage netting.

By the beginning of September the wall foundations were laid and the rail-link was in place. The first bombing raid on the bunker took place on 31 January 1944, by which time the roof was finished and the new extension almost complete. This gives some idea of the timetable for the changeover from the V1 to the V2 and these dates also coincide with the take-over of the V-weapons projects by the SS. PRO file AIR 40/2544 contains a page from a British military mission inspecting the large V-weapons sites in 1951, and confirms that the ramp exit 'C' could no longer have been used for a V1. The bombing campaign against Siracourt lasted until 6 July 1944, by which time 5,000 tons of bombs had been dropped on the site, including sixteen 12,000lb 'Tall Boy' bombs on 25 June. Despite this huge tonnage of bombs, the bunker survived virtually undamaged, although the construction site was no longer usable. Recently the earth blocking the entrances has been removed and access is now possible to the interior, although there is still a lot of soil under the roof.

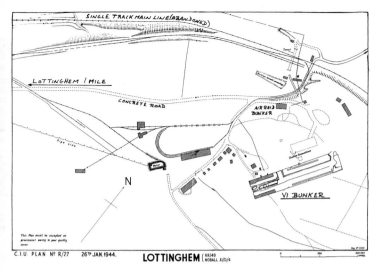

Lottinghen is about 20 miles inland from Boulogne and just north-east of Desvres. Because the site is fairly difficult to find, it is useful to have the IGN map for reference. To reach the site, follow the D254 out of Lottinghen towards Senlecques. After about ¾ mile the road passes over the abandoned railway and climbs first to the left, then to the right, and shortly afterwards there is a sharp right-hand bend. From this bend, the remains of a concrete road go off to the left across the fields and this is the main site access road. After a mile the road runs alongside the edge of the forest, Les Grands Bois, and crosses over the abandoned single-track railway in a ravine. This was the main unloading area for the site and sidings were built alongside the track. Work at Lottinghen started later than at Siracourt and when the first bombing raid took place on 24 February 1944 the roof was still unfinished. The last raid was on 30 April 1944 and by this time construction work had stopped. Within the forest are massive craters left by the bombing, and these give some indication of the scale of the attacks.

The bunker west wall has a V1 exit similar to that originally at Siracourt but there is no sign of an extension at the end. The largest structure still complete is an air-raid bunker on the edge of the forest and this survived undamaged. Only 600 tons of bombs were dropped on the site, but because the main bunker structure was incomplete, the effect of the attacks was enough to result in work stopping before the arrival of Allied forces. The site is a very attractive location and a day could easily be spent exploring the site and forest.

There are two bunker sites on the Cherbourg Peninsula:

(iii) Couville (Wasserwerk Cherbourg) *Michelin map No. 54; IGN map No. 1210 E.*

Take the D900/D904 from Cherbourg towards Les Pieux and 300yd past the village of Baudretot, turn left on to the D22. A mile along the D22 there is a turning to the right for St Luc and 250yd before this turning a track leads off to the left, through some trees. This is the most convenient entrance to the Couville site, as the building remains are across the field. Unfortunately, Couville bears little similarity to Siracourt or Lottinghen and, because the Allied bombing resulted in work being stopped very early in the construction programme, it is difficult to imagine what the final layout would have looked like. In addition, there are no surviving German plans for the site. We do know that a 35-

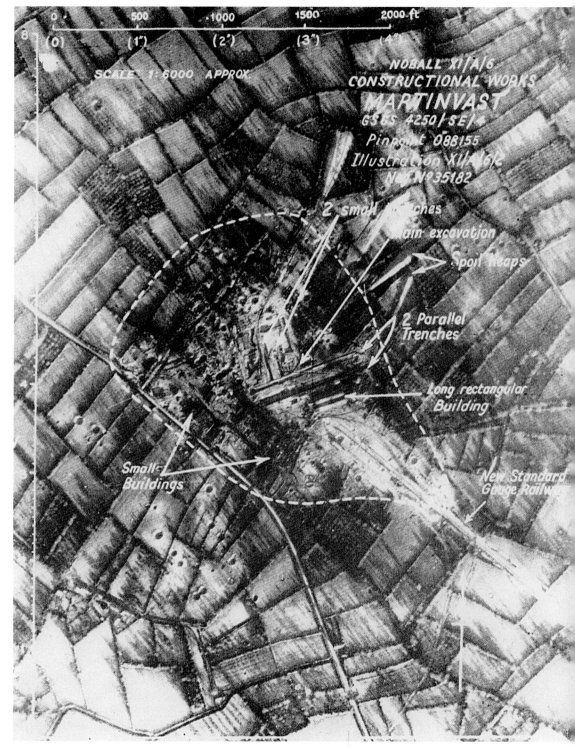

The V1 bunker at Couville (Martinvast). This PRU photograph of the site was taken after the first bombing raid on 11 November 1943. (PRO)

track sidings was being built adjoining the Paris main line, north of the site, and this gives an indication of the amount of rail traffic expected. A spur was taken from these sidings and run into the site and this was being used before work was abandoned. In addition, in order to provide building material, a quarry was opened near the station and a narrow-gauge track ran along the D22 into the site. The first bombing raid took place on 11 November 1943 and at this time construction was little more advanced than what can be seen today. The most obvious feature of the site are the two parallel walls, 512ft long, 4ft 6in thick and 28ft apart, but as they are only about 3ft above ground level, they are relatively inconspicuous. Between the walls the ground is excavated 5ft below ground level but the true height of the walls cannot be determined. The walls were clearly intended to support a roof but the overall layout of this section is puzzling, and what was intended is difficult to imagine. The main site workings before the bombing appear to have been at the southern end of the walls and it is probably here that the operational centre of the site was intended to be. Most of this area is now overgrown with brambles and gorse, and only a few of the features are visible. Between November 1943 and May 1944 some 500 tons of bombs were dropped on the site and this was enough for construction to be stopped in April. A large anti-aircraft flak battery was installed and some work continued as a ruse to attract further Allied bombs but all activity ceased in May 1944.

(iv) Tamerville (Wasserwerk Valognes) *Michelin map No. 54; IGN map No. 1210 E.*

Tamerville was intended to be a sister site to Couville, but construction only reached the ground preparation stage before the project was abandoned. A spur was taken off the main line north-west of Valognes and ran north-eastwards across the N13 into the fields below Château de Beaumont. Ground was cleared at the site for a large sidings, as shown on an ACIU photograph dated 20 January 1944 but that is as far as it went. With Couville already being bombed at this date, it is not surprising that work at Tamerville did not proceed. The influence of the SS and Kammler was making itself felt by this time and projects that had little or no chance of completion were quickly dropped from the V-weapons programme.

4.5 SPECIAL SITES

(i) Monterolier, Grotte de Clairfeuille, Beaumont I and II *Michelin map No. 52; IGN map No. 2010 E.*

From Monterolier take the D24 in the Beaumont direction for one mile and Beaumont II is 250yd on the left before the D41 crossroads. For Beaumont I, turn left at the D41 cross-roads and after ¾ mile turn left onto the D96, followed by a sharp left turn after 50yd and the site entrance is on the left, 250yd along the single track road.

We already know that versions of the V1 were designed to carry warheads other than those containing high-explosives. A diagram, dated 19 September 1944, shows the standard

Beaumont II V1 storage site – new organisation, Somme-Seine. The remains of one of the nine tunnel entrances, isolated by post-war quarrying, the tunnel blocked at the quarry face. (Author)

V1 warhead and detonator replaced with a container and a detonator corset, to ensure the container contents were release at the target. Germany had been the first to use poison gas in the First World War, the chlorine based 'mustard gas' and phosgene and both these chemicals had been manufactured in WW2. Both these gases are heavier than air, by a factor of 2.5 for chlorine and 3.5 for phosgene, ensuring they dispersed slowly when required. Phosgene only becomes gaseous above 46.8°F (8.2°C), hence a mixture of the two would be the most effective. If the weapons to deliver the alternative warheads were available together with one of the materials, then they also required a special site where these weapons could be prepared for use. By early 1944, due to Allied bombing, all the bunker sites, which would have been able to provide protection for these activities, were having to be written out of the equation. But at least one site did still exist where these special V1s were to be assembled, although due to the subterfuge adopted, not until the German retreat did the site become known to Allied Intelligence as Beaumont I. The excavations at Clairfeuille started late in 1943, using Russian Pows and continued into 1944. Unlike similar sites, every piece of debris was taken in lorries at night and dumped miles away, leaving no signs of the activity underground. Beaumont II may have been intended for a similar purpose, but its tunnels only extended a few yards when work was abandoned. The final result at Beaumont I was a tunnel complex with three entrances giving access to a herringbone system of tunnels, 13ft wide x 11.5ft high, total length 1.75 miles.

Neuf morts par asphyxie dans une grotte normande

Trois enfants puis les personnes qui s'étaient portées à leur secours ont été intoxiqués par de mys... ...ations de monoxyde de carbone.

Neuf personnes ont trouvé la mort hier, asphyxiées dans des galeries souterraines en...

L'autre mystère de la grotte

The most active V1 sites during the brief V1 offensive from June to September 1944 were in the Somme–Seine area, south of Dieppe. The forest areas provided ideal camouflage for the 'modified' V1 launch sites, seven were operational in a small area of the Foret d'Eawy, and therefore it would be logical if the site for these special V1s was close to this launch area. Between St Saëns and Aumale, Colonel Wachtel had 24 operational sites, a large percentage of the total available in the whole of northern France. A few miles behind St Saëns is the village of Monterolier and 2 miles from Monterolier are the caves of Clairfeuille. Today, as the photos show, it is hard to imagine what was being planned in this underground labyrinth, but the local people remember the V1s arriving after dark from the railway, after spending daylight hours in the nearby tunnel. There are no huge concrete installations at Clairfeuille, just a few yards of concrete off the road, enough for access and parking in front of the caves, it looks very innocuous. After the war, the caves were a favourite place for a few hours of excitement for the local children, often cycling from Monterolier. But in 1994, it all went wrong and within a short time, three children and six adults had discovered that the Germans had left a deadly legacy at Clairfeuille. On the morning of Tuesday, 21 June 1994, three children from the nearby town of Buchy cycled to

One of the partially blocked entrances to the tunnel at Montérolier. (Author)

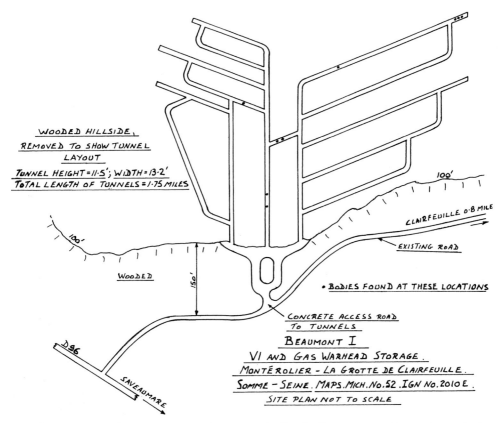

V1 warhead storage and servicing, Montérolier, Grotte de Clairfeuille, Beaumont I Somme-Seine. (Author)

Clairfeuille to spend the morning exploring the caves. Late in the afternoon when the children hadn't returned, a search started and two of the children's fathers went to the caves and found their cycles outside the entrances. Soon, men from the Buchy Fire Brigade arrived with a local doctor and an amateur caver. Four Buchy firemen plus the caver entered the tunnels, believing the accident to have been caused by a rock-fall; none of them were wearing breathing masks, presumably because there had never been any toxic gas problems at Clairfeuille. Two of the firemen quickly emerged complaining of nausea and close to collapse, but there was no sign of the others. Firemen from Rouen then arrived and a group of them entered the tunnels wearing masks, but three of them never returned. Whatever is lurking inside Clairfeuille is extremely volatile and deadly.

Eventually all the bodies were recovered by firemen wearing self-contained breathing apparatus and the investigation began. The 'official' story is that all nine were killed by carbon monoxide poisoning caused by the three boys lighting fires in the tunnels and with the ceiling vents blocked by undergrowth on the surface above, the gas had no way to escape. Carbon monoxide levels of 2,000 parts per million were said to have been found in the tunnels, twice the lethal dose, but compared to the volume of the tunnels, according to an independent report, that amount of gas would have required the burning of a pile of wood the size of the Arc de Triomphe. Not only that, but carbon monoxide is lighter than air and anyone collapsing from its effects would have fallen to the ground, into a supply of fresh air, enabling them to recover. So what really happened at Clairfeuille?

Did these three children discover some hidden cache of gas cylinders, supposed to have been removed by the French Army after the war? Clairfeuille was only one of hundreds of sites that had to be made safe after the Germans retreated, but this explanation is unlikely in view of the extensive inspection carried out. It is the case, though that on the Cherbourg Peninsula, some farm water supplies are still being contaminated by petrol, draining into the system from secret supply dumps buried by the Germans and in 2000, their location was still a secret!

It was suggested that if poison gas was stored at Clairfeuille then it was intended for the Normandy beaches, but they are a long way from Clairfeuille and there are many more convenient storage places in Normandy itself. Clairfeuille is also a long way from the expected landing beaches in the Pas de Calais. The Dieppe raid on 17 August 1942, using Canadian troops, was a costly failure and illustrated the problems of attempting a landing at a well-defended enemy port. It is unlikely that the Germans expected a repeat of Dieppe, two years later in 1944. What we do know is that in August 1944, both Beaumont I and II were inspected by RAF Intelligence Officers and beforehand both sites would have been thoroughly checked for booby-traps and mines. Their report, together with those on the other V-weapons sites, is included in PRO file AIR 40/1778. No mention was made of finding anything related to poison gas storage, apparently the tunnels had been completely cleared by the retreating Germans in July 1944. After the war the French Army inspected the sites and the tunnel entrances were blocked with rubble, although at Beaumont II, some quarrying work continued. For over 40 years the more adventurous local children used the tunnels as a playground, with no problems. It is extremely unlikely that suddenly on 21 June 1994, three children discover a cache of hidden gas cylinders, missed by previous children and the original military inspections. But there are two significant factors associated with the tragedy. Firstly, the bodies were widely distributed along all 1.75 miles of the tunnel network, but heavier than air chlorine or phosgene would have needed considerable forced air movement to distribute the gas along the tunnels. This implies that the gas supply was located at several places in the tunnels. Secondly, the date, 21 June 1994, is almost exactly 50 years to within a few days of the V-weapons troops, including the SS, leaving the site. During the Second World War, time delayed explosive devices had become scientifically sophisticated using a variety of materials and chemicals to produce the required delay factor. The author believes that the tunnels were probably booby-trapped with time capsules of poison gas, concealed in plastic containers in the roof and timed to start releasing their deadly contents as close to a macabre 50th anniversary as possible.

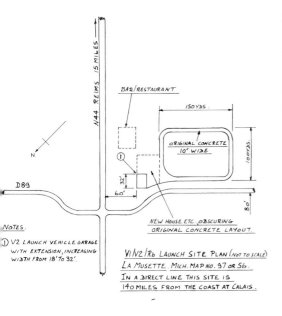

NOTES.

① V2 LAUNCH VEHICLE GARAGE
WITH EXTENSION, INCREASING
WIDTH FROM 18' TO 32'.

V1 /V2 /Rb LAUNCH SITE PLAN (NOT TO SCALE)
LA MUSETTE. MICH. MAP NO. 97 OR 56.
IN A DIRECT LINE THIS SITE IS
140 MILES FROM THE COAST AT CALAIS.

(ii) La Musette *Michelin maps No. 56 or 97.*

On the N44, 15 miles north of Reims and over 140 miles from Calais in a direct line, is a site at the N44–D899 crossroads. There is no record of a V1 or V2 launch site so far south and it was seen purely by chance en-route for the V1 storage site at Rilly la Montagne. On the right, the only visible feature from the road is the rear of a concrete building but it contain one of the unusual vents found at the rear of all the 'modified' V1 sites or V2 Striwas. A modern house has been built on the concrete apron at the rear of the site, but still visible is a large access road shaped in a loop. The surrounding area revealed no more clues, no trace of V1 compass or launch pads, so what was the purpose of La Musette? The site is at least 140 miles from Calais, putting it out of range of the V1/V2 or Rh, if it was to be used against England and certainly London. But is possible that it was intended to be used to bombard the Allied forces in northern France after the D-Day landings, or even used for the longer-range V1s and V2s being developed.

V2 launch vehicle garage or 'Striwa', at La Musette, nearly 150 miles from the channel coast. (Author)

CHAPTER 5

V2 Site Descriptions and Locations

5.1 INTRODUCTION

In May 1943 Dornberger, at this time still very much in charge of the V2 project, sent reconnaissance staff from Artillery Regiment 760 to northern France to select locations for the V2 field launch and storage sites, together with transit depots, main depots, and fuel production and storage sites. In charge was Oberst (Colonel) Hohmann. He and his staff must have been very busy in the summer of 1943 since they had to cover a huge area, from Calais to Cherbourg and inland up to 200 miles from the coast – an area of over 3,000 square miles. In the circumstances information about potential site locations must have been supplied in advance from the German forces already in occupation, otherwise the job would have taken years. Indeed, we know that the site locations for the original V2 organisation were already established before the German document referred to on page 35 was issued on 4 November 1943, which radically altered the site organisation and plans. The bunker sites such as Watten and Wizernes were already under construction by the summer of 1943, and it is clear that, although Peenemünde had been involved in the bunkers, orders for their inclusion in the programme had come from the very top.

5.2 ORIGINAL V2 STORAGE SITES

5.2.1 Main Storage Sites

Of the six main storage depots at Hollogne, Savonnieres, Méry-sur-Oise, Elbeuf, Haut Mesnil and La Meauffe, the author has visited the last four. Haut Mesnil and La Meauffe are described in 5.5. Elbeuf is now a very large, expanded town and modern developments also appear to have removed any traces of the V2. At Méry-sur-Oise, however, there are some very interesting remains from its wartime use and the site survived to be included in the new V2 organisation.

(i) Méry-sur-Oise
Michelin map No. 55 or 97.
Note, this site was divided into three sections for ACIU target information purposes, Méry-sur-Oise, Fôret de l'isle Adam and Villiers Adam.

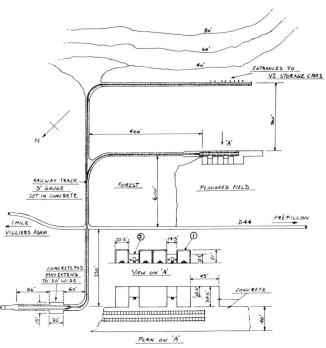

① V2 CHECK-OUT BUILDINGS; 4-OFF; CONCRETE TEST STAND IN MIDDLE OF FLOOR, 6'x6-8'x2' HIGH
  WITH 4-OFF 1·5" DIA. BOLTS. DOORS MISSING AT BOTH ENDS.
② TEST EQUIPMENT BUILDINGS, 2-OFF; ACCESS FOR CABLES ETC. TO CHECK-OUT BUILDINGS VIA 2 OPENINGS
  ON INSIDE OF EACH DIVIDING WALL, 6·6'x5' AND 19'x28".

Plan of the V2 storage site at Méry-sur-Oise, north of Paris.

Location: from Beauvais take the N1 for Paris and after 24 miles turn left on to the N322 for L'Isle-Adam. Pass through L'Isle-Adam and at Mériel turn left for Villiers-Adam. The site is on the left between Villiers-Adam and Frépillon, on the D44. The V2 test stand buildings are visible from the road, and until a few years ago a narrow-gauge railway crossed the D44 but this has now been covered in tarmac. Turn left along the barely recognisable concrete road and follow it round to the right. This brings you out at the V2 test stand buildings, open-ended for ventilation and electrical transmissions. The interiors are filled with soil, but they contain concrete plinths, still with their mounting bolts, for testing various sections of the V2. The smaller buildings linking the test stands would have been used for the equipment and instrumentation for the various test procedures.

A US soldier poses with a captured V2 site transport, probably at Méry-sur-Oise. This was the branch line to the V2 test stands. PRO

123

V2 Test Stand buildings at Méry-sur-Oise storage site, north-east of Paris. (Author)

The V2 was a very complicated weapon, as different from the V1 as a Model T Ford was from a Formula 1 racing car, and after the long journey from the production centre in Germany some V2s would have required considerable remedial work. There were valves of every type, transducers, servo motors, relays with hundreds of contacts, gyroscopes, radio equipment, five batteries for electrical power, including the control/guidance systems, and a host of other electrical/mechanical equipment. The full extent of the testing required before the rocket actually reached the launch pad is shown in the five volumes of procedures produced for the British-controlled V2 launches from near Cuxhaven in 1945, codenamed Operation 'Backfire'. These five volumes (PRO WO33/2555 to 2559) show what was required in the 'ideal' situation, but events in the V2 offensive from Holland meant that each rocket was reduced to the bare minimum of testing before use. This produced many failures, either at launch, during flight or with target accuracy.

In front of the test buildings are two rail tracks, of 3ft gauge, and this system was used to bring the V2s from the storage caves, although access to the caves is now blocked. The rails join to form a single track which crosses the D44 and it then runs for another 350ft before curving to the right and dividing into two sections at a concrete pad, the full extent of which is obscured by undergrowth. One section of the track ends in a pad, perhaps indicating that this was also a launch site. It may have been intended for V2s that were not suitable for further transportation, as the site is only 75 miles from the coast. Although Méry-sur-Oise was on the Allied target list, it appears to have led a charmed life as there are no obvious signs of bomb damage.

5.2.2 Field Storage Depots

Four forward field storage depots were included in the original V2 organisation, all in the Calais–Somme region. From east to west they were La Motte, Thiennes, Bergueneuse and Fransu, and the author has visited all four sites. The La Motte and Thiennes sites in the Forêt de Nieppe, were originally small storage areas, but the site was expanded into three storage areas under the general title of Fôret de Nieppe and this is described in 5.5.1. What has survived at Thiennes, as well as the numerous air-raid bunkers for the troops guarding the sites, is a miniature version of Watten, described later on pages 162–74. At Fransu, north-east of Abbeville, work did not proceed beyond initial site preparation, but as described in 4.1, the Conteville/Cramont site was probably intended to replace Fransu. Bergueneuse, however, is well worth a visit. A tunnel system built into a hillside, it has survived intact and most of the interior can still be inspected.

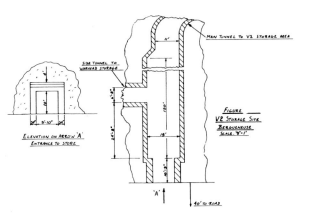

ELEVATION ON ARROW 'A'
ENTRANCE TO STORE

FIGURE
V2 STORAGE SITE
BERGUENEUSE
SCALE '8'-1'

(i) Bergueneuse *Michelin map No. 51; IGN map No. 2306 O.*

Bergueneuse is about 4 miles to the north-east of Sautricourt. Take the D343 to Anvin and either the D94 or the D97 to reach Bergueneuse. The site is located on a minor road off the D94, turn left before entering the village at the D71 junction. The site entrance is on the left a few yards from the road. The tunnel entrance is reinforced concrete, 10ft high x 9ft 11in wide, giving clearance for the V2 in transport mode. The main tunnel, opens out to 15ft wide some 10ft 9in from the entrance and then extends in a straight line for 150ft before the left-hand wall moves in to reduce the width to 11ft. Immediately the tunnel curves to the right at 45 deg. and extends for another 300ft before ending in a rock-face. The maximum tunnel height is 18ft and at regular intervals there are supports for lifting gear. The floor of the tunnel has 4ft-wide runways at either side. On the left-hand side of the main tunnel, 45ft from the entrance, is a 6ft 9in-wide side tunnel. This extends for 30ft before it also widens to 15ft. After a further 60ft this section is blocked by two massive steel doors, reaching 15ft to the ceiling. The whole interior is remarkably dry and well ventilated, providing good storage conditions. The main tunnel would have held at least ten V2s and the side tunnel was probably intended for warhead storage.

Bergueneuse was on the Allied target list but there are no signs of bomb damage and the tunnels themselves are bomb-proof. There were quarries outside the village and the new activity may not have been regarded as suspicious by Allied Intelligence until a definite link was established based on information from French agents. The nearest rail link is 2 miles away at Anvin and the new V2 storage site of Monchy-Cayeux is not far away, between Sautricourt and Anvin.

5.2.3 V2 Transit Depots

The original V2 organisation included six transit depots for rockets en route between main storage depots and the field launch sites. Here, the V2 vehicles would be parked up in a safe area and the journey continued the following day. Three of the six were in the Calais–Somme area, between Watten and St Pol, one between Bayeux and St Lô in Normandy, and two on the Cherbourg Peninsula. How many of these transit depots were built is not known but from the report described below it appears that work was only started when the new organisation came into being. Report A.I.2(g) 7X, PRO File AIR40/1219, covers V2 sites on the Cherbourg Peninsula and Normandy following a survey after D-Day using captured German information, and refers to the La Croix Frimot transit depot on the Cherbourg Peninsula. From another PRO file, ACIU report AIR20/5867, the progress of work at La Croix Frimot is described, and this shows that work at this original organisation site did not start until May 1944, but by 27 May the site had increased to an excavation 190ft long x 22ft wide. This means that at some of the transit depots, work was not started as part of the original organisation even though the locations had already been chosen. This is discussed in section 5.5.

5.3 ORIGINAL FIELD LAUNCHING SITES

Originally 45 field launching sites were planned for the V2. Each comprised concrete access roads and three concrete pads with parking for the various vehicles, including the fuel tankers. The 'three pads' concept is based on the fact that each launch Abteilung comprised three batteries and each battery could man three launching pads. Two of these sites were on the Cherbourg Peninsula, four in Normandy (Calvados) and the other 39 between Calais and the Somme. Another site was built in the entrance to the Château Molay, north-east of Cloay where there is a similar site; but nothing now remains of the concrete pads. The new site organisation dated 4 November 1943 makes no mention of field launch sites in Normandy, and thus can be taken as confirmation that the locations mentioned above were part of the original organisation. Judging by the state of one of these sites, Lison, it is likely that many of the original field sites were never completed. In the two other site areas, Calais–Somme and the Cherbourg Peninsula, it is also likely that the original field sites were started but never completed. Document A.I.2(g) 7X, an RAF Air Intelligence (Technical) report, also refers to the two launch site locations on the Cherbourg Peninsula, one near Beaumont, to the west of Cherbourg, and the other near Montaigu, to the south-east, which is also the location of a V1 'modified' site, number 18. Both of these V2 sites were reported as consisting of a ballasted roadway running parallel to an existing road and joining it at both ends. At neither site had any concrete been laid at the time of capture. Neither has been found by the author, and it is likely that they were been broken up for their materials. The same probably applies to those sites in the Calais–Somme area; some were started but never finished and the remains have now blended into the landscape. Descriptions have been included in the new V2 organisation, section 5.5.

5.4 BUNKERS

The four bunker sites all formed part of the original V2 organisation but their use was modified to suit the changed military situation from 1943 onwards, and eventually none of them played any part in the 'new' organisation.

(i) Watten (Kraftwerk Nordwest) *Michelin map No. 51.*
Watten is a few miles north-east of St Omer in the Pas de Calais and many of the roads in the area give directions to the site. In the last ten years Watten has become a popular destination for coach parties, but it wasn't always so. In the 1970s and 1980s the site was open to the public and was more or less as it was in 1944 when it was abandoned by the Germans. Today, less is accessible than previously and parts have been 'improved', but the site is still the most impressive of the bunkers to visit.

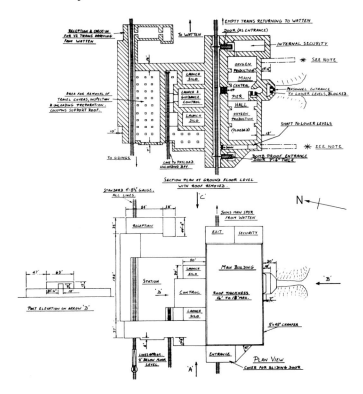

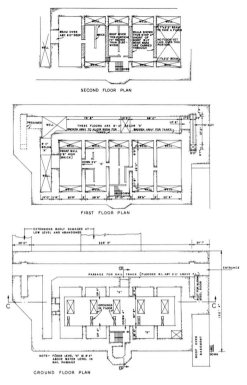

SECOND FLOOR PLAN

FIRST FLOOR PLAN

GROUND FLOOR PLAN

Details of the main buildings at Watten V2 bunker.

The area was inspected in December 1942 by officials from the War Ministry, Organisation Todt and Peenemünde. The site chosen was on the edge of the Forêt d'Eperlecques, at the base of a low escarpment and close to some quarries. Work started in March 1943 and it was planned that the base would be operational by October 1943 – a very tight schedule. Considering what was involved, even without the Allied bombing, it would probably have been late. Although the OT was experienced in large construction projects, from the autobahn to the fortifications of the West Wall, no single project had been as unusual and as complicated as Watten. To achieve the target date, PoWs from eastern Europe and Russia were brought in by Fritz Saukel's organisation, which was in charge of the foreign workers used by the Third Reich. Saukel was hanged for war crimes on 16 October 1946. At Watten two workers' camps were built a mile from the site and work continued seven days a week, 24 hrs a day, under the supervision of the OT and SS. During the six months that the site was under construction, over 35,000 workers passed through the camps. After the war Dornberger and von Braun both claimed to know very little about Watten, as they did for the underground V-weapons factory at Nordhausen, but in 1943 no one had a better understanding than the Peenemünde team of what was required.

Plans for the V2 and its larger developments meant that Watten had to be capable of handling rockets over twice the size of the V2 in a bomb-proof environment and this resulted in some unique construction problems. The OT had carried out tests on captured reinforced concrete bunkers and these showed that, with the correct thickness, a flat roof could be constructed that would withstand the heaviest bomb in the Allied armoury, which at the time was the 12,000lb Tall Boy. This 21ft-long bomb had an explosive weight of 5,400lb (2 tons). Its offset fins gave it a slow spinning motion to help accuracy and the streamlined casing was intended to ensure that impact occurred as close to Mach 1 as possible. The only aircraft capable of carrying the Tall Boy were Lancasters and these had to be specially modified to take the weight. Xaver Dorsch, the OT's construction chief, believed, not unreasonably, that this bomb was the heaviest that the Allies were going to use in the war. In fact, the Grand Slam at 22,000lb and over 25ft long was the largest single bomb carried in the Second World War and once again the Lancaster was the only aircraft able to lift it. The magic figure arrived at by the OT was 18ft and Dorsch was able to show that a flat roof of this thickness would provide protection from the Tall Boy. Using formulae taken from the American National Defense Research Council, using the dimensions and impact velocity of the Tall Boy, a figure of 9ft 10in is produced for the penetration depth and 18ft 5in for the scabbing depth. ('Scabbing' is when the roof is not physically penetrated but material is detached from the ceiling by the shock waves through the concrete.) To improve the scabbing protection for buildings, it was standard practice to build a steel mattress of girders into the underside of the roof, and the ceiling at Watten was provided with this extra protection.

From June to July 1944 four of the bunker sites – Watten, Wizernes, Siracourt and Mimoyecques – were targeted by a special bombing campaign using Tall Boys. Watten was subjected to an additional bombing raid in 1945 in which several US-designed hard-target bombs similar to the Grand Slam were dropped by the RAF. Early in this special bombing programme two raids were made on Watten, on 19 June and 25 July 1944, when a total of 32 Tall Boy bombs were dropped. Only one hit the main building, impacting near the centre of the roof on the south side and causing serious structural damage. A piece of concrete weighing several tons was blown off the roof, and inside the ceiling developed cracks, with a large section becoming detached – only the anti-scabbing mattress prevented it from falling to the floor below. This ceiling damage can no longer be seen because in the 1990s a false ceiling was added inside the main building. The 1945 attack using the US weapons also obtained only one hit on the main building, above the west entrance at one of its strongest points, the junction between the wall and the roof. Shock-waves from the explosion resulted in a number of the steel reinforcing bars being ejected and a large piece of the roof was removed, although this damage could have been repaired fairly quickly.

Watten V2 bunker, aerial view taken on 13 March 1944. By this date Watten had been bombed eight times; but the main bombing campaign started shortly after this photograph was taken. (PRO)

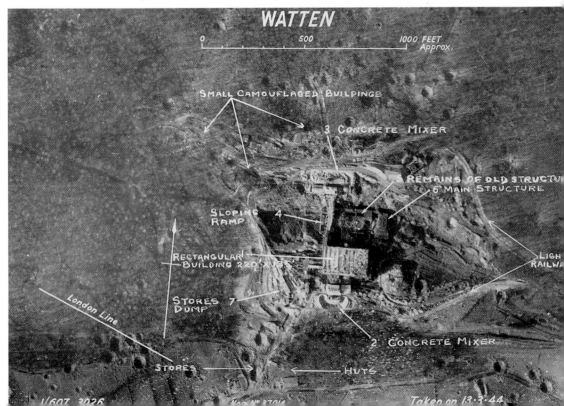

Mention must also be made of Project Aphrodite – a scheme to use as huge bombs time-expired Flying Fortresses packed with 22,000lb of explosives. The idea was that the crew would pilot the plane to the target, set the fuses and then bale out, with the Fortress's final dive on to the target being radio-controlled from an accompanying aircraft. Project Aphrodite was not a success and one of the aircraft exploded prematurely over the North Sea, killing Joseph P. Kennedy, brother of the future President.

Nearly 80ft above the ground, the finished roof weighed 50,000 tons and required some special high-level construction equipment. The problem was solved by the OT in a very unusual way. The walls were built up to a height of 15ft and the roof was added, with few access problems at this height. Then, using hundreds of jacks, the roof was raised, a few inches at a time, the walls underneath being built up to their full thickness of 18ft, as the roof moved upwards. To transport the huge quantities of cement, sand, gravel, steel and eventually rockets, a standard-gauge spur was taken off the main line at Watten with two narrow-gauge lines for the construction material running to a sidings on high ground behind the site. Material was loaded on to skips at the sidings and these were allowed to run down the incline by gravity, pulling the empty skips back to the top at the same time. From March until August 1943 work proceeded without hindrance and enough progress was made to be able to confirm that the target date of October 1943 would be achieved.

However, all this was to change very quickly. On the night of 17 August 1943 Peenemünde was bombed for the first time and on 27 August it was Watten's turn. The raid by 185 B-17 Flying Fortresses of the US 8th Air Force was a daylight raid at high level and hence accuracy was not very good for such a small target. The damage caused by this first raid was not serious but it was the start of an almost constant bombardment that lasted until August 1944, by which time over 4,000 tons of bombs had been dropped on the site in twenty-five air-raids. The main building escaped serious damage but some of the minor buildings were badly affected and more importantly the site generally became unusable owing to the numerous bomb craters and the destruction of equipment. A halt in the bombing from October 1943 to February 1944 gave both sides an opportunity to assess the situation. From the Allied point of view the bombing results at this time were inconclusive. The main building at Watten was still standing and there had been varying amounts of damage to the other buildings. Construction work had been badly disrupted but no one knew what was going on in the main building. In fact, in October 1943 Allied Intelligence still did not know what Watten was intended for, although agents' reports did refer to Watten as a rocket base. The only criterion had been that all large, new concrete structures in northern France within a 150-mile radius of London were to be bombed.

By October 1943 the influence of the SS was increasing, and after their take-over of the V-weapons site programme it was clear that a no-nonsense approach was going to be taken on what part, if any, the bunkers would play in the V-weapons offensive. The bunkers, especially Watten, had been approved by Hitler and as such they could not be abandoned out of hand, but changes were required. Obviously the halt in Allied bombing was not going to last and it was very likely to resume, probably on an even heavier scale,

The south wall of the main building at Watten V2 bunker. The air intakes were for the compressors producing liquid oxygen. The roof shows damage from 'Tall Boy' bombs. The 'octagon' was originally an entrance to the lower levels. (Author)

at some time in the near future. Work therefore continued at Watten but at a reduced pace and a variety of new plans were drawn up, showing alternative methods of using the main building in particular as a rocket base.

Watten is privately owned and open to the public during the summer, seven days a week; tours are self-guided and most areas are accessible. Unfortunately, since 1990 the guide-book has been amended to make it more politically correct and gone are references to the more unpleasant aspects of Watten, including the use of forced labour. In addition, the main building has been altered internally, including the addition of false ceilings and a reduction in access compared to 1980. The interior of the main building is still flooded to just below ground level and hence the lower levels cannot be inspected. At the west entrance the bomb-proof door, 7ft 6in thick, is now operating in its slot, protected above by a canopy similar to that at Siracourt. The main entrance at the eastern end is flooded but access can be made through the west door to the right where equipment for LOX production was to be installed, although the plinths and other features have now disappeared. Immediately to the right of the west door is a passageway which had a vertical shaft at the far end, giving access to the lower levels (flooded) and this shaft is also no longer visible. There were similar larger vertical shafts in the rocket unloading bay.

West railway tunnel entrance to the main building at Watten. The extension had a bomb-proof sliding door. The slots are 'dog-leg' ventilation ducts. Again, the roof shows Tall Boy bomb damage. (Author)

As originally planned, trains loaded with rockets would arrive at Watten from Germany and would first be stopped in the reception station, now accessible, where all documentation would be finally checked and the transportation covers removed. An inspection was made of the rockets and wagons for any signs of damage or other irregularities, including a check on radiation levels if such a cargo was included. Any non-essential supplies would be unloaded at this time and stored initially in the roofed-over section of the station. This initial check and inspection were an important part of the site procedures as the main building would have been regarded as a 'clean' area and no 'foreign' material would have been allowed to enter. A radiation leak, for example, in the lower levels could have been catastrophic. Once checked out the train moved forward to a sidings a few hundred yards to the west before being reversed back towards the main building. If the cargo included rockets, the train entered the main building through the west door, then both sliding doors were closed and the rockets unloaded. Height clearance here is about 60ft and originally runway beams for the lifting hoists could be seen above the track, but these are now hidden from view. The rockets were lowered down to the working areas before the east door was opened and the empty train returned to Germany. If the supply train had contained warheads, alcohol or other material, it would have entered the second unloading bay between the station and the main building.

This is a single-storey structure, as only normal headroom would be required. The train would have been unloaded and the contents transferred to the lower levels. LOX was to have been produced in the main building. When ready for launch, the rockets were raised almost to the surface at one of the silos via a lift system similar to that used in the US Minuteman ICBM silos. After final checks the countdown took place and the rocket was launched from just below the surface, the exhaust being vented at either side. Watten could easily handle rockets twice the size of the V2, with very large rockets arriving in sections both to avoid damage and to ease transportation difficulties. The launch silos have an opening measuring 30ft x 50ft, which would give ample clearance for the much larger versions of the V2.

(ii) Wizernes (Schotterwerk Nord-west) *Michelin map No. 51.*

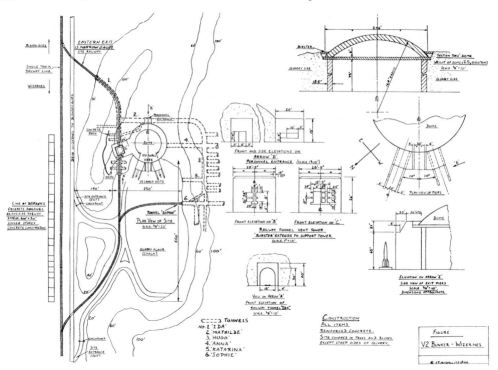

If Watten was intended to be the ultimate rocket base, it had a 'sister' only 10 miles to the south-west, in a chalk quarry near the town of Wizernes. This site was designed to a similar specification as Watten, to provide a secure bomb-proof environment for storing, servicing and launching V2 rockets and its larger developments. Liquid oxygen would also have been produced on site and accommodation provided for all the personnel involved in the operation of the site. There was even a hospital. At Watten no attempt was made to conceal the main building, and it stands out today as a massive monument in concrete. At Wizernes, however, the dome was covered in soil and it would have looked little different from any other chalk quarry.

Construction work started at Wizernes in July 1943, a few months later than Watten, and the method adopted by the Organisation Todt was similar to that used at Siracourt. At Wizernes the massive hollow concrete dome was built first, supported by the chalk underneath, chalk being the only local material capable of supporting the 25,000-ton weight. The dome has a maximum thickness of 16ft 6in, an internal diameter of 201ft and an internal height of 48ft. The dome was positioned at the west end of the quarry, which had already been excavated to a depth of over 100ft. There is very little published data on the effect of shells or bombs striking concrete at oblique angles, but it can be assumed that the dome would have provided protection at least as good as the flat roof at Watten. Under the dome the working area is an octagon with walls 5ft thick, extending from ground level to a 6ft 6in-thick floor under the dome. This gives a total working height of 75ft and this may have been the maximum size of the rockets that could be assembled at Wizernes. At the rear of the dome is a personnel entrance, probably intended for emergency use.

When the author first visited Wizernes in the 1970s the site was abandoned. The quarry floor still had the remains of the standard-gauge railway leading into the main tunnel ('Ida') and the side tunnel ('Sophie'). There was an iron grille over the entrance to 'Ida', but entry was possible and a short inspection of the tunnel was made but the water levels made any extended exploration dangerous. Twenty years later, in 1997, the site was opened to the public after a joint French and EC-funded project to turn it into a vast

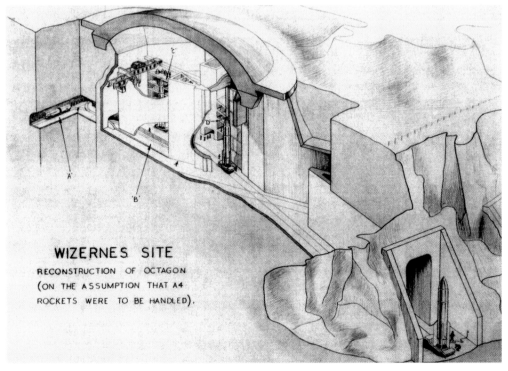

WIZERNES SITE

RECONSTRUCTION OF OCTAGON
(ON THE ASSUMPTION THAT A4
ROCKETS WERE TO BE HANDLED).

Wizernes V2 bunker. Artist's impression of the V2 assembly and launch area. (PRO)

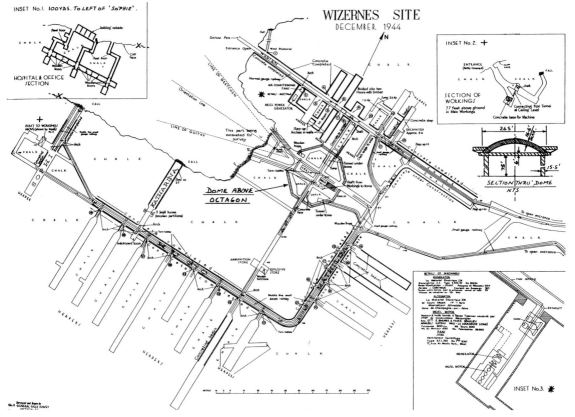

Wizernes V2 bunker. British Army plan of the site, December 1944. (PRO)

underground museum. Visitors now enter via the original railway tunnel 'Ida', although the rails have been removed and the floor levelled. On either side are short branch tunnels intended for storage and one still houses a large diesel generator, used in 1943/4. Partway along, headphones are available which trigger multi-language descriptions as visitors follow the marked route. A few yards further on 'Ida' is blocked by a rock-fall caused by British sappers in 1945 and the route turns right, joining up with tunnel 'Mathilde' later. Originally an unloading station was built at the 'Ida–Mathilde' junction and beyond here 'Ida' reduces in width; a narrow-gauge track was to have continued ahead until it reached the opposite exit. The supply trains would have returned the same way. From the unloading station, another narrow-gauge system ran along 'Mathilde', serving the remaining underground workings, and rejoining the main track at 'Sophie'.

On the surface, above the unloading station, there is a large concrete structure which served as a vent for the rail tunnel and the remainder of the tunnel systems. From the map, the huge scale of the southern tunnel system can be seen, providing an additional underground space approximately 1,500ft long by 15ft wide. The tunnel 'Sophie' is a large underground complex in its own right with a rectangular basement alone covering an area of 66ft x 40ft, a vertical shaft rising 77ft to the surface. The underground hospital and offices are only 100 yards further along the quarry and the position of these facilities, some distance from the main workings, may be significant, perhaps indicating that the work to be carried out here was especially hazardous.

Wizernes V2 bunker. This photograph shows the dome, the remains of rocket launching piers and the ventilation tower for railway tunnel 'Ida'. The site was opened to the public in May 1997. (Author)

Returning to the visitors' route, after several yards visitors enter a lift to the original floor under the dome. This floor now contains a large selection of Second World War material and regular filmshows take place here on the history of the V2 and related topics. The same lift is used for the return except that visitors leave by the opposite door and the route passes through the partially completed octagon walls, which can be seen disappearing into the darkness above. The exit route now rejoins 'Ida' at the headphones office and you leave at the entrance to 'Ida'. The tour takes two hours, depending on how much time is spent with the exhibits and filmshows under the dome.

Once rockets had been prepared for launch, they were to exit from the two piers 'Gustav' and 'Gretchen', which were partially completed but have now slipped out of alignment. In 1944 parts of the bomb-proof doors for the piers were found at Watten and their final height could have been 75ft, which gives an indication of the height available for assembling and launching rockets. The amount of forced labour used at Wizernes is not known but a great deal of manual work would have been needed during construction. Work carried on until March 1944, a full eight months, although the site had been photographed several times by Allied PRU aircraft.

On 11 March 1944 the first bombing raid took place and these continued on almost a weekly basis until July 1944, by which time a total of 3,200 tons had been dropped on the site. It virtually stopped all work. Originally a long line of single-storey concrete buildings ran alongside the main single-track railway line outside the quarry, covering an

Above: Wizernes V2 bunker, 6 July 1944. The dome is in the lower right-hand corner; the railway tunnel vent is at 5 o'clock; the dome personnel access at 10 o'clock; and the quarry floor at 12 o'clock. (PRO)

This amazing low-level PRU photograph shows the Wizernes V2 bunker, 16 March 1944. In the centre is the dome; left is the rail tunnel vent; centre-left is the rail tunnel entrance. (PRO)

Wizernes V2 bunker. The unloading station in railway tunnel 'Ida', showing the ventilation equipment, construction wagons and rock-fall caused by British Army demolition charges in 1944. (Author)

area of about 600ft x 30ft. These would have provided a similar function to that of the reception station at Watten. They were badly damaged in the bombing and their remains have now been removed. Wizernes had one major operational advantage over Watten, in that the pre-launch checks and the launch itself were both carried out at the same level, which meant that no complicated lifting gear was required to bring the rocket to the surface. In addition, there was more secure space available at Wizernes than at Watten, certainly enough for LOX production and the storage of alcohol and other essential materials, plus room for any nuclear activities that might have been planned.

The Wizernes tour is an experience not to be missed. Despite the 'improvements' for visitors, there is still an uneasy sensation inside the tunnels, a chill which is due not just to the damp atmosphere. The many tunnels still barred to visitors that disappear into the darkness raise questions about what was really going on in these dark recesses. Certainly the tour only scratches the surface of the real history of Wizernes.

(iii) Sottevast, Brix (German site name 'Reservelager West').
Michelin map No. 54; IGN map No. 1210 E.

Location: from Cherbourg take the N13 and 500 yards past the turning for Brix turn right on to the D262. Continue on the D262 for about 2 miles, ignoring the D262E branching off to the left. At the T-junction with the D50 turn right and after ¾ mile a narrow road goes off to the right for Les Fontaines. Take this road and after ½ mile park the car and the site is in the fields on the left. The original German access road survives, and where this can be found it provides a good indication of the site's location.

Despite the obvious advantages to be gained from building four similar facilities, which would have speeded up construction and meant only one design of internal equipment, the Germans decided on four completely different solutions to the problem of the storage, servicing and launching of the V2 and its derivatives. But although at both Watten and Wizernes the basic structure was completed and drawings exist which show the final form, at Sottevast the main structure was never finished and only a few incomplete drawings were found in a safe when the site was captured in 1944. Work started in March 1943, and by March 1944, when the first bombing raid took place, the main structure was only about a quarter complete – virtually in the state it is today.

We do know what the basic layout would have been. The main building was to have covered an area of 600ft x 109ft, larger than Watten, with the main entrance for rail traffic being 170ft long x 92ft wide, a spur being taken off the main line at Sottevast to supply the site. The map shows the extent of the standard-gauge and narrow-gauge track

Sottevast V2 bunker, 25 March 1944. 1: end of partly constructed rectangular building; 2: two trenches aligned on London; 3: curved cutting leading to north end of (2); 4: long building with rail access and camouflaged loading platform; 5: dump of timber and building materials; 6. deep rectangular hole. (PRO)

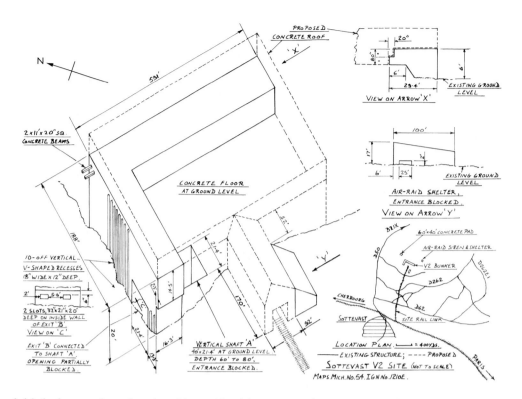

PROPOSED
CONCRETE ROOF

VIEW ON ARROW 'X'

20"

6'
23.4'

EXISTING GROUND
LEVEL

N

59'

2 x 11' x 20" SQ.
CONCRETE BEAMS

CONCRETE FLOOR
AT GROUND LEVEL

100'

17'

6'   25'

EXISTING GROUND
LEVEL

AIR-RAID SHELTER,
ENTRANCE BLOCKED.
VIEW ON ARROW 'Y'

PARIS

60' x 40' CONCRETE PAD

AIR-RAID SIREN & SHELTER

V2 BUNKER

D262

186'

10-OFF VERTICAL
V-SHAPED RECESSES
18" WIDE x 12" DEEP.

2'   5.6'

2 SLOTS, 32" x 21" x 20'
DEEP ON INSIDE WALL
OF EXIT 'B'.
VIEW ON 'C'

EXIT 'B' CONNECTED
TO SHAFT 'A'.
OPENING PARTIALLY
BLOCKED.

CHERBOURG

SOTTEVAST

D62

SITE RAIL LINK

VERTICAL SHAFT 'A'.
40' x 21.4' AT GROUND LEVEL
DEPTH 60' TO 80',
ENTRANCE BLOCKED.

LOCATION PLAN. ⊢⎯⎯⊣ = 400 YDS.
⎯⎯ EXISTING STRUCTURE; ⎯⎯⎯ PROPOSED
SOTTEVAST V2 SITE (NOT TO SCALE)
MAPS. MICH. No. 54. IGN No. 1210E.

laid during work at the site. Alongside this entrance is a concrete air-raid shelter, 100ft long x 31ft wide, now partially buried, for personnel working outside. Even if it had been finished, Sottevast would not have had the imposing presence of Watten. Its maximum height today is 20ft and it is likely that the roof would have been earthed over. One of the supporting walls is only 6ft above ground level. The plan shows the final layout of the main building as envisaged by Allied Intelligence, using drawings found at the site in 1944. At present, the structure resembles a giant 'L' laid on its side, partially enclosing an open concrete area. Missing are the two other legs of the 'L' which would have formed an enclosed rectangle and these four walls would have supported the outer, main roof. The open area inside the 'L' is actually the roof of the underground section of the main building. The only access to this is via the vertical shaft 'A' and exit 'B'. Shaft 'A' is now blocked with concrete beams and 'B' is blocked with soil but a local farmer said the entrances were very deep, at least 60ft.

The only other finished items at the site are a small bunker to the east, on which was mounted an air-raid siren, and a concrete pad, 60ft x 40ft, to the north. The author believes that shaft 'A' and exit 'B' were part of the launch platform: their alignment is north-west and the exit could have been for the rocket motor's exhaust gases. With sufficient height underground, rockets would have been moved vertically to shaft 'A' before launch. Exit 'B' can still be entered, just, as the soil does not quite reach the roof, and visible against the face of the inner wall are two rectangular slots. These may have been intended to provide supports for lifting gear or a door. The purpose of the V-shaped grooves on the outside wall is as yet unidentified. To the north of the main building is a

Sottevast V2 bunker, July 1944. This photograph shows Exit 'B'. (PRO)

concrete pad, 60ft x 40ft, without any signs of built-in anchor points of the type usually associated with anti-aircraft guns. This pad may have been a late addition to provide a V2 launch pad when Sottevast became a storage only facility. It is a great pity that the interior of Sottevast has not been made accessible, like Watten and Wizernes, as these rocket bunkers have considerable tourist appeal and more could be learnt about Sottevast's original operational use, not only with V2s but also with the Rheinböte and various larger developments.

(iv) Brécourt (Olkeller Cherbourg) *Michelin map No. 54; IGN map No. 1210 E.*

Brécourt led a charmed life, and was never bombed despite hundreds of air-raids on the other V1/V2 sites on the Peninsula and a file of photographs at the ACIU headquarters. Uniquely, this dual-purpose site has survived undam-aged and exactly as it was left by the retreating Germans in 1944.

In the 1920s France, like other modern countries, was busy converting its coal-fired warships to oil-burning. Cherbourg was then and still is a large naval base (all of France's nuclear submarines are built there), and it needed to be able to store a considerable quantity of heavy diesel oil for the ships in a secure location convenient to the base. Brécourt is 3 miles west of the port, a few hundred yards off the D90. Leave the D90 at the first junction on the left after the Hameau de Mer roundabout, on to the D16. At the next roundabout either the first or second exit will take you to the site, built into the hillside, by a ravine taking a stream down to the sea a few hundred yards away. In 1920 tunnels were cut into the hillside and work started on eight huge underground oil reservoirs, although the last two were never completed. The reservoirs, 240ft long x 50ft wide and 46ft deep, were made of concrete with a steel lining, and were open-ended at the top. The whole complex was connected by tunnels with accommodation for personnel and equipment, and a rail link ran into the site from the track running along the coast. The site is still under the control of the French Navy, although oil is now stored in above-ground tanks inside the naval base. With permission from the Naval Commander at Cherbourg, the author was taken on a guided tour of those areas still accessible, including Reservoir Number 3, the adjacent tunnels and part of the German additions to the site.

German forces arrived at Cherbourg shortly after the French capitulation in June 1940 and although Brécourt had already been replaced as an oil depot, the potential of the site for other uses must have been obvious. It is not surprising therefore that when suitable locations were being investigated for use as V-weapons bases, Brécourt was chosen on the basis that very little additional work was required.

Internally the changes amounted to the following. Reservoirs 1 to 6 were unchanged, while 7 and 8 were modified to provide offices and workshops for personnel. The various connecting tunnels and other underground areas were intended for storage for V-weapons, fuel, warheads and vehicles, and for LOX production. Each of the original reservoir entrances was served by the site's 24in narrow-gauge railway, most of which is still in place. The entrances in the hillside for reservoirs 1 to 3 were given increased security by the addition of bomb-proof doors, similar to those at Watten. The original French doors remained, and 30ft in from each entrance a recess was provided for a 12ft-thick steel and concrete sliding door. This feature was also intended to be added at the other entrances. Originally the site was to be used as a V1 base and at the north end of the site, two massive blast walls were built to protect the V1 ramp. For reasons unknown, but probably connected to the bombing of the original V2 bunkers, the role of Brécourt was changed, as at Siracourt, from a V1 to a rocket base, although all the alterations needed were not completed: the accommodation and equipment block behind the V1 ramp is not finished; there are remains of vertical, steel reinforcing bars on the roof (also shown in earlier photographs); and the two rectangular openings were probably intended for stairwells for an additional storey. The rocket exit point from the underground storage is now blocked off. Rockets would have emerged horizontally and some form of handling gear would have been required to swing them into the vertical position. Access is possible, but a few feet below ground everything is flooded. V2 exhaust gases would have been directed upwards by the surrounding structures. This is probably why the rocket exit is not roofed over.

Perhaps the most interesting feature at Brécourt is the 13ft-square angled rocket exhaust tunnel. The problem of damage and erosion to the launch pad and associated

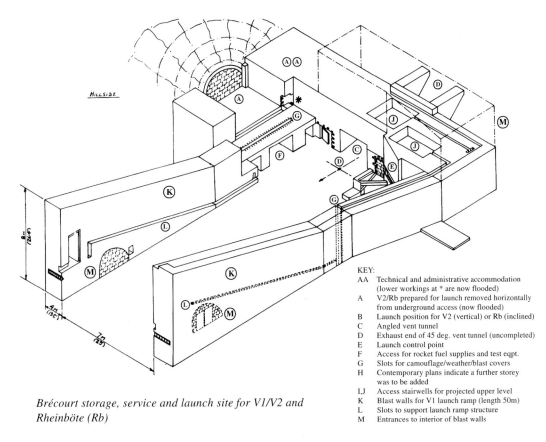

Brécourt storage, service and launch site for V1/V2 and Rheinböte (Rb)

KEY:
AA   Technical and administrative accommodation
        (lower workings at * are now flooded)
A   V2/Rb prepared for launch removed horizontally
        from underground access (now flooded)
B   Launch position for V2 (vertical) or Rb (inclined)
C   Angled vent tunnel
D   Exhaust end of 45 deg. vent tunnel (uncompleted)
E   Launch control point
F   Access for rocket fuel supplies and test eqpt.
G   Slots for camouflage/weather/blast covers
H   Contemporary plans indicate a further storey
        was to be added
I,J   Access stairwells for projected upper level
K   Blast walls for V1 launch ramp (length 50m)
L   Slots to support launch ramp structure
M   Entrances to interior of blast walls

equipment caused by the red-hot, high-speed exhaust gases was one that became more important as rockets became larger. By the 1960s larger rockets were being placed on raised launch pads and the motor exhaust went downwards before being deflected sideways by a water-cooled 'bucket'. By this method the launch pad and equipment could be used again within a short period of time. At Peenemünde the original launch pad had been a large elliptical area, with different locations used within the ellipse. In addition, a steel launch table was developed, nicknamed the 'lemon-squeezer', which deflected some of the gases away from the pad. At Brécourt a novel solution to the exhaust gas problem was in the process of being built. Tunnel 'C' is angled upwards at 45 deg., and when completed it would have directed the exhaust vertically. It was not intended for the V1 because it has no exhaust as such until it reaches the end of the ramp, nor for the V2, which was launched vertically. The only rocket in the German arsenal that was launched at an angle was the Rheinböte, usually at about 45 deg. for maximum range, and we know now that this weapon was regarded as a stand-by for the V1. This makes the Rh III, which had a warhead equivalent to that of the V1, a more serious project than previously thought, and the 8-ton Rh III would have produced considerable exhaust gases for a few seconds after the first stage of the solid-fuel motor ignited. The angled vent at Brécourt would have solved this problem.

The original use of Brécourt as a V1 base also resulted in some unusual features regarding the ramp blast walls. These are 13ft thick, far greater than anything built at other V1 sites, and this fact alone indicates that the V1s launched from Brécourt were to be given special pre-launch preparation and protection. In addition, the start of the ramp is protected by a wall height of 20ft, whereas at the ski sites the blast wall was level with the ramp at the start. The blast walls contain access passages and storage rooms and at one time the right-hand wall was connected directly to the hillside. All these features indicate that the Brécourt V1s had special warheads, either chemical, gas – or nuclear.

Brécourt was photographed from the air by PRU aircraft but the site was never bombed, even though the blast walls are clearly visible. Couville and Sottevast are only a few miles away and they were bombed on a regular basis, and it seems very strange that Brécourt should have escaped so lightly. Although permission to visit the site is required from the Cherbourg naval authorities, parts of it can be seen from the high ground opposite, and recently a V1 has been placed between the blast walls.

5.5 NEW FINAL V2 ORGANISATION, INCLUDING THE A9/A10

5.5.1 Storage Sites and Motor Transport Servicing Sites

Of the original organisation – which comprised seven main storage sites for the V2, four field storage depots and six transit depots – virtually everything had been written off by the end of 1943 and only three of the original main (rear) storage sites (Méry-sur-Oise, Tavannes and Hollogne) appear in the new arrangements. The only other named main storage site in the new system was Bar-le-Duc, but sites were also required for a further 500 V2s plus sites for spare parts and the repair and service of the special vehicles used in the field launch organisation, Meillerwagens, Vidalwagens, etc.

The final V2 storage organisation shown in Map and List 5, included locations that were nearly all new to the V2. Of the Forward Underground Storage sites, in the area from Calais to the Seine, Bergueneuse was an original site and evidence of tunnel widths of 10ft (3m) or greater plus concealed open-air storage, indicates that Lumbres; La Pourchinte; St Riquier; Pont Remy; Bois d'Etrejust; Inval Boiron; Agenville and Monville were intended for the V2, but of course they could also have provided storage for the narrower V1 and Rheinbôte. Raimbert and Salouel were not inspected and have not been visited by the author, but they have been assigned to the V2 because of the weapon's greater storage requirements.

(i) **Lumbres/La Pourchinte** *Michelin map No. 51; IGN map No. 2204 E.*

These two sites have been combined because they are adjacent and were intended to work together. From St Omer take the N42 towards Boulogne and Lumbres is 5 miles

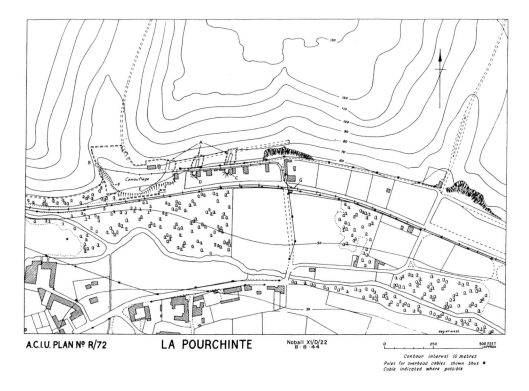

The V2 new field storage site at La Pourchinte, Pas de Calais, 8 August 1944. This ACIU plan of the site was based on aerial photographs.

along the D42. Turn left onto the D192 for Elnes and Wavrans and the site originally spread both sides of the railway (abandoned with the main section being in the wooded area on the left of the D192. ACIU aerial photos dated 6 July 1944 showed that the site was utilising existing French industrial buildings, especially north of the railway and in the far SW corner of the site with other areas extensively camouflaged and a new rail spur had been built in the wooded area. Lumbres would have provided the servicing and testing facility before V2s were transported to the field launch sites. Originally a branch of the railway ran along the D192 to Elnes and Wavrans and this branch was used for the La Pourchinte part of the site, only a few hundred yards from Lumbres. The plan of La Pourchinte is dated 8 August 1944. The site was to be the V2 storage for Lumbres with four tunnels 'A' and 'B', all served by a narrow gauge system off the main line at 'G'. The main tunnel was at 'B', narrow gauge lines are 'E' and 'F' and spoil heaps are 'C' and 'D', from the tunnel excavations.

Allied inspection of the site found evidence of its use as a storage base for the German Navy but the author believes that this was after its abandonment as a V2 site. A modern paper mill, 1967, has obscured the tunnel entrances but the forest area still has signs of its wartime use. Parts of the railway are still there, other sections towards Wavrans have been converted into a footpath.

(ii) St Riquier *Michelin map No. 52*

From Abbeville take the N25 for St Riquier, 6 miles. Before entering the town turn left onto an unmarked road and this road joins a track which was originally a rail spur serving the site from the main line. Carry on along the track for ½ mile until the start of a concrete road, providing access to the tunnels. Unfortunately the concrete access road is now flooded and this restricts inspection of the site, but at least ten tunnel entrances can be seen. Aerial photos taken in June 1944 show several tunnel entrances, possibly eleven, with a very wide (30ft) road and a looped vehicle turning point, midway along the site, obviously intended for a very long transporter. The tunnels were also served by a narrow-gauge system. The site was bombed in August 1944 but the raids were not continued, probably because the rocket threat appeared to be diminishing compared to the V1.

(iii) Pont Rémy *Michelin map No. 52*

Location: From Abbeville take the N1 for Pont Rémy, 5 miles. The site is in two sections involving the rail system and V2 storage. Between 17 March 1944 and 31 August 1944, ACIU interpreters established that a new railway turntable had been built in the station yard, on the site of a disused sidings. This turntable was 80ft in

St Ricquier V1/V2 storage site – final organisation, Pas de Calais. Entrance to one of the narrower tunnels, for the V1. The only tunnel not flooded out of at least 10. (Author)

Brécourt V1/V2 bunker. To reach their launch point, V1s exited from the lower tunnels in the hillside, V2s from the top. (Author)

diameter with a 9ft overlap all round and was connected to the main line at either end. At least five cranes, including two gantry type, were located on the main line and adjacent to the turntable. By August the whole facility was so well camouflaged that many of the features were impossible to identify. The turntable and lifting gear was intended to handle V2 rail transporters, the V2s being moved by rail on what became known to the ACIU as 'triple flats', carrying two V2s with their noses overlapping on the centre wagon, each 'triple' travelling as a single unit and they had a total length of just over 80ft. The turntable has now disappeared and the area is occupied by a scap metal yard. Access to the rocket storage areas is off the N1 from Abbeville. Before entering Pont Rémy, three minor roads go off on the LH side, to high ground overlooking the town. The site areas are about 300yd apart and ¼ mile from the N1. In each case excavations were carried out to provide above ground parking although – aerial photos taken in August 1944 show one possible tunnel entrance in the central site area. Very few signs now remain of the excavation work.

(iv) Bois d'Etrejust *Michelin map No. 52*

Location: From Pont Rémy take the N1 south through Airaines and after two miles turn right onto the D157. After a further two mile turn right for Etrejust. Aerial photos taken on 19 July 1944 and an Allied ground inspection revealed four excavations but with only the entrances completed, on a wooded slope 600yd to the right of the village. In a recent

Inval Boiron V1/V2 storage site – final organisation. A V2 tunnel with grille to allow bats access, one of 17 at the site. (Author)

visit, the author could not locate the actual site, which has poor road and rail access and this is probably the reason why the site was not completed.

(v) Inval Boiron *Michelin map No. 52*

Location: From Etrejust, head SW towards Avesnes and Arquel. From Arquel take the D521 towards Senapont and turn right in Inval towards the église (church). Follow the road towards the white cliffs and park just across the river. Aerial photos identified 20 galleries in the hillside, served by 17 entrances and a subsequent Allied inspection revealed tunnel lengths of 35 to 157yd. Several entrances are still visible, others have been blocked with rubble, but a species of protected bat has taken up residence in the tunnels and modern doors with grilles prevent access. Nevertheless, with its concrete access roads the site is impressive and was well advanced when work was abandoned.

(vi) Agenville *Michelin map No. 52*

Location: Agenville is close to the Domléger/Conteville/Cramont site complex. From Agenville turn left onto the C1 minor road for Jongleurs and after about one mile the site is on the right at the end of an unmade road. 200yd from the C1 a parking area has been excavated on the right and 100yd further two tunnel entrances are visible. Only one is accessible although partially blocked and the site is obviously unfinished, visible tunnel

Agenville V2 storage site – final organisation. One of the two unfinished V2 storage tunnels. (Author)

depth is about 30yd although the width is suitable for the V2. Rejoining the C1, turn left eventually onto the D933 for Mazicourt and after a few hundred yards, there are several excavated areas on the right against the hillside, intended for rocket and vehicle parking.

(vii) Monville *Michelin map No. 52 or 55*

Location: Take the N27 from Rouen towards Dieppe and after 5 miles turn right onto the D155 at Malaunay for Monville. A few hundred yards before Monville turn right onto a

minor road for Bois le Vicomte and the site is in a wooded area on the right after ¾ mile, parking is difficult due to the narrow road. Allied Intelligence identified at least five tunnels under construction, one with a width of 14ft and two gantry cranes with 50ft span were being erected at Monville station. Some of the tunnels are accessible with

Monville V1/V2 storage site, Somme-Seine. One of the V1 tunnel entrances. (Author)

difficulty due to the overgrown state of the ground and some concrete foundation platforms had been laid across the road. North of Monville, at Clères, an 80ft railway turntable was under construction, similar to that at Pont Rémy. Like Pont Rémy, the Clères turntable had disappeared although the area where it was built next to the station, can still be seen.

(viii) Salouel *Michelin map No. 52*

Location: Although Salouel was not inspected by Allied Intelligence and has not been visited by the author, a good aerial photo exists showing the site activities on 24 June 1944. Take the N29 from Amiens in the Rouen direction and Salouel is 2 miles off the road on the left. The site is ¼ mile north of the town centre, on the eastern side, in a wooded area. The ACIU aerial view shows evidence of at least two tunnels, new buildings and large camouflaged areas. It appears that work at Salouel may have started after the other new V2 sites and hence it was not far advanced when it was abandoned.

The final V2 Forward Underground Storage in Normandy comprised two sites, Haut Mesnil and La Meauffe, both part of the original storage arrangements but considerably reworked from late in 1943 onwards. Details of these sites are given in 5.5.5.

The last type of V2 storage was provided above ground and the final organisation had three sites. These were Foret de Nieppe, 30 miles SW of St Omer in the Pas de Calais. Monchy Cayeux, 5 miles south of Bergueneuse, Pas de Calais and Bois de Baugy, 10 miles SW of Bayeaux, Normandy. As we are already in Normandy, the Bois de Baugy site will be described first. This site was also inspected by RAF Intelligence officers as soon as the Germans had left the area. It covers a wooded area of 1,500 x 1,000yd and had not been completed. Decauville track had been laid along a number of branches, intersecting at a clearing in the woods, which in turn led off to 33 dispersed wooden storage huts with overall dimensions of 60 x 11.5 x 12ft high and 53 x 10.5 x 10ft high internally. A track had also been laid in the central clearing for a travelling gantry or crane, to transfer rockets to and from the trolleys found at the site. To visit the site, take the D572 from Bayeux and after 9 miles, 3 miles beyond Vaubadon, turn left onto the D13 through Balleroy and after 1.5 miles turn right onto the D116. The 'Bois' is on the left and the original unmade access road can still be seen, with its wide access radii. Unfortunately, nothing now remains of the V2 site, concrete bases for the huts are buried under 50 years of undergrowth.

The second site is in the Pas de Calais, Michelin map 51, IGN map No. 2305 O. Monchy Cayeux is very close to the V1 storage site of Sautrecourt and is ¾ mile, further north along the D343. About 200yd after the junction with the D98 on the left, turn left onto a wide concrete road leading into a wooded area, le Bois de Falimont, and the site is located among the trees. Appendix 1 describes the site and the high level of security which also probably applied to all parts of the final V2 organisation. Once again, apart from the spaces amongst the trees, nothing remains of its V2 usage.

The last site is Fôret de Nieppe, whose location has already been described. The site was expanded into three storage areas and when Allied officers inspected the site, their findings were as described below.

The forest covers an area of 6 x 2 miles and three sections were designed for rocket storage:

(i)   The western extremity near Thiennes
(ii)   The northern extremity, the Bois de la Motte
(iii) The SE extremity

Approximately 40 miles of Decauville track had been laid in the forest, connected to the main line near Thiennes and a loop ran through the forest, connecting to the main line again at Merville. Overhead gantries were provided for off-loading the rockets and it was estimated that the site could have handled at least 50 rockets per day with a total storage capacity of 300 V2s although up to three times this number could have been accommodated without causing congestion. Wooden storage shelters were provided for the rockets, similar to those at Bois de Baugy but in certain areas it was believed that the rockets were to lie in the open under camouflaged netting. The site was very damp in places and sections were liable to flooding and the whole area gave the impression it was more suitable for summer rather than winter use. A large number of concrete shelters were built on the fringes of the site, similar to those described at the Thiennes launch site, No. 28, and local inhabitants said that in the later stages of the site work, only SS personnel were employed. The forest is now a recreation area and all the original storage areas can be explored on foot. The site's location is the same as for Thiennes, No. 28.

Total storage capacity at these three sites was at least 363 V2s and from Appendix 1 we know that in late 1943, the Germans had planned storage for a total of 440 V2s above ground. These plans were unlikely to be the final arrangements and it is likely that Conteville/Cramont would have added at least another 100 V2s to this total

Of the original transit depots and motor transport (MT) sites, it appears that work may never have started, only the locations being designated. Allied Intelligence inspected many rocket sites on the Cherbourg Peninsula and Calvados as soon as they were cleared of German forces. Report A.I.2(g)7X dated 31 August 1944 gives some locations and these have been used in this section. Two Peninsula sites, La Croix Frimot and Theurteville-Bocage are locations given in the original V2 transit dump organisation hence it is likely that these sites were being reactivated for the new system.

La Croix Frimot is close to the La Vaquerie 'modified' V1 site (17). The remains of the concrete access areas are still visible. Returning to the D37 from La Vaquerie, turn right and 200 yards before the D318 junction turn left down a minor road. After a few yards the road changes to concrete under the tarmac. On the right a new industrial development may have used some of the hardstanding but in any case this type of V2 site had no above-ground buildings. The ACIU report BS 874 dated 23 August 1944 throws some light on the development of the V2 organisation.

First, the La Croix Frimot type of site had not been identified before and hence it shows that this part of the original V2 organisation had probably not progressed further than identifying suitable locations. Secondly, work at the site started between 27 April and 11 May 1944 and this date confirms that it formed part of the final organisation. The

V2 transit storage depot at La Croix Frimot. The site is located a short way along the first turning on the left, following the main road north. The two excavated loops are clearly visible. (PRO)

report gives no details about the depth of the transit parking areas but presumably they would have been deep enough to almost completely conceal a V2 on a Vidalwagen, with camouflage netting draped over the entire area. A second transit site is referred to at Teurtheville-Bocage, located not far from the La Capitainerie 'modified' V1 site (25). Using IGN map number 1310 O, return to the D24 and turn left, and after 1⅓ miles turn right on to the D119 for 2 miles, then turn left on to the D115. Teurtheville is a mile along the D115. This site has not been found by the author and it is not known how far advanced the excavation work was in 1944. The report also mentions another type of site, comprising V2 Motor Transport (MT) and Servicing Depots, and it seems reasonable to assume that these were included in both the original and the new plans. Originally each motorised Abteilung comprised three Companies, each with three Batteries, and each Batterie could man a launch site comprising of three launch pads. Each Abteilung had a complement of 560 motor vehicles, including fuel transporters and mobile workshops, as well as wagons for communications, medical, fire-fighting and security purposes, as well as mobile canteens. An armoured launch control vehicle was provided for each launch site, if there was no permanent launch bunker. Each field site of three launch pads had around 62 vehicles to service and maintain, of which probably at least 50 were permanently assigned to each Batterie. The logistics of the transportation problem were made even more difficult by Allied air superiority. What may have seemed perfectly feasible in 1942, with the skies virtually free of Allied fighter-bombers, was a nightmare by 1944 as anything moving on the roads in daylight was at risk. Nevertheless, this vast cavalcade of motor vehicles had to be serviced and the A.I.2(g) report refers to one servicing depot in Calvados, at Vaubadan, between Bayeaux and St Lô, and two on the Peninsula, at Château de Chiffrevast and Bourdonnerie. Despite several visits to the area, none of these sites has been found by the author but a site similar to that described at Bourdonnerie was found at Le Poteau near the V1 ski site at La Sorellerie (11). The buildings here were built of concrete, and were obviously intended for MT since they had long rectangular inspection pits in the floor.

Le Poteau: site No. 45

Location: from the ski site at La Sorellerie turn left on to the D56 and the MT site is a mile along on the right, almost at the end of the wooded section of the Forêt de L'Hermitage. The site comprises ten buildings, arranged in a herringbone fashion from a central concrete access road. There are four single-door buildings, two doubles and four comprising a triple unit joined together. The overall internal length is 32ft x 11ft wide,

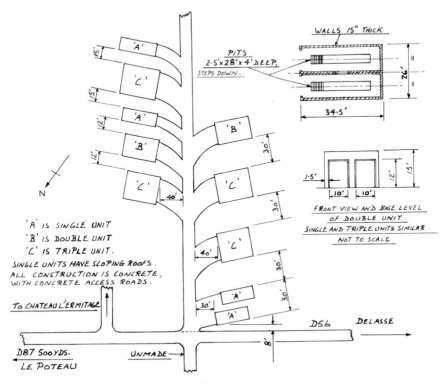

The V2 motor transport service/maintenance site.

V2 motor transport service/maintenance site at Le Poteau. (Author)

with entrances 10ft high. The dividing wall in the multiple units contains a 4ft x 3ft opening and each individual floor has a pit, 28ft long x 2ft 6in wide x 4ft deep, with steps at either end. This site could service twenty fuel tankers or the trailers of forty normal road vehicles or tractor units. The V2 road transportation Vidalwagen and some fuel tankers were towed by a six-wheeled multi-purpose tractor unit and these could be serviced individually, at least two per single unit. The site is well screened by mature trees, located as it is on the edge of the forest, and there are no signs of bomb damage, although the nearby ski site was bombed several times.

The Bourdonnerie MT site is something of a puzzle because there are two places with this name in the area. The northern one is off the D87 between the ski sites at Lorion (12) and La Flague (9). For the southern one, leave the N13 at the D146 for St Joseph, turn left and cross over the N13, staying on the D146. The hamlet of La Bourdonnerie is ¾ mile along the D146, 250yd off on the right. It seems strange that two MT servicing sites were built so close together but it is possible that La Bourdonnerie had been bombed and Le Poteau was built as a replacement. La Bourdonnerie was not marked on the captured German map that identified some of the sites in the A.I.2(g) report.

Le Poteau is located within a 'hot-spot' of V1 launching sites, both ski and 'modified', with a total of eleven sites all within a few miles, but the V1 required very little MT compared to the motorised V2 batteries. The ski sites were permanently manned and the only transport involved was the movement of V1s which arrived, often by train, fully fuelled and armed. The 'modified' sites were slightly different but here again a permanent staff would have been assigned to each site, including a security detachment. Both types of V1 site had ample concrete areas which allowed them to be used as V2 launch sites (see sections 5.5.2 and 5.5.3).

Of the liquid oxygen production, original German factories were still being used, as was one of the original LOX storage sites, Rinxent, and this was also now being used for production. But it is clear from the final plans that emphasis for LOX production had shifted from Germany to France. With Rinxent and the bunkers of Sottevast and Brécourt now being used, hope had not been completely abandoned for the battered but still standing main building at Watten. Reference at Watten is made to both old and new facilities, indicating the changes that had taken place and with five sets of LOX production equipment designated for the site, it was hoped that something might be salvaged from the ultimate white elephant.

Confirmation that LOX production had moved to France, logical considering the transport problems from Germany, are two huge new underground production centres near Rouen. Using Michelin map No. 55:

(i) Canteleu–Dieppedalle, German code name 'Granit'

This site is not mentioned in the Appendix 1 organisation, which indicates that these plans were still being updated. The site is to the west of Rouen, close to the River Seine and is completely underground. Internally it measures 340 x 190 x 23ft maximum headroom. It is served by road and rail, a single track line from Rouen enters the site on the LH side. There are six main galleries which contained five groups of compressors and all other equipment for LOX production and storage but two of the three entrances were dynamited by the retreating Germans. The site is now in private grounds and special arrangements are required for a visit.

(ii) Caumont, German code name 'Steinkohle'

The site is further to the west of Rouen, on the other side of the Seine and has road and rail access. Internally it measures 700 x 40ft with at least 30ft headroom and it appears to have utilised an existing cave system. Five groups of production equipment were installed and foundations were being prepared for a further five sets of equipment, indicating that the underground galleries could be extended.

These two sites would have been able to provide all the liquid oxygen requirements for the rocket offensive in the Dieppe and Calvados areas.

5.5.2 V2 Launch Sites – Introduction

With the V1, the final launch site organisation was clearly defined. The ski sites were virtually completely superseded by the 'modified' sites, principally because of the Allied bombing. It was a different story with the V2 for two main reasons, the Allied bombing and the influence of the SS. This resulted in changes being made.

The large bunker sites such as Watten and Wizernes were the type most favoured by Berlin, and although Dornberger had surveyed northern France in 1943 for forty-five field launch sites for V2s, it is likely that very little was done to implement this building programme. With the increasing intensity of Allied bombing, the V2 situation was quickly reviewed. The most badly damaged bunker, Watten, was abandoned as a launch site. Work on the other bunker sites continued, to an extent, because it was appreciated that they had a limited chance of being completed. As a potential back-up, work started on modifying Siracourt and Brécourt to enable them to launch V2s and Rheinbötes.

A small number of self-contained launch sites were built close to original field storage depots, especially if the latter were more or less intact. The author has found only one such site, in the Forêt de Nieppes near Thiennes in the Pas de Calais. The building at Thiennes was able to produce its own LOX, store alcohol and HTP, and also contained its own launch control point. With little done to implement the original plans to build forty-five field launch sites, a new plan was devised in which only twenty-seven field sites were required plus twelve others capable of withstanding a 1,200lb bomb. The latter sites were probably designed to use existing tunnels and caves where little new construction work was needed, or even some of the new underground storage sites. With increasing SS involvement, simplicity would be the overriding criterion, especially if the 'favoured' bunkers were experiencing serious problems.

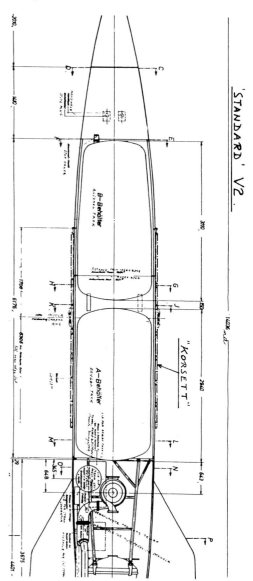

Details of a V2 with the fuselage 'Korsett', which finally cured the air-burst problem. (PRO)

These were the main factors influencing the V2 offensive that was due to start in the summer of 1944 from France. But another serious problem was also holding up the progress of the V2 to the operational sites in France, and it *had* to be solved. In early 1944 only one V2 in ten was completing its test flight, the remainder exploding a few thousand feet above the target area. Insulating the fuel tanks with glass fibre brought the success rate up to seven out of ten, but not until late 1944 did the Germans discover the eventual solution – reinforcing the outer centre-section of the fuselage. By then it was too late and the French launching sites had been lost.

5.5.3 Field Launching Sites

RAF Air Intelligence (Technical) produced a summary report on a survey of V2 sites in northern France based on information gleaned between August 1943 and September 1944, and the sections dealing with the field sites are reproduced below, ref: PRO AIR40/1219. The Air Ministry had been in charge of the V-weapons Intelligence campaign since 10 November 1943 when the original 'Bodyline' investigation with Duncan Sandys had been reorganised to bring in more specialised Air Intelligence personnel.

Information on the field sites was extremely important to Allied Intelligence in 1944. They knew from photographic evidence that the bunker sites were unlikely to play any part in the V2 offensive because of the damage they had suffered, but the field sites were a different matter. New field sites could be built very quickly anywhere in northern Europe, and hence it was vital to learn as much as possible about this aspect of the V2 organisation. In August 1944 the outcome of the war was still not a foregone conclusion.

One of the problems with this report is that at the time it was written very little was known about the overall V2 organisation, original or otherwise. Information was based on actual site inspections, captured maps and prisoner of war interrogations, but crucially no senior rocket personnel had been captured at the time. From the following extract it is clear that the Allies recognised that any future V2 offensive using field sites would be difficult both to detect and to destroy. Part of this report referring to firing (launch) sites is quoted below, ref: PRO AIR40/1777:

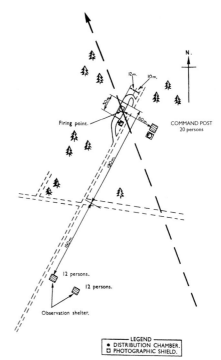

V2 field launch site details. There is some similarity of layout to a number of the modified V1 site access/parking roads.

(b) Firing sites

These may be constructed in several different forms and their dimensions vary within fairly wide limits but all have the common characteristics of being of simple construction, well concealed from observation from the air, accessible to road vehicles and situated some 5 to 10 miles from the storage sites. It is not necessary for the firing platform to be orientated on the target.

The following types of site have been examined:

(i) A group of three T-shaped concrete slabs measuring 67ft by 33ft constructed in three parts of which that forming the head of the T is reinforced and is the actual firing point.

(ii) A group of three concrete slabs some 33ft square and served by loops of corduroy road.*

(iii) A group of three concrete slabs of irregular but generally rectangular shape approximately 59ft by 33ft served by loops of corduroy or ballasted road.

(iv) Concrete slabs some 83ft by 33ft surrounding a level platform of steel box girders laid on four longitudinal lines of similar girders. The steel platform measures 70ft by 14ft 7inches and the slabs are served by ballasted tracks.

In addition to these permanent structures there is evidence that a heavy though portable platform some 15ft square of timber and steel construction can be set up on any level piece of road or hard standing and used for the launching of the rocket. It is this type of platform that it is believed has been used in Holland for firing rockets against this country.

4. Rocket Firing Areas

It would appear that it was the intention to confine rocket operations in France to the Calvados area and to the Pas de Calais area north of the Somme. Ground inspection is, however, as yet by no means complete. If it is subsequently proved that these two areas only were to be used for firing rockets, then it would seem that it was not intended that they should be fired at a range of more than 150 miles.''

A second Air Intelligence report, already referred to regarding the transit depots and MT service/maintenance sites, also discussed the launching sites between Cherbourg and Falaise in Normandy. The report is dated 25 August 1944 and was updated on 31 August 1944:

(* Authors' note: 'corduroy road' is a road made from logs laid lengthways against each other. 'Ballasted road' is a road made of loose stone pieces with the top surface compacted and level.)

(2) Launching Sites

Launching sites which have been examined differ somewhat in details, but all have the characteristics of rapid and simple construction and virtual invisibility from the air.

The more complete sites, apparently indicated by a filled red circle on the captured map, were found at Le Molay (map ref. T/649783) and Château du Cloay (map ref. T/561718). Both sites have similar characteristics and the concrete slabs are constructed on, and level with, existing tree-lined roads or avenues, all evidence of the work being carefully covered. No firing control point (or 'Striwa') was found at either site. The shape of the slabs is thought to be intended as an aid to the correct and rapid positioning of the various vehicles for the fuelling and preparation of the projectiles.

Three other sites have now been examined, all indicated by two concentric red circles on the captured map. None of these appears to be in a very complete condition. One of these near Lison (map ref. T/529766) is shown [below]. This consists basically of three concrete slabs, 18–19ft square, set in a stony field.

What probably was a survey peg was found in-line with the slabs, suggesting that they had been surveyed into position. Access is provided from a nearby road. These slabs consist of non-reinforced concrete poured direct on to a rock foundation, and varying in thickness from about 7in to as little as 4in. The nature of the surrounding field appears to be such that vehicle movement would be possible over it without further preparation. The two other sites, also indicated by two concentric red circles on the captured map, were near Beaumont Hague (map ref. O/013228) and near Montaigu (map ref. O/294132). Both these sites consisted essentially of a ballasted roadway constructed parallel to, and some 100yd away from, an existing road, and connected to it at both ends. No concrete slabs had been built at either site at the time of capture. At the site near Beaumont Hague a sunken concrete

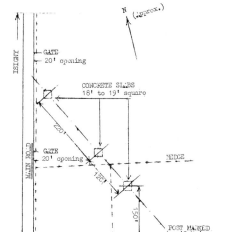

V2 field launch site near Lison, Calvados, Normandy.

pillbox was under construction about 100yd away from the ballasted road. This pillbox was four-sided, being some 12ft square with heavily reinforced 4ft thick walls. On the side facing the ballasted road three pipes, 2½in diam., entered the wall at floor level. These may be for cables, and in general the building suggests the 'Striwa' or fire control hut described by P/W, except that it had four walls and could not therefore be meant to house a road vehicle.

Finally a third report, quoted below, describes a V2 field site discovered in the Pas de Calais, near the V1 ski launching site No. 11, Fôret Nationale de Tournehem. Ref: PRO AIR40/1764.

La Wattine – V2 Firing Site. Location. Lat.50°45`N. long. 02°03`E. Map ref. Sheet 50, point 999546

A rocket firing site was inspected at La Wattine. This site, situated in the southernmost tip of the Forêt Nationale de Tournehem, was so well camouflaged as to be hardly recognisable, even when standing on the spot. A sleeper road led up into the wood and branched off into two loops serving the firing platforms. Only one of these latter could be identified for certain, by an adjacent survey mark, but there were probably others, and in any case rockets could perfectly well have been fired from any level point on the two road loops. A dug-out was provided in the middle of the site for housing the control vehicle.

Eventually a total of nine Wattine type of field launch sites were found in the Pas de Calais. Two, Bullescamps and Bouvelinghem by photo reconnaissance and La Wattine, Foret de

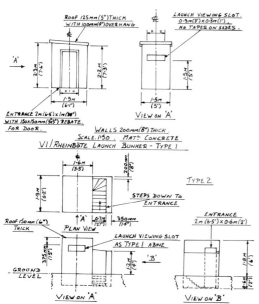

Vignercourt, Lignereuil, Hermanville, Noyelle Vion, Lambus au Bois, and Bois de Dompierre, by inspection. This compares with 18 such sites planned for the area, as stated in Appendix 1.

These three reports probably refer to every type of field site built in France between 1943 and 1944 for both the 'original' and 'new' V2 organisations. The Cloay, Molay, Lison, Beaumont Hague and Montaigu sites were all part of the original organisation and, regardless of their completion, the German strategy appears to have been that if they

Details of the two types of launch bunker found at V1 modified sites.

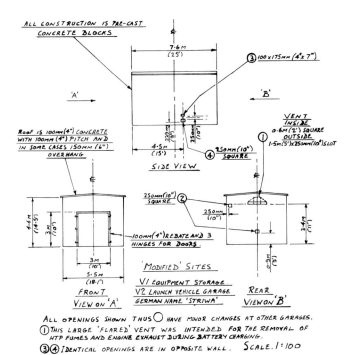

ALL CONSTRUCTION IS PRE-CAST CONCRETE BLOCKS

7·6M (25')

③ 100 x 175MM (4" x 7")

'A'

'B'

VENT INSIDE
0·6M (2') SQUARE
OUTSIDE
1·5M (5')x250MM (10")SLOT

ROOF IS 100MM (4") CONCRETE WITH 100MM (4") PITCH AND IN SOME CASES 150MM (6") OVERHANG

4·5M (15')

229MM (9")

250MM (10")

① 250MM (10") SQUARE

④ 250MM (10") SQUARE

SIDE VIEW

250MM (10") SQUARE ②

250MM (10")

4·4M (14·5')

3M (10')

100MM (4") REBATE AND 3 HINGES FOR DOORS.

3·4M (11')

0·9M (3')

'MODIFIED' SITES

V1 EQUIPMENT STORAGE
V2 LAUNCH VEHICLE GARAGE
GERMAN NAME 'STRIWA'

REAR
VIEW ON 'B'

3M (10')

5·5M (18·1')

FRONT
VIEW ON 'A'

ALL OPENINGS SHOWN THUS ◯ HAVE MINOR CHANGES AT OTHER GARAGES.
① THIS LARGE 'FLARED' VENT WAS INTENDED FOR THE REMOVAL OF HTP FUMES AND ENGINE EXHAUST DURING BATTERY CHARGING.
③ ④ IDENTICAL OPENINGS ARE IN OPPOSITE WALL.   SCALE. 1 : 100

Details of the garage at modified launch sites. Such buildings could also house the V2 launch vehicle, and in this role the garage was known as a 'Striwa'.

were available in 1944 they were inspected to see if they were still suitable for incorporating into the new organisation. (This is despite the report on page 35 which states that there were no field launching sites in the Calvados region.)

PoW interrogations for the second report indicate that there were two types of firing control point. One was a small bunker, as at Beaumont Hague, and the other, described by prisoners as a 'Striwa', was capable of housing a road vehicle. This final point is significant. The only road vehicle that was of importance at the field sites was the armoured half-track, used as a mobile launch point. The only building at any launching site in 1944 that could house this armoured half-track was the garage at the 'modified' V1 launch sites. This establishes a link between the 'modified' V1 sites and the new V2 field sites, following the strategy already established at Siracourt and Brécourt of using *any* site for the V2, regardless of its original role.

On the Cherbourg Peninsula there are two V1 'modified' sites close to the Montaigu site referred to in the second report, at Montaigu la Brisette (18) and Les Semis (19). At both of these sites there is a concrete road running parallel to an existing road and joined to it by loops, as described in the report. Both these V1 sites have a remarkable resemblance to the V2 launch site details. The common factor of two parallel roads joined by loops appears also at the 'modified' V1 site at Rauville la Bigot III (30) on the Cherbourg Peninsula.

The third report on La Wattine appears to refer to the type of firing point noted in sections (ii) and (iii) of the first report. This very simple form of construction was

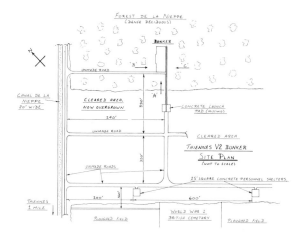

FOREST DE LA NIEPPE
(DENSE DECIDUOUS)
BUNKER
CANAL DE LA
NIEPPE
20' WIDE
CLEARED AREA,
NOW OVERGROWN
UNMADE ROAD
240'
UNMADE ROAD
CONCRETE LAUNCH
PAD (MISSING)
CLEARED AREA
Thiennes V2 Bunker
Site Plan
(NOT TO SCALE)
UNMADE ROADS
25' SQUARE CONCRETE PERSONNEL SHELTERS
THIENNES
1 MILE
200'
600'
PLOUGHED FIELD
WORLD WAR 1
BRITISH CEMETERY
PLOUGHED FIELD

probably the final attempt to produce a V2 launch point that was impossible to detect from the air. At Blizna the launching platforms at the north site were described in the Sanders Report as being constructed of logs, 18ft square, with a steel base plate, and a total of fifteen were available. As soon as one pad became too badly burnt to use, launches were transferred to another. These pads are very similar to those described at the end of section (iv) in the first report, describing the type believed to have been used in Holland. If the majority of the 'new' launch sites were constructed as described at La Wattine, after nearly sixty years they would be completely invisible, reclaimed by nature.

Thiennes Launching Site, Forêt de Nieppe Michelin map No. 51; IGN map No. 2304 E.

Thiennes is near the La Belle-Hôtesse 'modified' V1 site (23) in the Calais–Somme area. Using this as a starting point, take the D238 towards Thiennes, turning left on to the D122 for Thiennes. Follow the D122 into Thiennes and turn left, 250yd after the sharp right-hand bend in the village. Cross the railway on to an unmade road following the

Thiennes V2 bunker, Pas de Calais. Close up of the partially blocked V2 fuel hose outlets, the Decauville narrow gauge track for the V2 trolley runs alongside and 6 ft. from this wall. (Author)

canal and turn right before the start of the forest. Parking is available by the path to the British cemetery. The site is only a few hundred yards inside the forest and in what was a cleared area are two concrete personnel shelters. The forest covers an area of about 20 square miles and a branch was taken off the main railway line to serve the nearby V2 storage sites. The Thiennes site is unique in that it resembles a miniature version of Watten – and like Watten it contained all the equipment for launch, LOX production and fuel storage. The building is 112ft x 43ft x 18ft high and is constructed from reinforced concrete and blocks 20in x 30in. At the front entrance facing the launch area is a 9ft wide recess with a steel framed observation port and a doorway into the interior. Most of the interior can be inspected with a good torch, although some rooms are flooded.

Along the LH wall there are wooden shutters over the air intakes and this section would have contained the compressors, coolers, filters and so on for producing LOX from the outside air, together with nitrogen as a by-product, used for pre-launch testing and purging. Judging by the size of this room, it was probably capable of producing about 2 tons a day. The V2 required 4.9 tons at launch, but because of evaporation losses from storage it would have required three days' continuous operation to produce enough for one launch, unless this was supplemented by supplies from other sources. It is unlikely therefore that Thiennes was expected to launch V2s regularly.

Other rooms would have contained the storage tanks for LOX and possibly alcohol, HTP, the catalyst and nitrogen. On the outside RH wall near the end are two staggered, funnel-shaped openings, pointing downwards, and along this wall is a 24in-gauge rail track set in concrete. The funnel-shaped openings were intended for the fuel hoses of the V2 fuel tanks, which could be fuelled either here or closer to the firing point from rail-mounted tanks. The launching point was about 100ft from the edge of the forest. The records of Operation Backfire, the British-controlled V2 launches from Altenwalde near Cuxhaven in 1945, show that for field launches the V2 countdown was of relatively short duration, as most of the testing had already taken place in the workshops and test stands. This was probably intended to reduce the length of time that the V2 was in the open during this critical period. The countdown procedure in a secure environment, such as Watten, would have been as follows:

–3 hours: Warhead removed from container and attached to main fuselage in a horizontal position, detonators fitted.

–2 hours: Rocket elevated to vertical position and placed on launch table.

–1.5 hours: Clamps removed from trim tabs on fins, four batteries fitted, 2 x 27v, 1 x 36v and 1 x 50v, for internal power, fuel tanks pressurised at 30lb psi, to check for leaks and the complete fuel system purged with nitrogen.

–1 hour: Rocket filled with fuel in the following order: alcohol 8,750lb; LOX 11,000lb; HTP 370lb; calcium or potassium permanganate catalyst 30lb. The venting system allows 5–10lb of LOX to evaporate a minute, depending on outside temperature. Four steerable graphite fins fitted below motor exhaust. Top-up LOX supply connected.

–30mins: External power supply connected via umbilical cable, trajectory checked using accurate bearings of site and target, gyros set to correct vertical and horizontal reference axes using readings from a collimater on the launch pad, initial system checks carried out on guidance, control and motor circuits. Launch area cleared of personnel.

−10 mins: Final run through of all system switches, relays and valves in their firing and operational sequence, pressures and temperatures checked.

−3 mins: All gyros start running.

−2 mins: Final checks completed. LOX vent closed and supply disconnected, gyros uncaged.

−1 min: Black powder igniter lit under rocket motor, main LOX and alcohol valves opened allowing 20lb of fuel per second to flow by gravity into combustion chamber.

−20 secs: Visual observer confirms fuel has ignited, HTP system initiated and turbines start rotating to power both fuel pumps and associated systems.

−10 secs: Turbines now running at maximum revolutions, external power supply switched off, internal batteries on, initial thrust stage starts.

−5 secs: Thrust now at 8 tons and all systems working.

Zero: Main thrust stage of 25 tons starts and all systems now GO.

+8 secs: External power supply jettisoned, all systems now running on internal power, thrust increases to 25 tons.

+10 secs: Lift-off. Trajectory timing sequence starts, rocket vertical axis still at 90°.

+14 secs: Rocket starts inclining from vertical.

+25 secs: Speed of sound reached, Mach 1.

+35 secs: Mach 2.

+54 secs: Maximum rocket angle of 49 deg. reached.

+60 secs: HTP turbines stopped, fuel pumps stopped. Zero thrust, height 20 miles. Rocket continues as a ballistic missile, reaching a maximum height of 50 to 60 miles and velocity of Mach 5 before impacting 150 to 250 miles down range, at Mach 3.

The warhead was armed by two fuses initiated by two electrical contacts, A and B, powered by a 36v battery. Forty seconds after motor propulsion started, switch A closed. Switch B closed at sixty seconds and the warhead was then armed. If the motor stopped before forty seconds, switch B closed, isolating the fuse system. This prevented the warhead detonating and ensured the safety of the launch site and personnel.

As soon as the rocket left local air space the site was rapidly cleared of equipment and returned to its camouflaged state. Local defence measures, including fighter cover, were stood down. All the clerical work associated with the launch was completed, and records made of any problems, readings and observations. All this was sent to operational HQ near Paris before being forwarded to Peenemünde. The tracking radar stations stayed in contact with the site until the rocket was out of range, at twenty-five to thirty-five seconds after launch, to confirm the initial trajectory was satisfactory.

5.5.4 *The Hottot Sites*

Early in 1944, from photo coverage of northern France, the ACIU interpreters discovered a new type of site, first identified near the village of Hottot les Bagues, 8 miles SW of Caen, on the D9. The original ACIU description of the site was that it comprised an irregular strip of concrete, with no buildings and, as no further developments took place, and with no reports from French agents, its purpose was a mystery. The capture of enemy documentation at Villers-Bocage produced more information on the sites, including 8 more locations, 4 in Calvados and 4 in the Pas de Calais. The site locations in Calvados were Hottot les Bagues; Claironde Ferme; Château de Beaumont; St Croix-sur-Mer; Bois de Villers.

In the Pas de Calais they were Le Veram; Le Breuil; Hames Boucres; Bois de Rossignol.

Significantly, all the sites were marked on a map of the projected rocket organisation captured at Villers Bocage. After the Allied inspection, the sites were described as a shallow excavation and rough clearing of the open ground, concreted to form a tapered strip with its broader end pointing towards England, although apparently not oriented on any particular location. In many cases road access to the site was poor. The concrete strip was made up of rectangles, each one narrower than the strip ahead, approximate dimensions overall being 170/180ft long, width 25ft, narrowing to 10ft. Attached to the rear was a platform, slightly raised and probably made from earth excavated in clearing and levelling operations. Its dimensions varied from 40ft square to 50/60ft x 55ft, depending on location. Usually a path led off at right angles from this platform, behind which at some sites was another platform 70ft square. No attempt was made to camouflage any of the concrete. Along the tapering strip, four rows of wooden stakes were driven into the ground, protruding about 6in above ground level. There were no buildings within the site area and it is believed the work on these sites started in early March 1944 and ended in April.

So, what was the purpose of the Hottot sites? The overall length of the strip, 170 or 180ft, is similar to the length of the ramp plus loading pad of the V1 ski sites. The outer width of the ski ramp concrete varied from 20ft to 25ft at the launch end, again similar. But there were no signs of any means of attaching the heavy ramp/firing tube structure to the concrete strip, which was an essential factor, Regarding the V2, the sites were marked on the captured rocket organisation map but there is no resemblance between the new field launch sites described in 5.5.3 and the Hottot sites.

Then, there is the Rheinbote, a weapon that required the least complicated launch pad and equipment of either the V1 or V2. The Rh was transferred to the launch site in two separate sections, each one about 22ft long, hence transportation was not a problem. As the Allied report says, in many cases road access was poor.

The author believes that the Hottot sites were intended to be a multi-role launch site for all three weapons, but initially the V2 and Rh. It is known that a V1 was being developed which used two solid-fuel detachable booster rockets, attached either side of the fuselage. These were to provide acceleration of the V1 along the ramp and replaced the complicated HTP/steam system. This in turn would have meant that a lightweight ramp could have been used, without the massive firing tube and piston. Such a ramp would have required virtually no attachments to the concrete base and could have been assembled in minutes rather than hours. The possibility of them being decoy V1 sites also has to be considered but they lack so many features of these sites that it is unlikely that the Allies would have switched bombing effort from the known sites to the Hottot type.

The Château Beaumont site in Calvados has been visited and all traces of concrete have disappeared. Parts of the adjacent ruins of the château were rebuilt by the Germans to provide accommodation, blending in with the original structure. From the size of these modifications, it indicates that a substantial number of personnel were allocated to the site, in which case it is unlikely that it was intended purely as a decoy site.

5.5.5 The America Rocket Sites and Regenwurm (earthworm)

With the A9/A10 becoming operational later in 1944 or early 1945, sites would be required to store, service and launch the rocket and France was the logical choice. Geographically, the further west the launch sites were, the greater availability of targets in the USA, even 300 miles would make an important difference.

The rocket organisation was based in France and some sites still had the potential to provide the required facilities for the new weapon. Sites such as Watten had by now been written out of the programme and realistically, also due to Allied bombing, Wizernes was now rapidly approaching the same situation.

In these circumstances, clearly the new sites had to have the following qualifications:
(i)   They should be untouched by Allied bombing
(ii)   They should be capable of remaining undetected from aerial reconnaissance
(iii) They should be as far west as possible
(iv)   They should also have the development potential to provide a secure bomb-proof environment for the new rocket as well as the V2.

Only two sites in NW France fulfilled these requirements, Haut Mesnil south of Caen and La Meauffe, NE of St Lô, both in Normandy. Both were quarry sites which had been operating since before the war. In 1942 they had been chosen as V2 forward storage sites in the original rocket organisation but little work appears to have been carried out up to late 1943. By early 1944 however, work at both sites suddenly accelerated in preparation for their new role as bases for the V2 and A9/A10. All of this, of course was unknown to Allied Intelligence and only D-Day on 6 June 1944 changed the course of events. Even so it was not until August 1944 that Allied Intelligence Officers were able to inspect rocket sites in Normandy. The task of determining exactly what the rocket threat comprised of was helped by the capture of German personnel who had been involved in the construction work plus the capture at Villers-Bocage, SW of Caen, of documents relating to the rocket organisation in Normandy. This information was reported in PRO files AIR 40/1777 and 1778 and although the original German documents were not included , a summary report was provided of the documents relating to Haut Mesnil and La Meauffe.

For Haut Mesnil the captured documents showed:

   (i) The road and rail facilities, a spur line from the Caen-Falaise mainline was taken into the site, plus the sites Decauville track system and plans of the looped galleries (tunnels).

  (ii) Details of the rocket loading equipment in those tunnels built with 50ft (15m) radius curves, giving 'an indication of the shape of the projectiles to be stored.'

 (iii) Details of the 100ft (30m) radius curves in other tunnels with different loading equipment for the projectiles.

 (iv) Details of the massive buttresses, walls and sliding doors built at the entrances to some tunnels.

  (v) At two of the entrances, the buttresses varied in detail.

 (vi) Details of the entrances to three tunnels.

 (vii) A plan of a 'presumed underground M/T park.'

(viii) A sketch of a T-shaped launching platform.

 (ix) Details of a 16.5ft square timber base plate intended for firing the rockets.

  (x) Details of three light wooden huts on the floor of the quarry with Decauville track running through them, thought to be for testing, maintenance and assembly of the rockets.

 (xi) V2 trolleys similar to those found at Bois de Baugy were found at the site.

RAF Technical Officers are not involved in speculation, they are only concerned with the facts but reading through the report, one gets the impression that they realised there was something strange about Haut Mesnil. For the 50ft radius tunnels with their handling gear, they go as far as mentioning that this indicated the shape of projectiles using these particular tunnels. But when it comes to tunnels with 100ft radius and different loading gear, there is no comment and the silence is significant. It does not need to be said because it is so obvious, if the 50ft tunnels were for the V2 then the 100ft tunnels must have been for a rocket about twice the length of a V2. Dr R.V. Jones, in his book *Most Secret War*, mentions that a dummy white-painted V2 was found in the tunnels at Haut Mesnil, to provide experience in handling the rocket round the bends in the tunnels.

Without fuel the V2 weighed 4 tons compared to the A9/A10s 24 tons, so different loading gear was definitely needed, and it was probably only days away from being fitted. The logistics of transporting the V2 from Germany to France were well organised to suit the rail network. With the fins at 45 deg., giving a maximum width of about 9ft, two V2s could be transported using the triple flats system. For the A9/A10, the maximum distance over the fins was 29.7ft at 90 deg. and 21 ft at 45 deg., which meant that the fins had to be removable for transportation and refitted before launch. A simple model test on a drawing board shows that with a 10ft wide tunnel a horizontal V2 can safely negotiate a 50ft curve. For the A9/A10 and a 100ft radius curve, the width of the tunnel needs to be at least 23ft.

The author has recently visited Haut Mesnil. The quarrying work has finished but the site is being redeveloped as a landfill site for Caen. Fortunately the rocket tunnels were built to pass under or adjacent to the main N158, Caen to Falaise road, some 100ft above the quarry floor. This situation stopped any further postwar excavations and hence the tunnel entrances have survived almost intact. The original number of entrances appears to have been eight, three V2 tunnels on the north quarry face, now blocked, and five on the east face under the N158. Of these, three were for the V2 and two for the A9/A10. Four of the five were inspected, the most southerly tunnel was fenced off and appeared to be used for vehicle storage. Photographs show one of the V2 tunnel entrances and the A9/A10 tunnel entrance and interior. All four tunnels were linked by a side gallery for personnel, a few feet from each entrance. The V2 tunnels were not as complete as the A9/A10 tunnel, which had concrete walls and floor with massive steel beams in the roof. Unfortunately, although the tunnels were originally looped, all are now blocked after about 100yd. This was a recent developement due to subsidence concerns when the N158 above the tunnels was widened into a dual carriageway. The A9/A10 entrance is 24ft wide and 26ft high, giving adequate clearance for the A9/A10 with fins aligned at 45 deg. Haut Mesnil can be found on

SECRET

STORAGE & LAUNCHING OF A.4. ROCKET PROJECTILE
(BASED ON AVAILABLE INFORMATION)

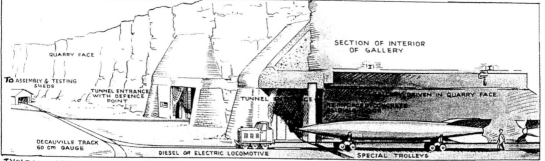

TYPICAL UNDERGROUND STORAGE.

TYPICAL DISPERSED SURFACE STORAGE

British Intelligence August 1944 sketches. Top – rocket/storage launch site, at Haut Mesnil (Regenwurm) and bottom – above ground rocket storage as Bois de Baugy, Monchy Cayeux and Thiennes. Both of these are part of the final V-weapons organisation as directed by Himmler's SS General Kammler. (PRO)

Michelin map No. 54, 6.5 miles south of Caen on the N158 Falaise road. Recent road improvements mean that you have to turn right off the N158 for Cintheaux and negotiate the new roads which enter at the rear of the quarry.

According to the PRO report, the captured German documents only refer to the defences at La Meauffe, but as it was mentioned in the same package as Haut Mesnil, I think we can assume that they were related. La Meauffe was also visited using Michelin map No. 54 and IGN map No. 1312 E. Take the N174 from St Lô north towards Carentan. Three miles from St Lô turn right before Pont Hebert onto the D92 and the main entrance to the quarry, now disused, is on the left after ¾ mile. The quarry is in two sections, left and right of the D92, the road being about 100ft above the quarry floor. Unfortunately the RH excavation is completely flooded and the LH side partially, as previous visits, but a local farmer provided some interesting background information. The quarry was operating before the war and a rail link from the nearby main line entered the LH section of the quarry, parts of the track and original buildings are still visible. Water had always been a problem at La Meauffe and this was pumped into a specially built canal, emptying into the River Vire. Quarry work stopped when the Germans arrived in 1943 but not until 1944 was there a sudden increase in activity. Security was always very strict and new tunnels were excavated in both LH and RH sides of the quarry. The RH section was only accessible via a tunnel from the LH side, under the D92. Farmhouses on the access roads to the main workings on the left were emptied of their inhabitants and turned into fortifications. Although the quarry was worked for a time after the war, the drainage canal has now become blocked, allowing both sides of the main workings to flood. A large section of the LH side can still be explored and some of the tunnel entrances are visible above the water line, as is the connecting tunnel under the D92.

Amongst the Villers-Bocage documents was a reference to the code name 'Regenwurm', earthworm, and there was enough information to establish that this referred to a rocket base combining both storage and launch facilities, using tunnels in quarry faces. The only sites which have these features are Haut Mesnil and La Meauffe. A tunnel at Wizernes was designated for Regenwurm, but this was on a German drawing dated 1 August 1944, by which time Wizernes was only days away from being captured by Allied forces.

CHAPTER 6

Rheinböte

Despite the fact that the Rheinmetal-Borsig weapon had lagged behind the other V-weapons, especially since the V1 had proved to be a success (and as we know now, the Rheinböte was developed as a back-up to the V1), by late 1944 it was ready for operational use in its four-stage Z-61/9 version. It is also likely that the Rh III, the warhead of which was comparable to that of the V1, was being flight-tested, especially since General Kammler had showed some interest in the overall project. The problem with the Z-61/9 version was the limited weight of its warhead – 55lb. Its effectiveness with a high-explosive filling was minimal – but with chemicals, gas or nuclear waste it certainly had a military use. Like the V2, the Rheinböte was intended to be launched by motorised troops but it could also be launched from static sites. In its mobile role it needed a special organisation with dedicated equipment, and by 1944 this equipment should have been at the manufacturing stage, but this had not happened and as an ad-hoc replacement a V2 Meillerwagen was adapted for the Rheinböte. This was not ideal as the 42ft 6in, pencil-slim Rheinböte had no guidance system and needed an accurate launch if it were to impact anywhere near the target after a 150 mile flight. This was not what the Meillerwagen was designed for, and at launch the nose of the rocket was probably swaying in an arc of several degrees.

What we do know about the Rheinböte's deployment is that on 12 July 1944, at a conference at the Führer's headquarters to discuss the HDP and Mimoyecques site, it was decided, among other things, that two Rheinböte launchers would be positioned outside the south tunnel entrance. What launch equipment was to be used was not recorded. There were other options for the Rheinböte. The Siracourt bunker, for example, was being modified for the V2 and the changes would also allow the Rheinböte to be launched from the bunker roof. Brécourt was also being modified and the changes here looked as if they had been specifically designed for the larger version of the Rheinböte, the Rh III. Both Siracourt and Brécourt had dual functions, and there was another site only a few miles along the coast from Brécourt that also fell into this category.

In 1924 the French Navy had ordered several 13.4in (34cm) turret-mounted guns from the arms manufacturer Schneider. The guns were to be added to naval bases on the coasts of Tunisia and Algeria and further south at Dakar. In addition, two similar guns in twin turrets were to be added to the coastal defences around Cherbourg and the site chosen was Castel-Vendon, 5 miles west along the coast from Cherbourg. The guns arrived at Cherbourg in 1928 but because of cuts in defence spending they were put into storage at the naval base. In 1935, as war clouds began to gather over Europe, France rapidly began to strengthen its defences and work started at Castel-Vendon. Two concrete silos were built on the cliffs, connected by tunnels and with underground accommodation for personnel and munitions for the guns stored at Cherbourg. The work had not been

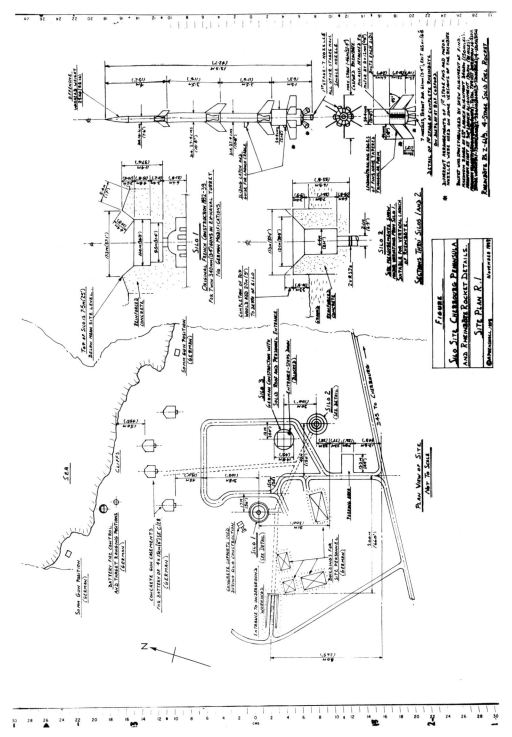

The silo site at Castel-Vendon, Cherbourg Peninsula.

finished and the guns not yet installed when the German forces arrived at Cherbourg in July 1940. Referring to the site plan on page 171, Silo 1 was complete, Silo 2 was partially complete and the underground workings were about 75 per cent finished. In 1942 the Germans started work at the site, initially as part of the West Wall, and added a battery of four Skoda 6in SKC/28 guns in separate concrete casements, together with two 2in guns and fire control and range-finding bunkers on the edge of the cliffs. The main battery was between the silos and the cliffs. The Schneider guns and turrets, by then outdated, were probably melted down for scrap.

Since the Second World War Castel-Vendon has been under the control of the French Navy, but on the author's first visit in 1974 it appeared to be abandoned and the fencing had disappeared in large sections. Some dimensions were obtained for Silos 1 and 2 and the initial figures appeared to show that both silos would accommodate a V2 vertically, although at the time the author was not aware of the pre-war history of the site. In addition, note was made of a third silo. This was of similar dimensions but was roofed over at ground level with access steps leading downwards at one edge, now blocked with rubble. Further investigations in the 1980s and 1990s, during which the early history of the site was established, culminated in another inspection of the site in 1996 accompanied by staff from the naval base. This detailed inspection provided the following information:

(i)   Silo 1 could not accommodate a V2 vertically because, although it was wide enough, it was only 37ft 7in deep, compared to the V2's 45ft height.
(ii) Silo 2 could not accommodate a V2 because, although it was deep enough at 55ft 10in, the lower 19ft 10in had a diameter of only 7ft – too narrow for a V2 with fins fitted. The lowest level of this silo was blocked with two steel beams, effectively providing a floor at the 55ft 10in level.
(iii) Silo 3 was no longer visible under twenty years of overgrowth, but French plans of the site do not show a third silo and therefore it was assumed to have been added by the Germans.

There is no doubt that the site was inspected by the Germans after July 1940 and the original French work would certainly have been of interest, as it was at Brécourt. From 1943 suitable V-weapons sites were being inspected in northern France and there is a good chance that Castel-Vendon was noted for inclusion in the site building programme. The presence of the coastal battery provided perfect camouflage, since Allied Intelligence was concerned with V-weapons and so showed no interest in additions to the West Wall fortifications. The differences between Silos 1 and 2 raise the question of why they had different dimensions when the two turrets they were originally intended for were presumably identical. The existence of Silo 3, with a similar outer diameter to the other two silos but not shown on French plans, indicates that something other than West Wall fortifications were planned for the site.

A Rheinböte is the only rocket that would conveniently fit the dimensions of Silo 2 and the Rheinböte could be launched vertically (although this reduced its range to less than 100 miles). By the 1950s silo-based ICBMs were the mainstay of the US nuclear deterrent and even in the 1990s America, Russia, France and China were all still using silos, although where possible they had been replaced by a mobile deterrent in the form of nuclear-powered submarines. The final Rheinböte site has already been mentioned in the 'modified' V1 sites section.

By late 1943, the initial competition between the German army and the Luftwaffe, each developing their own V-weapon, had been overwhelmed by the stark reality of the deteriorating military situation, and inter-service competition now took a back seat to the operational use of the weapons that had taken so many years to develop. Details of the concrete pad immediately in front of the ramp at the 'modified' V1 launch sites have already been mentioned. On each side of the HTP wash-down sump is a row of twelve 0.8in (20mm) diameter bolts set in concrete pockets, and these bolts were used for a rail system to ensure the correct alignment of the V1 when it was secured on to the lower end of the ramp. The transfer of the V1 from the compass pad to the ramp was the most vulnerable stage of the whole operation, and with the skies full of Allied planes speed was essential. However, the rails shown on the German drawing are far stronger than would be required simply for the movement of the V1 and it is possible that they were also intended to be used for the Rheinböte. A mobile Rheinböte launcher could have been clamped to the rails very quickly, and the V1 ramp support blocks already in place provided an accurate alignment guide for positioning the Rheinböte on the same target bearing as the V1. Given the dual purpose of other sites, it would make sound operational sense to apply the same philosophy to the new 'modified' V1 sites. Access and security was already guaranteed by the V1 organisation and the modifications were minimal.

From the information we now have, it seems that the V1 and Rheinböte were designed to fulfil the same role, and this adds support to the notion that the 'modified' sites were intended for a dual role. This means that all the 'modified' V1 sites already described were also potential Rheinböte launching sites. Particularly good examples on the Cherbourg Peninsula are at Hameau de Haut (21), La Capitainerie (25) and Tonneville-Le Manoir (14).

CHAPTER 7

Mimoyecques and the Hochdruckpumpe

Mimoyecques *Michelin map No. 51; IGN map No. 2103 ET.*

Location: from Calais take the A16 autoroute towards the Eurotunnel but carry on past the Tunnel leaving points and leave the A16 at Junction 9. Turn left on to the D244, through Wadenthun, and turn right on to the D243 before reaching Pihen-lès-Guines. At Landrethun-le-Nord, turn right on to the D249 and the Mimoyecques site is ½ mile on the right, clearly signposted and only a few yards from the road. The underground parts of the site are open during the summer, although access inside is restricted by rockfalls caused by Allied bombing and demolition charges.

Work started at Mimoyecques in April 1943, virtually the same date as Watten, and one must admire the persuasive powers of Herman Rochling who managed to get

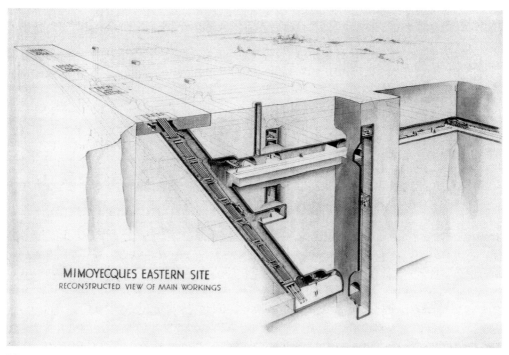

Mimoyecques HDP bunker: artist's impression of the interior. (PRO)

Main railway tunnel showing off loading deck on left hand side.

Rectangular slot through concrete slab above inclined shaft.

Mimoyecques HDP bunker: a view of the Eastern site, showing the railway tunnel and surface slab with opening for five barrel nozzles. (PRO)

Hitler's approval for a project, that many thought was ridiculous. The reasons for choosing the location at Mimoyecques can be summed up as follows:

(i)   For protection and operational reasons the 450ft-long barrels of the HDP had to be buried in the ground and aligned precisely on London, and the high ground of Le Mont Roland (518ft), was the only suitable site in the area that could offer the minimum range for the trajectory.

(ii) Railway access was excellent, as the nearby main line already had a loop going to the quarries at Ferques and any other additions to the rail network in the area would not raise any suspicions despite the regular flights of the Allied PRU aircraft.

(iii) Security in the area was as strict as anywhere in northern France, with the coast only 3½ miles away and the long-range cross-Channel batteries at Cap Gris Nez and Blanc Nez nearby.

Originally twenty-five barrels were planned for the site, set in groups of five, but by the time construction work got under way this figure had been reduced to fifteen barrels in three groups of five. The drawing on page 176 shows details of the underground workings based on a British Mission sent to investigate the results of the Tall Boy bombing, while an artist's impression from the Sanders Report (opposite) shows how the site would have functioned. Trains entered the main tunnel at the south entrance, unloaded supplies in the centre, as in the photograph, and these would be conveyed along eleven 160ft-long side tunnels, on the left. These side tunnels connected via lifts to a

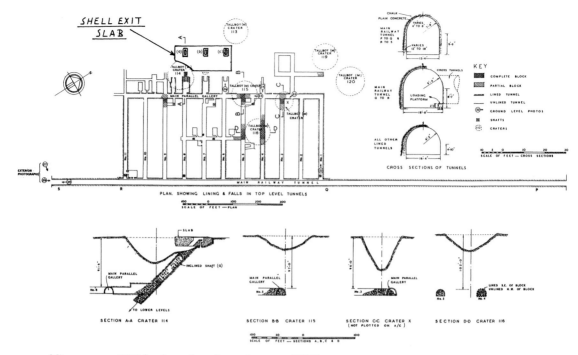

Mimoyecques HDP bunker: plan of tunnel system. (PRO)

main gallery running parallel to the main rail tunnel, the main gallery being only 91ft 6in from the surface above. Side branches 6, 7 and 8 contained the breeches for the fifteen 450ft-long barrels, which were inclined at approximately 45 deg., with the exit nozzles built into a massive concrete slab on the surface, 228ft x 98ft and 17ft 6in thick at its maximum point.

By the summer of 1943 construction work at Mimoyecques had reached the stage where the concrete slab on the surface above the workings was finished and three dummy haystacks had been erected over the openings for the barrel nozzles. Back in London the debate regarding German secret weapons had reached the stage where Lord Cherwell, Churchill's chief scientific adviser, was arguing, with some authority, that any German rockets would need sites in France that resembled something like giant mortars buried in the ground, with their alignment on London, and served by a large, new rail link. Unfortunately for Mimoyecques, the longitudinal axes of the rectangular openings in the concrete slab on the surface were aligned precisely on London – a fact that could be easily verified from the air – and there was also a new rail link. Consequently on 1 November 1943 the bombing raids started, and were to continue until 27 August 1944, by which time 4,100 tons of bombs had been dropped on the site. This massive destructive force was exceeded at only one other site, Siracourt. The raid on 6 July 1944 included seven 12,000lb Tall Boy bombs, four of which caused extensive rock-falls within the tunnel complex and damaged the exit slab on the surface. Despite the bombing, Berlin was reluctant to abandon the project but the results of trials had also shown problems with the shell design. On 12 July 1944, after a meeting on the future of Mimoyecques, Hitler signed an order which produced several important changes. First, only one shaft was to be used for the HDP with a total of five barrels, instead of fifteen. Secondly, the other two shafts were to be used for two Krupps K5 11in artillery pieces known as 'Schlanke Berta' ('Slender Bertha'). The barrels were reamed out to 12.2in with a smooth bore, and it was intended to use new shells developed at Peenemünde in which a rocket motor boosted the shell's range. Thirdly, two Rheinböte launchers, codenamed 'Meteor', were to be positioned in front of the main tunnel entrance.

However, German forces were being pushed back along the Channel coast far faster than expected and on 30 July 1944 the order came for all work to be stopped at Mimoyecques. An alternative site was being considered in the nearby quarry at Hydrequent, as some of the tunnels there had already been modified for two railway guns and it appeared that it might be possible to move the whole HDP operation to the new location. But events were now moving so quickly that even these plans had to be scrapped and on 27 September 1944 Canadian troops found the site intact but stripped of all equipment, including the HDP barrels. On 9 and 14 May 1945 British Army sappers detonated 36 tons of explosives inside the tunnels, putting an end to Mimoyecques. But

Mimoyecques 'super gun' site, 2 March 1944. Visitors enter by main tunnel south entrance, bottom LH, Black rectangle, centre-left, is concrete slab for 15 barrel nozzles, aligned on London. (PRO)

it was not quite the end for Hitler's super-gun. By the end of November General Kammler and his forces had managed to assemble two shortened barrels on the banks of the River Ruhwer, near Trier, just across the German border, north-east of Luxembourg. Kammler's move to the Luxembourg area was significant in that the German Ardennes Offensive, known to the Allies as the Battle of the Bulge, started on 16 December and Luxembourg was the southern boundary of the German thrust which Hitler hoped would cut the Allied forces in two and lead to the capture of their main supply port at Antwerp. The Luxembourg area was held by the US Third Army and an effective bombardment of this sector would have reduced the ability of the Americans to defend the southern boundary of the German offensive. These same US forces were later able to relieve the US 101st Airborne Division at Bastogne, which had been surrounded by German armour for over a week.

On 30 December 1944 the first HDP shells were fired towards the Third Army in Luxembourg at a range of over 27 miles, and eventually over 180 shells were fired up to 22 February. The failure of the German offensive resulted in the continued advance of the Allies and the guns were dismantled and moved further back into Germany. Plans to erect a third barrel had been cancelled because of the chaotic situation but the military effect of the HDP appears to have been zero. Modified versions of the other three V-weapons became part of the 'arms race' of the late twentieth-century, but it was not until 1991, during the Gulf War, that the reincarnated HDP appeared as Saddam Hussein's 'super-gun'. 'Project Babylon' was intended to install a 3ft-bore 580ft-long version of the gun on a 45 deg. hillside near Baji, 130 miles north of Baghdad. The gun would use rocket-boosted shells, carrying conventional or chemical/nuclear warheads, and the barrel was aligned on Israel, 500 miles away.

CHAPTER 8
Prédefin and Rocquetoire

Rocquetoire (Umspannwerke C) *Michelin map No. 51; IGN map No. 2305 O.*

Some 7 miles inland behind Test Stand VII, the 'elliptical test stand' at Peenemünde, and directly in line with the normal trajectory of V2s fired along the Baltic coast, was a Würzburg Riese (Giant) radar set. The Würzburg had been developed by Telefunken as an aid to detecting aircraft and with its 10ft-diameter dish it could scan through 360 deg., and from −5 deg. to +95 deg. in elevation. Operating on what was for 1939 the very high frequency of 560 megacycles, it could plot the range and height of aircraft to within a few feet at ranges of up to 25 miles. As aircraft performance increased, there was a need to improve the radar's detection capabilities and in 1941 Telefunken took the most obvious route. The ability to plot aircraft accurately depends on two main variables: the

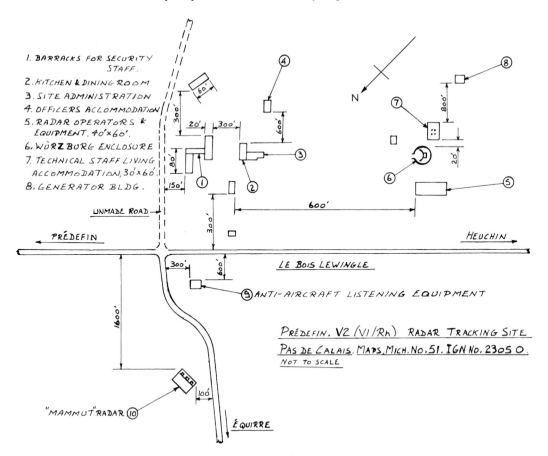

1. BARRACKS FOR SECURITY STAFF.
2. KITCHEN & DINING ROOM
3. SITE ADMINISTRATION
4. OFFICERS ACCOMMODATION
5. RADAR OPERATORS & EQUIPMENT. 40'x60'.
6. WÜRZBURG ENCLOSURE
7. TECHNICAL STAFF LIVING ACCOMMODATION, 30'x60'.
8. GENERATOR BLDG.

PRÉDEFIN. V2 (VI/Rh) RADAR TRACKING SITE PAS DE CALAIS. MAPS, MICH. No. 51. IGN No. 2305 O. NOT TO SCALE

9 ANTI-AIRCRAFT LISTENING EQUIPMENT

"MAMMUT" RADAR 10

Plan of the Prédefin V2 radar tracking site, Pas de Calais

179

frequency of the transmitted signal and the diameter of the dish. By increasing the Würzburg dish to 25ft diameter, the range improved to 50 miles in the general scanning mode and 37 miles in the direction-finding mode.

The main disadvantage of the new Giant Würzburg was its narrower beam width and hence reduced general surveillance capability. In addition, because of its increased size and weight, it required a fixed emplacement, unlike the original mobile version. The Würzburg at Peenemünde was used for plotting the initial trajectory of rockets, with a string of Würzburgs along the coast covering the remaining flight and impact. The Peenemünde Würzburg also performed two other trajectory requirements. One was beam guidance: as soon as the rocket was detected as straying from the Würzburg's beam, signals were sent by radio to correct the deviation. The other was motor cut-off, after which the rocket became an unguided ballistic missile. To achieve the required target accuracy, it was essential that combustion was terminated at precisely the right moment. The Würzburg performed both these functions during the initial part of the trajectory. In France the same requirements existed, but they were complicated by the fact that launches had to be monitored from two rocket sites, Watten and Wizernes, which were some miles apart. Unlike at Peenemünde, trajectories here would vary.

The site chosen to provide radar coverage was next to the village of Prédefin, about ten miles north-east of St Pol. From the V2 storage site at Bergueneuse, take the D71 for Heuchin and 250 yards before the D94/D92E junction turn left on to an unmarked road. After a mile or so, the site is on the right with the accommodation blocks in a slight hollow; turning left, the remains of the 'Mammut' radar are on the right. At Prédefin, two types of radar were installed: a giant Würzburg for initial coverage and a Telefunken 'Mammut', FuMG 52, which controlled the later part of the flight. The 'Mammut' had a rectangular aerial 100ft wide x 33ft high, and although it was fixed it could scan electronically through a 100 deg. arc over ranges up to 186 miles and heights up to 82,500ft. Prédefin had more buildings than standard radar stations in northern France, for communications equipment and personnel. According to a local farmer the site had a total of 150 personnel, of whom 100 were concerned with security. The extra protection would have been necessary to safeguard the information relating to the rocket sites. The additional buildings caused a problem to Allied Intelligence since it was obviously not a standard radar station, of which there were many in northern France, and the site was put on the Crossbow target list as a V1 launching site. On 19/20 June 1944 the site was attacked three times by the US 8th and 9th Air Forces and the results were described as 'one direct hit and two near-misses to the launching point (P)'. From the air the accommodation blocks resembled a launch ramp. In addition to the radars, a sound-listening device, like a large pair of ears, was located on the opposite side of the road from the Würzburg.

Although Peenemünde would have preferred the V2 to be independent of ground signals, the state of the art in gyros and accelerometers meant that the rocket's guidance and control system could not guarantee impact at the target area. For Watten, a cable trench was dug in a 100 deg. arc, 7.5 miles behind the site, which would encompass every possible target location in the UK. The Leitstrahl beam guidance and Brenschluss motor cut-off equipment would be plugged in at the appropriate location in the arc that aligned the equipment with Watten and the target in a straight line. For Wizernes, the provisions were more sophisticated and a concrete bunker, Station C, was built in the village of Rocquetoire, 6 miles behind the site. This bunker, on the edge of the village, is 105ft x 64ft x 21ft high and housed the generator and transmitting equipment for the Leitstrahl and Brenschluss systems (see below). The bunker's location is such that a straight line can be drawn from central London through Wizernes to Rocquetoire. To reach the site, take the N43 from St Omer and Arques and about 4½ miles beyond Arques, Rocquetoire is signposted on the right-hand side. The village is 2 miles from the N43. The actual bunker lies partially in the garden of a modern bungalow and the lady owner allowed the author to climb on to its roof via the original steel access ladders.

The field sites were to be provided with Leitstrahl equipment, and this was located up to 28 miles behind the launch point (see page 182).

The front of the beam guidance bunker at Rocquetoire. This would have tracked and guided V2s which were planned to be launched from Wizernes. (Author)

MOST SECRET   TARGET PREDEFIN.

            NO   XI/A/175 3   TYPE CONSTRUCTIONAL.

DATE	TIME	FORCE	COMMAND or GROUP	ESCORT	BOMBS	RECONNAISSANCE RESULT	LINY HEIGHT	P.R.U. ASSESSMENT RELEASE.
19.6.44		36 Fortresses.	EIGHTH AF.	Yes	75 tons.	36 Attacked. Results unobserved.		I.R. SA. 2105 dated 20.6.44. Attack by 20 A/C dropping 700x100 lb GP at 1020 hours. (a) Bombs are seen falling, but no bursts are visible through 10/10 cloud cover. (b) TARGET STILL IN CATEGORY "D".
20.6.44	1107	36 Marauders	9th AF		499x250 GP	GOOD		
20.6.44		24 Forts. and Libs.	EIGHTH AF.		80.7 tons GP.	32 A/C attacked. (includes 9 A/c despatched on BLANGERMONT).		
		SIGNAL DATED 23.6.44. Report on damage up to 1510B hours on 20th June 1944. Many craters are seen in the target area. There is one direct hit and two near misses to the launching point (P). A rectangular building (Probably r1) shows severe roof damage and there are four hits on the road passing through the site. TARGET IS NOW NOBALL DAMAGE CATEGORY A1.						

Report of the bombing raid on Prédefin radar site, which was mistaken for a V1 launch site. (PRO)

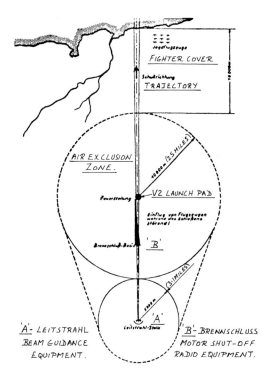

V2 field launch site, showing location details of the 'Leitstrahl' beam guidance and 'Brenschluss' motor cut-off equipment.

CHAPTER 9

Blizna

Peenemünde was bombed for the first time on 17 August 1943 and events moved very quickly after its vulnerability to air attack had been exposed. On 19 August Himmler flew to Hitler's Rastenburg headquarters in East Prussia to discuss the V-weapons projects. One of the results of these discussions was that a large part of the V2 test programme, including operational training and testing using live warheads, was transferred to the SS training camp at Heidelager, otherwise known as Blizna (see Map 9). Located between Cracow and Lvov in Poland it was beyond the range of Allied bombers flying from England. The SS would provide the security, and with the other SS involvements, including the Nordhausen underground factory, the process was beginning that would see the SS in complete control of all the V-weapons projects. The man chosen by Himmler, and approved by Hitler, to represent the SS was the ubiquitous General Hans Kammler. Included in the work transferred to Blizna in the autumn of 1943 was the V1 field training work that had previously been carried out at Zinnowitz and Zempin, along the coast from Peenemünde. As can be seen from Map 9, the Blizna site covered a large area, the outer perimeter enclosing an area of at least 10 square miles. Both the V1 and V2 arrived at Blizna by rail, with live warheads packed separately, and then they were transferred to the 24in narrow-gauge 'Decauville track' system that served the whole site. The map was produced by a British Army team led by Colonel T.R.B. Sanders, which also produced the Sanders Report on the V1/V2 bunker sites in France.

Key to the map (page 195):

A   = Officers quarters
B   = V1 buildings
C1   = Main workshop for V1/V2
C2   = Large open garage for road vehicles
C3   = Loading platform
D   = Wooden building for storing V1/V2 at night
E   = Some living quarters, Flak towers, others not known
K   = barracks/living quarters for troops including lecture rooms
L2, 4, 5 = V2 firing areas, a total of at least fifteen firing platforms. Launch direction was north-west, with the target area being Sarnaki at a range of 155 miles
R1, 2   = V1 launch ramps. (R2 was not completed.) Launch direction as for the V2, with the target area being Sawin at a range of 100 miles

The V2 firing platforms were constructed of logs, and were 18ft square with a steel baseplate on top. The control post, a dug-out reinforced with timber, was situated 40 yards away. As soon as one firing platform was badly burnt, a new one was used. The description of the firing point closely resembles that found at Wattine on the Pas de Calais.

A mobile communications and tracking post was situated at Niwisha, 3 miles north-west of Blizna.

By July 1944 the relentless advance of the Russian forces had made Blizna untenable and at the end of July the site was abandoned, with equipment and personnel moving north-westwards to 'Heidekraut', a site at Tuchel Heath, Tuchola, mid-way between Danzig and Bydgoszcz in Poland. In January 1945 it was Heidekraut's turn to be evacuated and virtually all the V-weapons work moved to Thuringia, close to the vast underground cities built to house the political and military headquarters of the Third Reich.

The final V2 organisation as far as the UK was concerned was Operation 'Backfire', the test launching of V2s from Altenwalde near Cuxhaven, in the autumn of 1945. Even in defeat the German rocket troops could not resist the old routines and they called themselves Altenwalde Versuchs Kommando, AVKO for short. Using a hotch-potch of recommissioned equipment, some of it salvaged from lakes and pits, they eventually assembled several V2s which were tested and, under British Army control, launched over the North Sea. The events leading up to the launch and the work involved in getting the V2s ready are described in five volumes of archive material.

CHAPTER 10
Italian Sites

From June to August 1944 Allied forces advanced from Rome along the 'leg' of Italy until the German resistance started to stiffen as they approached the Gothic Line, the line of defences stretching from north of Pisa on the Mediterranean to Pesaro on the Adriatic. The capture of the port of Leghorn (Livorno) south of Pisa considerably eased the Allied supply situation for the final offensive to strike into northern Italy. To deny the Allies access to this port or to render it unusable would be a crucial factor in holding up any further advance into Italy. With the topic of secret weapons already in the news following the V1 offensive against the UK, it was not surprising that reports started arriving in London about V-weapons sites in Italy. The first reported site was in the La Spezia area, based on local information supplied to Allied Intelligence.

(i) La Spezia

La Spezia was north of the Gothic Line and was an important German base for the defence of the Mediterranean side of Italy. Two reports are reproduced in Appendix 2 which describe construction work in the La Spezia area. Italian sources seemed to be convinced that this work was related to either the V1 or the V2. Unfortunately no photographs were supplied with the reports but the sources repeatedly refer to ramps. Reference to five ramps is puzzling because no sites in France or Germany had more than two ramps but the covering quoted, of approximately 50ft, is a possible ramp length for the improved version of the V1 as used in Holland. One important factor about this information is that La Spezia is only about 125 miles from Leghorn, well within the range of the V1 or V2, and the south-south-easterly direction referred to would be the correct launch direction from La Spezia to Leghorn. From the reports there is no doubt that some important, secret work was being carried out in the area under specialist German supervision.

Details of the second site were provided to the author by an Italian group interested in the history of the Second World War.

(ii) Ghedi-Montechari Air Base

This air base, 8 miles south of Brescia in northern Italy, was occupied and improved by the Luftwaffe from 1943 onwards. At one end of the airfield, building work was started and some parts of the incomplete structure resemble the V1/V2 bunkers in France. The information is claimed to come from an Organisation Todt engineer working at the airbase until the German surrender in 1945, from a local farmer who used some of the steel after the war and from a serving Italian Air Force officer. Photographs show parts

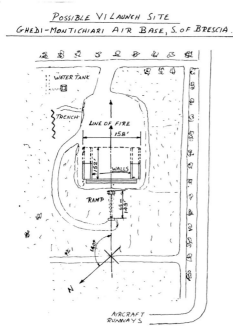

POSSIBLE V1 LAUNCH SITE
GHEDI-MONTICHIARI AIR BASE, S. OF BRESCIA.

WATER TANK

TRENCH

LINE OF FIRE
158'

152'

WALLS

RAMP

149'

140'

N

AIRCRAFT
RUNWAYS

of the 20ft-thick supporting walls for the roof, which was never added, and the overall length of the completed section of the walls is 76ft, with foundations for an additional 76ft making a total length of 152ft, the overall width being 158ft. Although the evidence at Ghedi is compelling, the main problem is the alignment shown for the ramp which would produce a line of fire to the south-east. To the author's knowledge, there are no targets in this direction within range of the V1/V2. If the alignment had been to the south-west it would just about have been possible for a weapon to have reached Leghorn, but there is still a question about the site's location.

To summarise, there is conflicting evidence about possible V1/V2 sites at both locations in Italy. The La Spezia site is in the right location but the evidence is sketchy that V-weapons sites existed there, and the Ghedi-Montechari site has convincing evidence for weapons but the location of the site is questionable.

Possible V1 site, Ghedi-Montichiari Air Base, south of Brescia, Northern Italy. (Author)

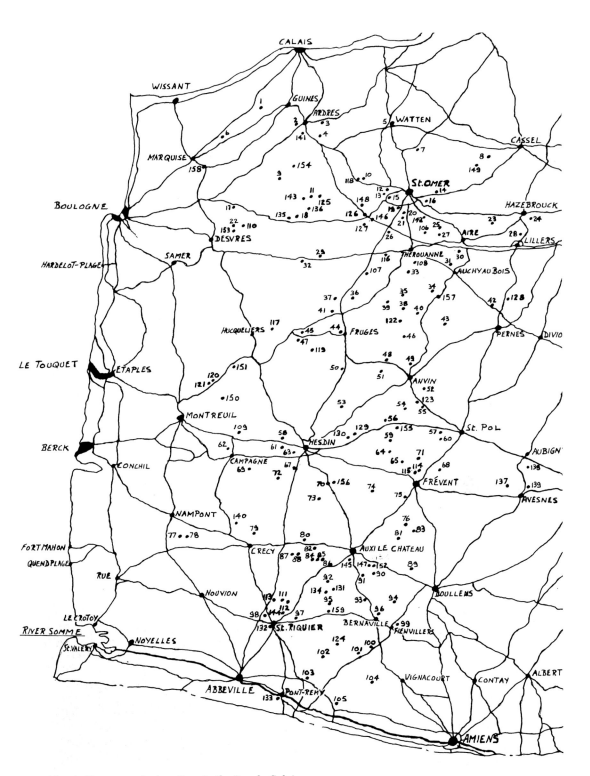

Map 1: V-weapon site locations in the Pas de Calais.

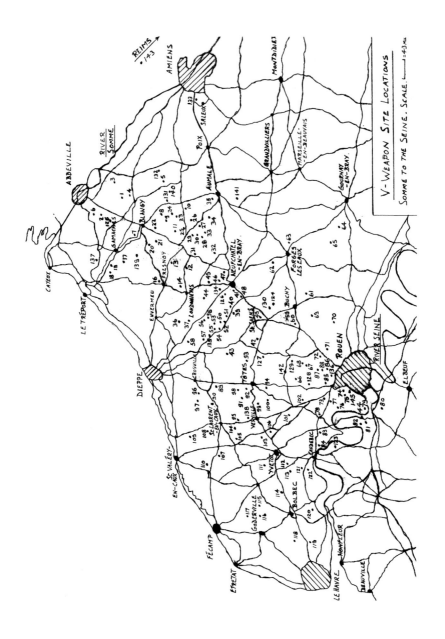

Map 2: V-weapon site locations, Somme to the Seine.

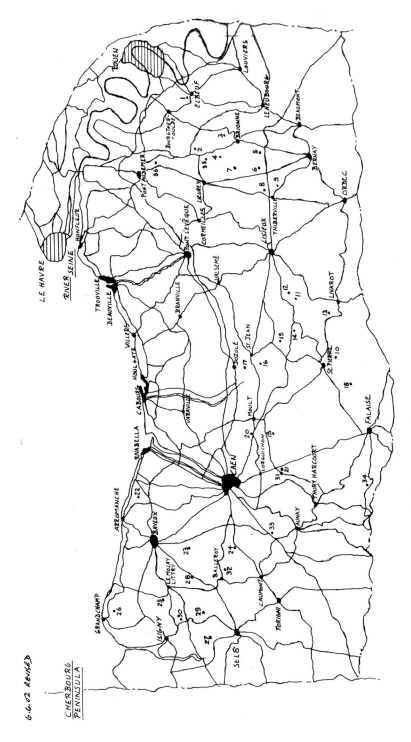

Map 3: V-weapon site locations, Seine to the Cherbourg Peninsula.

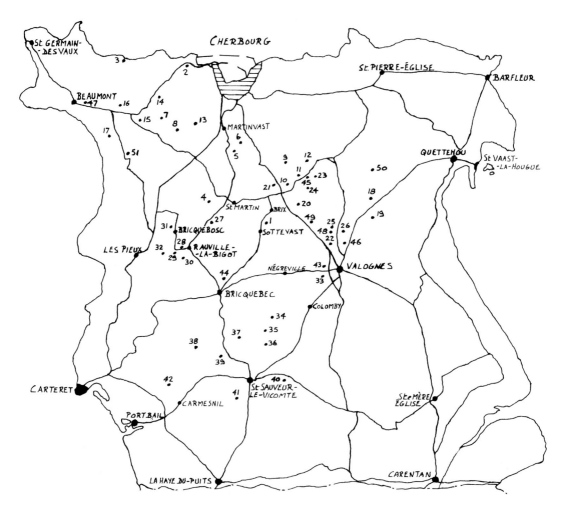

Map 4: V-weapon site locations, Cherbourg Peninsula.

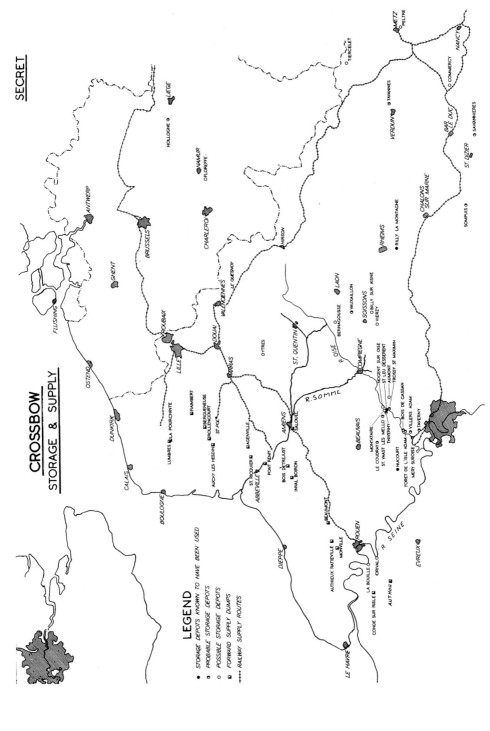

Map 5: V-weapons storage, rear. Final organisation.

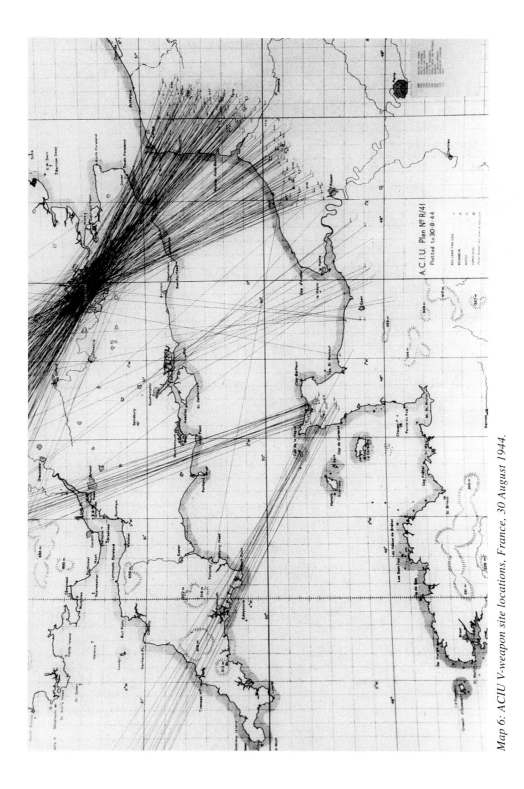

Map 6: ACIU V-weapon site locations, France, 30 August 1944.

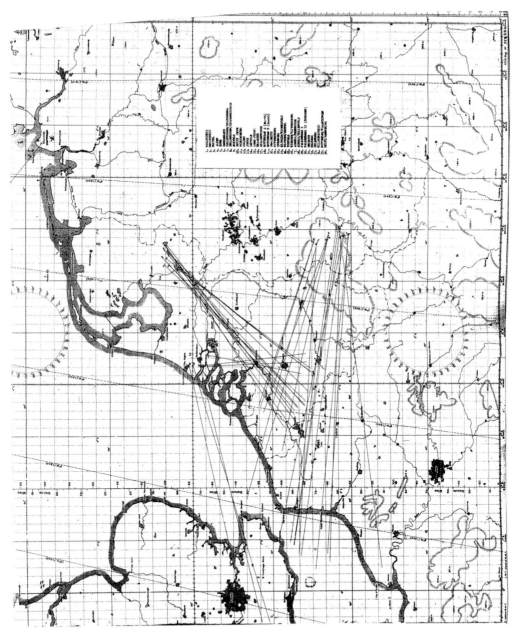

Map 7: ACIU V1 Launch site locations, Holland & Germany, 1944–45.

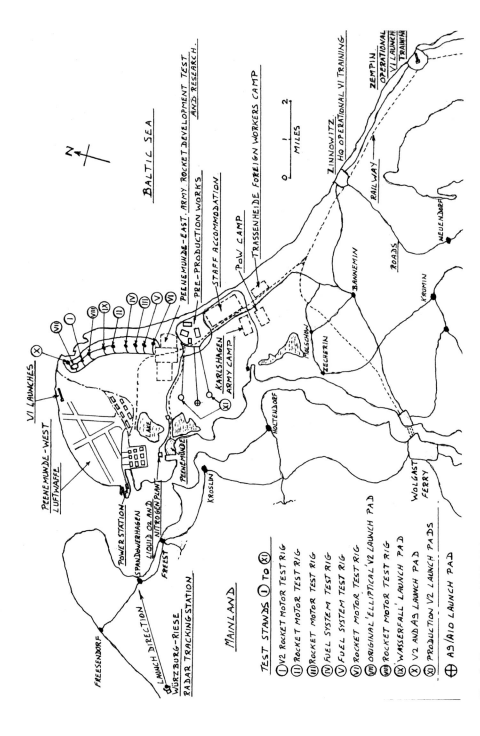

Map 8: Peenemünde, 1936–1945.

BALTIC SEA

PEENEMÜNDE-EAST. ARMY ROCKET DEVELOPMENT TEST AND RESEARCH.

PRE-PRODUCTION WORKS
STAFF ACCOMMODATION
POW CAMP
TRASSENHEIDE FOREIGN WORKERS CAMP

HQ OPERATIONAL V1 TRAINING

ZINNOWITZ

ZEMPIN
OPERATIONAL
V1 LAUNCH
TRAINING

RAILWAY

ROADS

NEUENDORF

BANNEMIN

KRUMIN

OLSCHON

ZECHERIN

KARLSHAGEN
ARMY CAMP

HOLTENDORF

0   1   2
MILES

V1 LAUNCHES

PEENEMÜNDE-WEST
LUFTWAFFE

LAKE

PEENEMÜNDE

KROSLIN

WOLGAST
FERRY

POWER STATION

SPANDOWERHAGEN

LIQUID O2 AND
NITROGEN PLANT

FREEST

FREESENDORF

LAUNCH DIRECTION

WÜRZBURG-RIESE
RADAR TRACKING STATION

MAINLAND

TEST STANDS Ⓘ TO ⓍⒾ

Ⓘ V2 ROCKET MOTOR TEST RIG
Ⓘ Ⓘ ROCKET MOTOR TEST RIG
Ⓘ Ⓘ Ⓘ ROCKET MOTOR TEST RIG
Ⓘ Ⓥ FUEL SYSTEM TEST RIG
Ⓥ FUEL SYSTEM TEST RIG
Ⓥ Ⓘ ROCKET MOTOR TEST RIG
Ⓥ Ⓘ Ⓘ ORIGINAL 'ELLIPTICAL' V2 LAUNCH PAD
Ⓥ Ⓘ Ⓘ Ⓘ ROCKET MOTOR TEST RIG
Ⓘ Ⓧ 'WASSERFALL' LAUNCH PAD
Ⓧ V2 AND A9 LAUNCH PAD
Ⓧ Ⓘ PRODUCTION V2 LAUNCH PADS
⊕ A9/A10 LAUNCH PAD

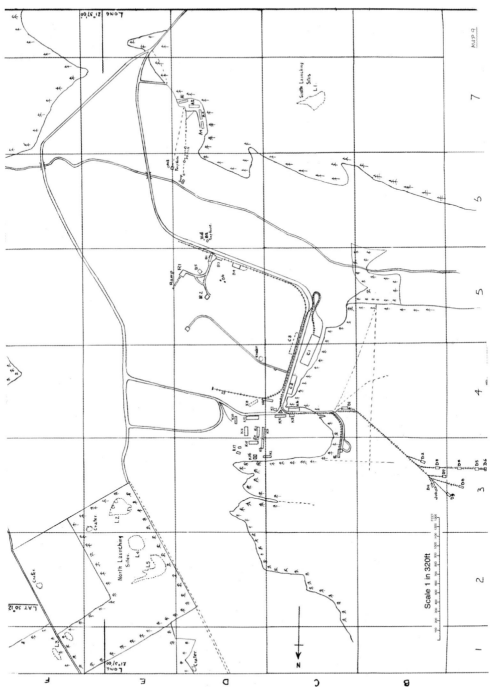

Map 9: Plan of the V2 site at Blizna, Poland.

Appendix 1

Ref : A.1.2.h/108/6

Wing Commander Mapplebeck

MONCHY CAYEUX

This place has been reported by ground sources as a secret weapon emplacement (December 1943, a large munition depot (February 1944), platforms for a battery of heavy artillery (January 1944), and finally in August 1944 as "mysterious operations – even military personnel are forbidden to enter – drivers have to remain outside while officers drive their vehicles in."

Its position is in a small wood to the East of the main railway line from ST. POL to HESDIN (via ANVIN), on GSGS.4040 Sheet 72/123177. It is about 1 mile from the old supply site at SAUTRECOURT (on the other side of the road, railway and river). One mile to the West lies an active flying bomb site (FLEURY). One mile to the East, in a wood, lies an inactive ski site (BOIS DE LA JUSTICE). Three miles to the North beyond ANVIN is a forward Crossbow Storage Depot (BERGUENEUSE), and approximately four miles to the South there is the heavy site at SIRACOURT, and considerable activity, probably of a storage nature in the woods at BOIS DE BELIEUL and RAMECOURT. It will be seen that the site lies in the midst of an area which is well studded with other forms of Crossbow activity.

From photographic reconnaissance, very little can be seen. A tree lined avenue leaves the main road at right angles running South West for 200 yards, where it enters a wood rectangular in shape (approx. 600 yards x 300 yards). The road continues through the full length of this wood, and rises in all approx. 120 feet from the main road. The wood itself slopes upwards gently on either side of the road, giving the impression that the road runs in a small reentrant. there may be some tunnelling.

The avenue from the main road is heavily covered with camouflage netting, and has been so covered since January. Nothing was visible here at the end of November, so it may be assumed that work started between that time and the end of January. Little activity could be seen under this camouflage, but there was considerable excavational activity in the wood during February and March, which culminated in the erection of buildings just off either side of the road. These buildings are of a rectangular shape of various sizes, and detailed interpretation is made very difficult by the density of the trees. It is thought however, that the majority of them are 58' x 17',

/The ...

The site is provided with either (or both) power and water. There is no noticeable change in the state of the site since that date, but the fact that it is active is shown by vehicles moving on cover of 12 May, and the appearance of wire, which completely surrounds the wood and neighbouring flak site on cover of 11 August.

From the foregoing information, no concrete suggestion as to the purpose of the site can be put forward. Although much smaller in size, the layout of the site is reminiscent of the rocket storage depot at Bois de Baugy, and the Foret de Nieppe. The buildings are of a size that compares well with the former, and their setting (as far as can be seen) at an angle from the roadway is also similar. The whole site is much smaller, but appears possible that it could be used for a similar type of storage. From a more general point of view, however, the site would appear to be a profitable target, as it is in an area where it is unlikely that the Germans would undertake anything that was not now of importance to them; it is active and probably occupied. And from ground sources, mentioned above, there are indications, albeit not very specific ones, that the work or storage there is highly secret and important. The sources quoted, are in addition, usually fairly reliable.

Target material has been given full distribution. It is recommended for immediate attack.

A.I.2(h)
23.8.1944

(Sgd.) D.H. Price
Squadron Leader

Monchy Cayeux, 'final' V2 Field Storage Site, Pas de Calais. ACIU report on the history of the site, 23 August 1944.

Appendix 2

28 January 1945

The following information has been received from a worker employed on V-1 and V-2 launching sites in the **LA SPEZIA** area

In the period between May and July 44 Germans worked on some existing tunnels in the SPEZIA area. This was suspended end of July for reasons unknown. Work resumed 24-25 Dec on tunnels, one Western part of LA SPEZIA at approx P.651091, and one Eastern part of gulf at approx P.702089.
14 Jan approx 300 Italian specialist workers under the supervision of 20 Or 22 Germans who wore civilian clothing. There were 300 Italians working two shifts, 12 hours each, but being switched from one tunnel to the other, to keep them confused as to the type of work. In the arsenal there are 5,000 Italian labourers, but seem to have little to do.
14 Jan 45. Tunnel East of SPEZIA has entrance of 30 metres. Interior has 5 ramps, each separated by a stone wall 6/10 – 8/10 metres high, length of tunnel unknown, but they are making the tunnel longer. The floor of each ramp is reinforced concrete : the tunnel is protected by about 25 metres of rock, the entrance is hidden by a wooden structure. Other tunnels East of LA SPEZIA with same specification has four ramps with overhead covering of approx 15 m.
It is believed that the existing tunnel known as Galaria Compando Arsenala will be used as a dump for the flying bomb. The only machinery seen in this area is only local machinery known to the workers. It is believed that several train-loads of machinery and material is to be used for the installation of the flying bomb and have arrived in SPEZIA by rail and will be sheltered at some of the tunnels. An electric power station is in the vicinity of the arsenal RR station. Will be used to produce power needed for launching or production of flying bombs. All these installations were to be ready for use on 28 Jan. Some of the targets were to be LEGHORN and FLORENCE. German technicians in charge live at SIRENZE Hotel, LA SPEZIA, 150 metres S.W. of Rly station on main roads. All the work concerning the flying bomb Installation has been kept under strict surveillance. Arsenal workers are not allowed to leave LA SPEZIA.

<u>S E C R E T</u>

HEADQUARTERS
15TH ARMY GROUP
APO 777

9 February 1945

SUBJECT : Reported V-1 and V-2 Sites

1.   Information was received recently from a Source concerning the possible existence of V-1 or V-2 Sites at SPEZIA .

Source supplied rough plans showing the position and layout.

Air photographs taken over a period were examined and conclusions arrived at are mentioned below :

(a)   <u>SITE 1 – (P 6908)</u>

<u>1.</u>   The existence of a <u>"barracks"</u> or large building at the S.W. extremity of MONTE della CHIESA is confirmed.

<u>2.</u>   Source shows a <u>"ramp"</u> built beneath this building and pointing approximately 140°. This is heading S.S.E. down the harbour, and would be clear of obstructions.

This cannot be confirmed from vertical photographs.

(NOTE – Clear oblique angle photos taken from the appropriate position might confirm whether a tunnel or ramp exists.)

No signs of activity have been noticed here.

<u>3.</u>   Entrances to tunnels or underground workings at P 697086 referred to by Source as <u>"flying bomb store"</u> is also confirmed, but no recent activity is visible here.

<u>4.</u>   Conclusion

There is no evidence to confirm the existence of a V-1 or V-2 Site and it is thought unlikely that one exists here.

(b)   <u>SITE 2 – (P 6509)</u>

1.   Source shows <u>"Electrical substation in reinforced building."</u>

It is confirmed that numerous small buildings exist here which might also be used as a substation.

<u>2.</u>   <u>"Tunnel with capacity of 8000 tons".</u>   The existence of a large tunnel or underground storage at this point is well known, and is amply confirmed by photographs – the entrances and spoil removed from inside being clearly seen.   Tip trucks are visible, and two small huts have been built recently near one of the entrances.

<u>3.</u>   The <u>"Launching site for V-1 bombs."</u>   From the photographs available, no such site can be seen at the point indicated, neither can any object resembling a V-1 launching ramp.   (NOTE – Clear, larger scale oblique angle photos of this pinpoint taken in certain weather conditions would be necessary for a more careful examination.)

<u>4.</u>   A possible Site for V-2 launchings is the partly destroyed SAN VITO works at P 644092.   No major clearance of damaged buildings or debris has been carried out here but one large building has been two thirds stripped of its roof.

S E C R E T

- 2 -

5.   A large covered R/R truck about 40/50 feet long was standing near this building on a spur run from the main sidings.   This was on 28 January.   The next photo coverage revealed that the truck had been moved and was not visible elsewhere.   The sidings are standard gauge and are serviceable and active as previously reported.

6.   "Arsenal Command Offices in Tunnel"

What is believed to be the Command Post is located in approximately the position indicated by Source.

A small amount of constructional activity has been noticed here in recent weeks, probably a concrete wall in course of erection.

7.   Conclusion

There is no visible evidence on these photographs of the existence of a V-1 launching ramp and it is thought that this is an unlikely site for V-1.

Apart from the small amount of activity mentioned above there is no evidence of the existence of a V-2 Site, but it is considered possible if certain modifications to local R/R tracks were carried out. There is no evidence of this at present.

For the Assistant Chief of Staff, G-2 :

R. H. WINDSOR *capt SS*
F/Lt.
G-2, (G.S.I.(a)5)

DISTRIBUTION :

A.C. of S., G-2, AFHQ
A.C. of S., G-2, Headquarters Fifth Army
G.S.I. Main Headquarters Eighth Army
G-2, (G.S.I. (Tech)
G-2, (G.S.I.(a)
G-3   Plans   )
G-3   Ops   )   1
R.A.
R.E.

British Army reports on suspected V-weapons sites at La Spezia, Italy, dated 28 January 1945 and 9 February 1945.

Bibliography

Only one book has previously been published which covers both the V1 and V2 site organisations in detail. This book, *The Defence of the United Kingdom* by Basil Collier, was published in 1957 by Her Majesty's Stationery Office (HMSO) and it describes the measures taken during the Second World War to defend the UK on land, sea and air, against attack by the Axis powers. Unfortunately the declassified archive material available in the 1950s was limited. Hence the book contains little or no information on how the V1 and V2 site organisations developed from 1943 to 1945, on the HDP 'super-gun' or the Rheinböte rocket, and German work on unconventional warheads.

A large amount of British Intelligence information related to the V-weapons is now available in the Public Record Office, Kew, London, and much of this is from the records of the ACIU and the RAF Technical Intelligence Organisation, A.I. 2(g). The following PRO references were all used by the author in producing this book and many of them deal with actual site locations in northern France.

ADM 223/674, 675

AIR 2/8415, 8416

AIR 14/2505, 2642, 2753, 2953, 3808, 3809, 3722, 3723, 3724, 3725, 3726, 3727, 3755, 3756

AIR 20/1661, 1667, 1695, 2629, 2644, 3398, 3428, 3440, 4039, 4132, 4262, 4263,5865, 5867, 5869, 5870, 5876, 5878, 5879, 5884, 5885, 5898, 5899, 5902, 5906, 5907, 5910, 5912, 5913, 5919, 5921, 5929, 5937, 5943, 5945, 5950, 6253, 7699, 8124, 8138, 8158, 8199, 8217, 8773, 8972

AIR 34/80, 109, 110, 117, 119, 121, 123, 131, 132, 134, 232, 241, 429, 624, 625, 695, 718, 750, 838, 841, 844, 846, 850, 851

AIR 37/370, 429, 832, 899, 1015, 1270, 1272, 1275, 1277, 1278, 1280, 1290, 1294, 1295, 1298, 1299, 1300, 1304, 1310, 1314, 1323, 1338, 1340, 1342, 1343, 1348, 1353, 1355, 1356, 1359, 1360, 1363, 1368, 1369, 1374, 1378, 1384, 1390, 1393, 1396, 1404, 1409, 1413, 1414, 1417, 1418, 1421, 1422, 1430, 1431

AIR 40/98, 158, 540, 579, 604, 655, 656, 658, 674, 888, 1011, 1036, 1039, 1084, 1219, 1283, 1457, 1678, 1718, 1762, 1763, 1764, 1773, 1777, 1778, 1824, 2114, 2161, 2332, 2333, 2517, 2520, 2524, 2527, 2528, 2537, 2541, 2542, 2544, 2545, 2572, 2665

AIR 51/351

AVIA 7/2133, 2134

AVIA 40

WO 33/2554, 2555, 2556, 2557, 2558, 2559

WO 106/2817, 2818, 2824

WO 109/1103
WO 199/889, 890, 891, 1104, 1610
WO 204/5950, 6748
WO 208/3143, 4334
WO 219/2165, 3365, 4929, 4937

The following books are related to the V-weapons subject:

Dornberger, W. *V2*, The Scientific Book Club, London, 1952

Holsken, D. *V-Missiles of the Third Reich*, Monogram Aviation Publications, Sturbridge, Mass. USA, 1994

Irving, D. *The Mare's Nest*, William Kimber, London, 1964

Young, R.A. *The Flying Bomb*, Ian Allan, London, 1978

The following three books were published in France and cover certain aspects of the V-weapons sites:

Hautefeuille, R. *Constructions Speciales*, Published by the author, Paris, 1995. (This book deals with the history of the construction by the Organisation Todt of the nine large sites: Watten, Wizernes, Siracourt, Lottinghen, Mimoyecques, Brécourt, Sottevast, Couville and Tamerville. In addition it includes archive information on the history of the V1, V2 and HDP.)

Grenneville, R. and L. *Les Armes Secretes Allemandes. Les V1. Normandie 1944*, Editions Heimdal. Bayeux, 1985. (This book covers the V1 sites on the Cherbourg Peninsula.)

Dufour, N. and Doré, C. *L'Enfer des VI en Seine-Maritime*. C.E.P.S.N.A., Saint Nicholas d'Aliermont, 1993. This book covers the use of the VI in the Somme-Seine area from the French viewpoint.

Index